CAMBRIDGE LIBRARY COLLECTION

Books of enduring scholarly value

British and Irish History, Seventeenth and Eighteenth Centuries

The books in this series focus on the British Isles in the early modern period, as interpreted by eighteenth- and nineteenth-century historians, and show the shift to 'scientific' historiography. Several of them are devoted exclusively to the history of Ireland, while others cover topics including economic history, foreign and colonial policy, agriculture and the industrial revolution. There are also works in political thought and social theory, which address subjects such as human rights, the role of women, and criminal justice.

Menasseh ben Israel's Mission to Oliver Cromwell

Controversial Jewish journalist and political lobbyist Lucien Wolf (1857–1930) co-founded the Jewish Historical Society of England in 1893, editing this work in 1901. It comprises a series of pamphlets and tracts written by Menasseh ben Israel (1604–57). An Amsterdam rabbi and founder of the city's first Hebrew publishing house, Menasseh was well regarded among non-Jewish theologians. As an advocate of messianic tradition, he sought to scatter the Jews across the world, leading him to England in the 1650s to campaign for their readmission following Edward I's edict of expulsion in 1290. The material presented here is chiefly concerned with Menasseh's interactions with Oliver Cromwell and shows the rabbi taking advantage of the contemporary drive for reinstatement for reasons of religious toleration as well as practical politics. The work includes the famous petition from the Jewish community and offers valuable insight into the history of the Jews in England.

T0381854

Cambridge University Press has long been a pioneer in the reissuing of out-of-print titles from its own backlist, producing digital reprints of books that are still sought after by scholars and students but could not be reprinted economically using traditional technology. The Cambridge Library Collection extends this activity to a wider range of books which are still of importance to researchers and professionals, either for the source material they contain, or as landmarks in the history of their academic discipline.

Drawing from the world-renowned collections in the Cambridge University Library and other partner libraries, and guided by the advice of experts in each subject area, Cambridge University Press is using state-of-the-art scanning machines in its own Printing House to capture the content of each book selected for inclusion. The files are processed to give a consistently clear, crisp image, and the books finished to the high quality standard for which the Press is recognised around the world. The latest print-on-demand technology ensures that the books will remain available indefinitely, and that orders for single or multiple copies can quickly be supplied.

The Cambridge Library Collection brings back to life books of enduring scholarly value (including out-of-copyright works originally issued by other publishers) across a wide range of disciplines in the humanities and social sciences and in science and technology.

Menasseh ben Israel's Mission to Oliver Cromwell

Being a Reprint of the Pamphlets Published by Menasseh ben Israel to Promote the Re-admission of the Jews to England, 1649–1656

EDITED BY LUCIEN WOLF

CAMBRIDGE
UNIVERSITY PRESS

CAMBRIDGE UNIVERSITY PRESS

Cambridge, New York, Melbourne, Madrid, Cape Town,
Singapore, São Paolo, Delhi, Mexico City

Published in the United States of America by Cambridge University Press, New York

www.cambridge.org
Information on this title: www.cambridge.org/9781108053808

© in this compilation Cambridge University Press 2012

This edition first published 1901
This digitally printed version 2012

ISBN 978-1-108-05380-8 Paperback

This book reproduces the text of the original edition. The content and language reflect
the beliefs, practices and terminology of their time, and have not been updated.

Cambridge University Press wishes to make clear that the book, unless originally published
by Cambridge, is not being republished by, in association or collaboration with, or
with the endorsement or approval of, the original publisher or its successors in title.

MENASSEH BEN ISRAEL'S

MISSION TO

OLIVER CROMWELL

Menasseh ben Israel.
from an Etching by Rembrandt

MENASSEH BEN ISRAEL'S

MISSION TO

OLIVER CROMWELL

Being a reprint of the Pamphlets published by
MENASSEH BEN ISRAEL to promote the
Re-admission of the Jews to England
1649–1656

Edited with an Introduction and Notes

By LUCIEN WOLF

*Past-President and Vice-President of the Jewish Historical Society of England
Co-Editor of the " Bibliotheca Anglo-Judaica," &c. &c.*

PEREGRINANDO QUAERIMUS

Published for the
Jewish Historical Society of England
By MACMILLAN & CO., LIMITED, LONDON

1901

TO MY WIFE

PREFACE

HE Jewish Historical Society of England, soon after its establishment, resolved on the publication of the present volume as a memorial of Menasseh ben Israel, whose name must always hold the chief place on the first page of the history of the present Anglo-Jewish community. The Society did me the honour of entrusting me with the preparation of the work.

Menasseh's tracts have been printed in facsimile. They have not been reproduced by any photographic process, but have been entirely reset in types similar to those employed in the original. Thanks to the resources of the printing establishment of Messrs. Ballantyne, Hanson & Co. of Edinburgh, and the taste and care they have devoted to the work, a much finer effect has been produced than would have been possible had photography been employed, while exact fidelity to the originals has not been sacrificed.

To me the preparation of this volume has been a labour of love. Nothing in the whole course of a very varied literary career, extending over nearly thirty years, has fascinated me so much as the story of the Return of the Jews to England. Its mysteries belong to the highest regions of historical romance, and it forms a page of history which is a real acquisition both to the annals of the British Empire and to that wider and more thrilling panorama of human activities which depicts the fortunes of my own co-religionists. I have not, however, spoken the last word on this subject in the present volume, which is chiefly concerned with the transaction with Oliver Cromwell in 1655–56 and its proximate causes. I hope to tell the whole story in detail in another volume, which I have long had in preparation for the " Jewish Library."

The preliminary essay on the Return of the Jews to England is in no sense a *réchauffé* of the papers on the same subject contributed by me to various periodicals during the last fifteen years. Those papers were written at successive stages of an uncompleted investigation. The present essay is a re-study in the light of all the facts, and it will be found that some of my former judgments have been modified, and a few even reversed.

I have to thank many friends for their assistance. Mr. Israel Abrahams very kindly relieved me of the labour of reading the proofs of the tracts, and made many valuable suggestions which have added to the completeness and beauty of the volume. Mr. B. L. Abrahams was good enough to revise my introduction, and thus saved me from not a few slips of style and memory. The Rev. S. Levy has given me useful assistance in preparing the annotations, and Dr. S. R. Gardiner was good enough to place at my disposal his unrivalled knowledge of the politics of the Commonwealth in solving some of the difficulties in the negotiations of 1655. My acknowledgments are also due to Miss S. R. Hirsch for the excellent index she has compiled. Finally, Mme. de Novikoff kindly obtained for me from the Hermitage Collection at St. Petersburg an excellent photograph of the alleged portrait of Menasseh ben Israel by Rembrandt, which I have reproduced, together with two other better known and more authentic portraits.

L. W.

LONDON, *December* 1900.

CONTENTS

INTRODUCTION

THE RETURN OF THE JEWS TO ENGLAND

I. Days of Exile

HROUDED in the fogs of the North Sea, the British Isles were, for two centuries after the Great Expulsion by Edward I., little more than a bitter memory to the Jewish people. In other lands they came and went, but England was as securely closed against them as was the Egypt of Danaus to the Greeks. With the exception of a few adventurous pilgrims who trickled into the country to enjoy the hospitality of the Domus Conversorum, they ceased gradually to think of the land which had been so signal a scene of their mediæval prosperity and sufferings. The Jewish chroniclers of this period, while dealing with the politics of other European countries, have scarcely a word to say of England.

Towards the beginning of the sixteenth century the fogs began to lift, and England once again appeared as a possible haven to the "tribe of the wandering foot and weary breast." The gigantic expulsions from Spain by Ferdinand and Isabella had created a new Jewish Diaspora under conditions of the most thrilling romance. The Jewish martyrs "trekked" in their thousands to all the points of the compass, fringing the coasts of the Mediterranean with a new industrious population, founding colonies all over the

xi

Levant as far as the Mesopotamian cradle of their race, penetrating even to Hindostan in the East, and throwing outposts on the track of Columbus towards the fabled west. But this was only the beginning of a more remarkable dispersion. The men and women who took up the pilgrim's staff at the bidding of Torquemada could only go where Jews were tolerated, for they refused to bear false witness to their ancient religion. They left behind them in Spain and Portugal a less scrupulous contingent of their race—wealthy Jews who were disinclined to make sacrifices for the faith of their fathers, and who accepted the conditions of the Inquisition rather than abandon their rich plantations in Andalusia and their palaces in Saragossa, Toledo, and Seville. They embraced Christianity, but their conversion was only simulated, and for two centuries they preserved in secret their allegiance to Judaism. These Crypto-Jews, in their turn, gradually spread all over Europe, penetrating in their disguise into countries and towns and even guilds which the Church had jealously guarded against all heretical intrusion. It was chiefly through them that the modern Anglo-Jewish community was founded.[1]

The Iberian Crypto-Jews, or Marranos,[2] as they were called, represented one of the strangest and most romantic movements in the religious history of Europe. Marranism was an attempt by the Jews to outwit the Jesuits with their own weapons. Both sides acted on the principle that the end justified the means, and each employed the most unscrupulous guile to defend itself against the other. The Inquisition was ruthless in its methods to stamp out Judaism,

[1] Wolf, "Crypto-Jews under the Commonwealth" (*Trans. Jew. Hist. Soc.*, vol. i. pp. 55 *et seq.*); "The Middle Age of Anglo-Jewish History" (*Papers read at the Anglo-Jewish Historical Exhibition*, pp. 53-79).
[2] The origin of this name is obscure. There seems to be little doubt that it was originally a nickname, seeing that the classical name for the converts was *Nuevos Cristianos*, or "New Christians." Graetz believes that Marrano is derived from Maran-atha, in allusion to 1 Cor. xvi. 22, "If any man love not the Lord, let him be Anathema Maran-atha" (*Geschichte der Juden*, vol. viii. p. 73).

Introduction

the Marranos were equally unprincipled in preserving their allegiance to their proscribed religion. Abandoning their ceremonial, abandoning even the racial limitation on marriage, the Jewish tradition was maintained by secret conventicles chiefly composed of males, and thus Jewish blood and the Jewish heresy became distributed all over the peninsula, and crept into the highest ranks of the nation. The Court, the Church, the army, even the dread tribunals of the Holy Office itself were not free from the taint.[1] A secretary to the Spanish king, a vice-chancellor of Aragon, nearly related to the Royal House, a Lord High Treasurer, a Court Chamberlain, and an Archdeacon of Coimbra figure in the lists of discovered Marranos preserved by the Inquisition.[2] At Rome the Crypto-Jews commissioned a secret agent supplied with ample funds, who bribed the Cardinals, intrigued against the Holy Office, and frequently obtained the ear of the Pontiff.[3] Some idea of the social ramifications of the Marranos is afforded by the careers of the early members of the Amsterdam Jewish community. Many of them were men of high distinction who had escaped from Spain and Portugal in order to throw off the burden of their imposture. Such were the ex-monk Vicente de Rocamora, who had been confessor to the Empress of Germany when she was the Infanta Maria; the ex-Jesuit father, Tomas de Pinedo, one of the leading philologists of his day; Enriquez de Paz, a captain in the army, a Knight of San Miguel, and a famous dramatist; Colonel Nicolas de Oliver y Fullana, poet, strategist, and royal cartographer; Don Francesco de Silva, Marquis of Montfort, who had fought against Marshal de Créqui under the Emperor Leopold; and Balthasar Orobio de Castro, physician to the Spanish Court, professor at the University

[1] Kayserling, *Juden in Portugal*, p. 327.
[2] Graetz, vol. viii. pp. 309-11; Ehrentheil, *Jüdisches Familien Buch*, p. 326.
[3] Kayserling, p. 139.

of Salamanca, and a Privy Councillor.[1]   It was by Jews
of this class that the congregations of Amsterdam, Hamburg, and Antwerp were founded, and it was largely through
them that those towns in the sixteenth and seventeenth centuries were enabled to wrest from Spain her primacy in the
colonial trade.

At a very early epoch Marranos reached England.   We
hear of them, almost immediataly after the expulsion from
Spain, figuring in a lawsuit in London.[2]   In 1550 a Marrano physician was discovered living in London.   Another,
Roderigo Lopes, was court physician to Queen Elizabeth,
and the original of Shakespeare's Shylock.[3]   When the Earl
of Essex, after the sacking of Cadiz in 1596, brought the
Spanish Resident, Alonzo de Herrera, a prisoner to England,
he turned out to be a Marrano.   After his liberation, this
descendant of the great Captain Gonsalvo de Cordova proceeded to Amsterdam, entered the synagogue, and spent
his old age in the compilation of cabalistical treatises.[4]
Amador de los Rios states that the Marranos founded secret
settlements in London, Dover, and York;[5] and it has been
shown that they possessed a secret synagogue in London
early in the seventeenth century, if not before.[6]   As in
Amsterdam and Antwerp, they were largely concerned in
the development of the Spanish trade, in the importation of
bullion, and in the promotion of commercial relations with
the Levant and the New World.

While the people of England were unconscious of this
immigration, it could not have been altogether unknown in
the continental Jewries.   That no trace of this knowledge

[1] Graetz, vol. x. pp. 195, 196, 200; Da Costa, *Israel and the Gentiles*,
p. 408; Kayserling, p. 302.
[2] Graetz, vol. viii. pp. 342-43; Colonial State Papers (Spanish), vol. i.
pp. 51, 164.
[3] Wolf, *Middle Age*, pp. 64, 67-70; S. L. Lee in *Gentleman's Magazine*,
Feb. 1880.
[4] Wolf, *Middle Age*, p. 68; Graetz, vol. ix. p. 494.
[5] *Historia de los Judios de España*, vol. iii. p. 357.
[6] Wolf, *Crypto-Jews*, loc. cit.

Introduction

is to be found in printed Hebrew literature is not strange, since the keeping of the secret was a common Jewish interest. It no doubt helped to stimulate Jewish hopes of a return to England, which more public circumstances had already founded. The Reformation in England first turned Jewish eyes towards the land from which they had been so long excluded. They were especially interested by Henry VIII.'s appeal to Jewish scholars during his conflict with the Papacy in regard to his divorce from Catherine of Aragon.[1] Still more deeply must their feelings have been stirred by Elizabeth's struggle with Spain. All over Europe, indeed, Jewish sympathies were with Elizabeth. The secret negotiations carried on by Roderigo Lopes, through his influential Marrano relatives, with the Grand Turk and with the Hebrew bankers of Antwerp and Leghorn, have yet to be made public; but it is certain that they played an important part in the story which culminated in the confusion of the Great Armada. But it was the increasing Hebraism of English religious thought, as represented by the Puritan movement, which chiefly attracted the Jews. This movement sent not a few Englishmen and Englishwomen to the continental ghettos to seek instruction at the feet of Hebrew Rabbis, and even to obtain entrance to the synagogue as proselytes.[2] When the Commonwealth, with its pronounced Judaical tendencies, emerged from this movement, the Jews could not fail to be impressed. The more mystical among them began to dream of the Golden Age. Indeed the doctrines of the Fifth Monarchy Men, carried to Smyrna by Puritan merchants, paved the way for the rise of the pseudo-Messiah, Sabbethai Zevi.[3] The more practical saw that the time had arrived when it might be reasonably hoped to obtain the revocation of Edward I.'s edict of banishment.

[1] Wolf, *Middle Age*, pp. 61–63.
[2] De Castro, *Auswahl von Grabsteinen*, Part I. p. 28.
[3] Rycaut, *History of the Turkish Empire* (1687), vol. ii. pp. 174, *et seq.*

Towards the end of 1655, the question of the readmission of the Jews to England was brought to a climax by Menasseh ben Israel's famous mission to Oliver Cromwell. The story of this mission has been briefly narrated by Menasseh himself in the *Vindiciæ Judæorum*, one of the tracts printed in the present volume.[1] As my object in this preliminary essay is to set forth the story more fully, and to endeavour to elucidate its obscurities, I cannot do better than take as my text this authoritative, though somewhat vague, statement by the chief actor in the events with which I am dealing. Here is what Menasseh wrote under date of April 10, 1656 :—

"The communication and correspondence I have held for some years since, with some eminent persons of *England*, was the first originall of my undertaking this design. For I alwayes found by them, a great probability of obtaining what I now request, whilst they affirmed that at this time the minds of men stood very well affected towards us, and that our entrance into this Island would be very acceptable and well pleasing unto them. And from this beginning sprang up in me a semblable affection, and desire of obtaining this purpose. For, for seven yeares on this behalf, I have endeavoured and sollicited it, by letters and other means, without any intervall. For I conceived that our universall dispersion was a necessary circumstance, to be fulfilled before all that shall be accomplished which the Lord hath promised to the people of the *Jewes*, concerning their restauration, and their returning again into their own land, according to those words, *Dan.* 12, 7 : *When we shall have accomplished to scatter the power of the holy people, all these things shall be finished.* As also, that this our scattering, by little, and little, should be amongst all people, from the *one end of the earth even unto the other*, as it is written *Deut.* 28, 64 : I conceived that by the *end of the earth* might be understood this *Island*. And I knew not, but that the Lord who often works by naturall meanes, might have design'd and made choice of me for the bringing about this work. With these proposals therefore, I applyed my self, in all zealous affection to the *English Nation*, congratulating their glorious liberty which at this day they enjoy ; together with their prosperous peace.

<hr />

[1] *Infra*, pp. 143-145.

Introduction

And I entituled my book named *The Hope of Israel,* to the first Parliament, and the Council of State. And withall declared my intentions. In order to which they sent me a very favorable passe-port. Afterwards I directed my self to the second, and they also sent me another. But at that juncture of time my coming was not presently performed, for that my kindred and friends, considering the checquered, and interwoven vicissitudes, and turns of things here below, embracing me, with pressing importunity, earnestly requested me not to part from them, and would not give over, till their love constrained me to promise, that I would yet awhile stay with them. But notwithstanding all this, I could not be at quiet in my mind (I know not but that it might be through some particular divine providence) till I had anew made my humble addresses to his Highnesse the Lord Protector (whom God preserve), and finding that my coming over would not be altogether unwelcome to him, with those great hopes which I conceived, I joyfully took my leave of my house, my friends, my kindred, all my advantages there, and the country wherein I have lived all my lifetime, under the benign protection, and favour of the Lords, the States Generall, and Magistrates of *Amsterdam , in fine* (I say) I parted with them all, and took my voyage for *England.* Where, after my arrivall, being very courteously received, and treated with much respect, I presented to his most Serene Highnesse a petition, and some desires, which for the most part, were written to me by my brethren the *Jewes,* from severall parts of *Europe,* as your worship may better understand by former relations. Whereupon it pleased His Highnesse to convene an Assembly at *Whitehall,* of Divines, Lawyers, and Merchants, of different persuasions, and opinions. Whereby men's judgements, and sentences were different. Insomuch, that as yet, we have had no finall determination from his most Serene Highnesse. Wherefore those few *Jewes* that were here, despairing of our expected successe, departed hence. And others who desired to come hither, have quitted their hopes, and betaken themselves some to *Italy,* some to *Geneva,* where that Commonwealth hath at this time, most freely granted them many, and great privileges."

II. The Hope of Israel

The first point in Menasseh's story which needs elucidation is his statement that he was originally induced to move in the question of the resettlement of the Jews by the assurances of "some eminent persons of England," that "the minds of men stood very well affected towards us." How had this philo-Semitic sentiment arisen, and who were the men who had communicated it to the Amsterdam Rabbi?

The evolution of English thought which rendered Menasseh ben Israel's enterprise possible is of considerable complexity, but its main features are easily distinguishable. The idea of Religious Liberty in England was due, in its broader aspects, to the struggle between the Baptists and the Calvinists. The Reformation established only a restricted form of Religious Liberty, and it was not until the Baptists found themselves persecuted as the Reformers had been before them, that the cry arose for a liberty of conscience which would embrace all religions. In the Separatist Churches, founded by English refugees in Amsterdam and Geneva, the idea grew and strengthened. The earliest noteworthy tract on the subject—Leonard Busher's "Religious Peace, or a Plea for Liberty of Conscience," published in 1614—was written under the influence of these exiles, and it is noteworthy that already in that work the extension of religious liberty to Jews was specifically demanded.[1] Amsterdam was at that time the seat of a flourishing Jewish community, some of whose members came into contact with the philo-Jewish refugees. In this way they probably learnt to understand the political significance of the successive rise of the Puritans and Independents, for at the very beginning of the Civil War the Royalist spies in Holland noted that the Jews sympathised

[1] Tracts on Liberty of Conscience, 1614–1661 (Hanserd Knollys Soc.), pp. 28, 30–31, 47, 71.

with the Republicans, and even alleged that they had offered them "considerable sums of money to carry on their designs."[1]

The progress of Religious Liberty in the seventeenth century reached its highest point, when in 1645 the Independents captured the Army under the scheme known as the "New Model." Meanwhile Roger Williams, the famous Baptist, who had already founded in America a community based on unrestricted liberty of conscience, had published his "Bloudy Tenent of Persecution," in which he generously pleaded for the Jews.[2] In 1646 a reprint of Leonard Busher's pamphlet was published in London, much to the joy of the Separatists in Amsterdam,[3] and a year later Hugh Peters, one of Cromwell's Army Chaplains, wrote his "Word for the Army and Two Words for the Kingdom," in which he proposed that "strangers, even Jews [be] admitted to trade and live with us."[4] The question of the readmission of the Jews was, however, still far from taking practical shape. Although frequently referred to, it had only been raised incidentally as an illustration of the advanced tendencies of the advocates of Religious Liberty.

In December 1648, the Independents contrived the famous "Pride's Purge," which put an end to the Presbyterian domination of Parliament. The hopes of the advocates of Religious Liberty ran high, and the Jewish question at once came to the front. The Council of Mechanics, meeting at Whitehall, marked their sense of the meaning of the *coup d'état* by immediately voting "a toleration of all religions whatsoever, not excepting Turkes, nor Papists,

[1] Hist. MSS. Com. Rep. VII., MSS. of Sir F. Graham, pp. 401–403.
[2] See reprint by Hanserd Knollys Soc., p. 141. For Roger Williams's services to the cause of Jewish Toleration, see Wolf, "American Elements in the Resettlement" (*Trans. Jew. Hist. Soc.*, vol. iii. pp. 77–78), and Straus, "Roger Williams, the Pioneer of Religious Liberty," pp. 172–178.
[3] Edwards, *Gangræna*, Part III. p. 103.
[4] Art. 10. See also his "Good Work for a Good Magistrate" (1651), pp. 53, 90.

nor Jewes."¹ To this the Council of Army Officers responded with a resolution, the text of which has, unfortunately, not been preserved, in which they favoured the widest scheme of Religious Liberty. It was, indeed, rumoured at the time that the Jews were specifically mentioned in the resolution.² However that may be, it is certain that in the following month two Baptists of Amsterdam, Johanna Cartwright and her son Ebenezer, were encouraged to present a petition to Lord Fairfax and the General Council of Officers, in which they asked that "the statute of banishment" against the Jews might be repealed. The petition, we are told, was "favourably received, with a promise to take it into speedy consideration when the present more public affairs are dispatched.³

Unfortunately, the "more public affairs" obstructed the triumph of Religious Liberty, and with it the Jewish cause, for a good many years. In the same month that Mrs. Cartwright's petition was considered, Charles I. was beheaded, and the chiefs of the Revolution, with a great work of reconstruction before them, felt that they must proceed cautiously. Toleration of the Jews meant unrestricted liberty of conscience, and this was held by the extreme Independents to imply not only the abolition of an Established Church, but a licence to the multitude of sects—many of them of the maddest and most blasphemous tendencies—which had been hatched by Laudian persecution and the reaction of the Civil War. Cromwell and his advisers were resolved to pursue a more conservative policy, and the toleration plans of the Independents were accordingly shelved. For a hundred years—until, indeed, Pelham's "Jew Bill" in 1753—they were not heard of in this purely secular shape again.

¹ *Mercurius Pragmaticus*, Dec. 19-26, 1648.
² Firth, "Notes on the History of the Jews in England, 1648-1660." *Trans. Jew. Hist. Soc.*, vol. iv.
³ "The Petition of the Jews for the Repealing of the Act of Parliament for their Banishment out of England" (Lond., 1649).

Introduction

The cause of Religious Liberty was, however, not the only force which was working in the country for the re-admission of the Jews. The religious fervour of the nation had been stirred to a high pitch, and there were few men whose minds had not become influenced by Messianic and other mystical beliefs. It is curious indeed to note that this current of thought ran parallel with the evolution of the secular idea of Toleration. Seven years after the first publication of Leonard Busher's famous Toleration pamphlet, Mr. Sergeant Finch wrote anonymously a book entitled "The Calling of the Jewes" (1621), with a prefatory epistle in Hebrew, in which he invited the children of Israel to realise the prophecies by asserting their national existence in Palestine. At the same time he called upon all Christian princes to do homage to the Jewish nation. This early manifestation of Zionism did not meet with much sympathy in high places, for James I. was so incensed at it that he clapped its publisher into jail.[1] The book, however, was a symptom, and the movement it represented only derived strength from persecution. The gloomier the lot of the sectaries, the more intense became their reliance on the Messianic prophecies. Even after the triumph of the Puritan cause, the sanest Independents held to them firmly side by side with their belief in Religious Liberty; and in the Cartwright petition we find both views expounded. Extremists like the Fifth Monarchy Men made them the pivots for fresh outbursts of Sectarianism. Judaical sects arose, the members of which endeavoured to live according to the Levitical Law, even practising circumcision. Prosecutions for such practices may be traced back to 1624.[2] Some of the saints, like Everard the Leveller, publicly called themselves Jews;[3] others went to Amsterdam, and were formally received into the synagogue.[4] Colchester was the

---

[1] Fuller, "A Pisgah-sight of Palestine," Book V. p. 194.
[2] Calendar State Papers. Dom. 1623-25, p. 435.
[3] Whitelock, "Memorials," p. 397.
[4] De Castro, *Auswahl*, loc. cit.

headquarters of one of these Judaical sects, but there were others in London and in Wales.[1] The practical effect of this movement was not only the production of a very wide-spread philo-Semitism, but a strong conviction that, inasmuch as the conversion of the Jews was an indispensable preliminary of the Millennium, their admission to England, where they might meet the godliest people in the world, was urgently necessary.

It was this feeling which, on the collapse of the Toleration movement in 1649, began to make itself most loudly heard. Edward Nicholas, John Sadler, John Dury, Henry Jessey, Roger Williams, and even Thomas Fuller, who was far from being a mystic, urged this view on the public, and an agitation for the Readmission of the Jews, as a religious duty outside the problem of Religious Liberty, was set on foot. This mystical agitation found a response in what to us must at first sight appear a strangely inappropriate quarter. It brought forth from Amsterdam a Latin pamphlet, entitled "Spes Israelis," with a prefatory address "To the Parliament, the Supreme Court of England," the author of which was Menasseh ben Israel, one of the Rabbis of the congregation. This pamphlet illustrates the inception of the enterprise for the Resettlement of the Jews in England, which its author endeavoured to carry out six years later.

Menasseh ben Israel was the son of a Marrano of Lisbon, who had suffered at the hands of the Inquisition, and had, as a result, taken up his abode in Amsterdam. Menasseh was educated under the care of Rabbi Isaac Uziel, and, at the age of eighteen, was ordained a Rabbi. He was an indefatigable student, became a mine of learning, an accomplished linguist, a fluent writer, and a voluble preacher. His attainments made considerable noise in the world, at a time when public attention was riveted on Biblical prophecy,

---

[1] Edwards, *Gangræna*, i. p. 121 ; ii. pp. 26, 31 ; "Middlesex County Records," vol. iii. pp. 186-87 ; *Anabaptisticum Pantheon*, p. 233 ; Hickes, *Peculium Dei*, pp. 19-26. There are many other scattered references in the literature of the period to this curious movement.

Introduction

and the question of its fulfilment through the Jews. His voluminous writings obtained for him a high reputation as a scholar, and the readiness with which he afforded information to all who corresponded with him made him many influential friends, who spread his fame far and wide. The secret of the distinction Menasseh secured for himself, in spite of the weaknesses of his character and the eccentricity of his mental tendency, lies in the fact that the world in which he lived was very largely given over to philo-Semitism, and to the special form of mysticism to which he had yielded himself. His alliance with a scion of the Abarbanel family, in whose tradition of Davidic descent he was a firm believer, inspired him with the idea that he was destined to promote the coming of the Messiah ; and hence the wild dreams of the English Millenarians appealed to him with something of a personal force. It was not, however, until the triumph of the Republican cause in England that he resolved to throw in his lot with the Puritan mystics, and even then he had some difficulty, as we may readily believe, in adopting an attitude which would at once conciliate the English Conversionists, and harmonise with his allegiance to the synagogue.[1]

At first his sympathies, like those of most of the leading members of the Amsterdam community, seem to have been Royalist, for in 1642 we find him extolling the queen of Charles I. in an oration.[2] In 1647 he was still far from recognising in the Puritan revolt a movement calling for his Messianic sympathy ; for, writing to an English friend in that year, he described the Civil War, not, as he afterwards believed it to be, as a struggle of the godly against the

---

[1] A good life of Menasseh ben Israel has yet to be written. Short biographies have been published by Kayserling (English translation in *Miscellany of Hebrew Literature*, vol. ii.) ; the Rev. Dr. H. Adler, Chief Rabbi of the British Empire (*Trans. Jew. Hist. Soc.*, vol. i.) ; and Graetz (*Geschichte der Juden*, vol. x.). None of these is exhaustive, or based on bedrock material.

[2] "Gratulação ao seren. Raynha Henri. Maria, dignissima corsorte ao august ; Carlo, Rey da Grande Britannia, Francia e Hebernia" (Amst., 1642).

ungodly, but as a Divine punishment for the expulsion of his co-religionists from Britain in the thirteenth century.[1] This letter is interesting as showing that his mind was then already beginning to be exercised by the Resettlement question; but he evidently had as yet no definite idea of taking any practical action. In the autumn of 1649 a method of action was suggested to him by a letter he received from the well-known English Puritan, John Dury, whose acquaintance he had made in Amsterdam five years previously.

A friend of John Dury, one Thomas Thorowgood, was deeply interested in the missionary labours of the famous evangelist, John Eliot, among the American Indians; and in order to prevail upon the philo-Jewish public to provide money for the support of the mission, had compiled a treatise showing that the American Indians were the Lost Tribes. This work was largely founded on the conjectures of the early Spanish missionaries, who had up to that time a monopoly of this solution of the Ten Tribes problem. It was written in 1648, and dedicated to the King, but the renewal of the Civil War in that year prevented its publication.[2] Thorowgood thereupon sent the proofs of the first part of the work to John Dury to read. It happened that Dury, while at the Hague in 1644, had heard some stories about the Ten Tribes which had very much interested him. One was to the effect that a Jew, named Antonio de Montezinos, or Aaron Levy, had, while travelling in South America, met a race of savages in the Cordilleras, who recited the *Shema*,[3] practised Jewish ceremonies, and were, in short, Israelites of the Tribe of Reuben. Montezinos had related his story to Menasseh ben Israel,

[1] Harl. Misc., vol. vii. p. 623; *infra*, p. lxxvii.
[2] Thorowgood, "Jews in America" (1660), Postscript to the "Epistle Dedicatory."
[3] The Declaration of the Unity of God, the fundamental teaching of Judaism (Deut. vi. 4-9). *Shema* means "Hear," and it is the first word of verse 4: "Hear, O Israel; the Lord our God is one God."

Introduction

and had even embodied it in an affidavit executed under oath before the chiefs of the Amsterdam Synagogue. As soon as Dury received Thorowgood's treatise, he remembered this story, and at once wrote to Menasseh ben Israel for a copy of the affidavit. The courteous Rabbi sent it to him by return of post,[1] and it was printed for the first time as an appendix to an instalment of Thorowgood's treatise, which, at Dury's instance, was published in January 1650.[2]

This incident, coupled with some letters he received from the notorious Millenarian, Nathaniel Holmes, came as a ray of light to Menasseh. For five years he had had Montezinos's narrative by him, and had not regarded it as of sufficient importance to publish. He had, perhaps, doubted the wisdom of publishing it, seeing that it tended to substantiate a theory of purely Jesuitical origin, for which no sanction could be found in Jewish records or legend. Moreover, he had no strong views on the prophetical bearing of the question, as we may see by a letter he addressed to Holmes as late as the previous summer, in which he stated that he had grave doubts as to the time and manner of the coming of the Messiah.[3] Now, however, the question began to grow clear to him, and it dawned upon him that the long-neglected narrative of Montezinos might be used for a better purpose than the support of Christian missions in New England. The story was, if true, a proof of the increasing dispersion of Israel. Daniel had foretold that the scattering of the Holy People would be the forerunner of their Restoration, and a verse in Deuteronomy had explained that the scattering would be "from one end of the earth even to the other end of the earth." It was clear from Montezinos and other travellers that they had already reached one end of the earth. Let them enter England

[1] Dury, "Epistolary Discourse to Mr. Thomas Thorowgood" (1649).
[2] Thorowgood, "Jews in America" (1650), pp. 129 *et seq.*
[3] The text of the letter has not been preserved, but its contents are summarised in Holmes's reply, printed in an appendix to Felgenhauer's *Bonum Nuncium Israeli.*

and the other end would be attained. Thus the promises of the Almighty would be fulfilled, and the Golden Age would dawn. " I knew not," he wrote later on, " but that the Lord who often works by naturall meanes, might have design'd, and made choice of me, for bringing about this work."[1] In this hope he wrote the famous מקוה ישראל which in 1650 burst on the British public under the title of the " Hope of Israel."

The central idea of this booklet did not occur to Menasseh immediately on receiving John Dury's letter. His first intention, as he explained in a letter dated November 25, 1649, was to write a treatise on the Dispersion of the Ten Tribes for the information of Dury and his friends. The volume, however, grew under his pen, and a week later he announced to Dury his larger plan. His letter gives a complete synopsis of the work, and he finishes up by informing Dury that " I prove at large that the day of the promised Messiah unto us doth draw near."[2] Thus he had already made up his mind on a question which, only a few months before, he had assured Holmes was " uncertain," and was intended to be uncertain. Holmes was at the time unaware of his conversion, for, on December 24, he wrote to him an expostulatory letter, in which, curiously enough, he advised him to study the Danielic Prophecies.[3] Still, Menasseh does not seem to have fully grasped the application of his treatise to the Resettlement question, for neither in the body of the work nor in the Spanish edition does he refer to it. It was only when he composed the Latin edition that his scheme reached maturity. To that edition he prefixed a dedication to the English Parliament, eulogising its stupendous achievements, and supplicating " your favour and good-will to our nation now scattered almost all over the earth."

[1] *Vindiciæ Judæorum, infra,* pp. 143–144.
[2] Dury, "Epistolary Discourse." For text of the letters, see *infra,* p. lxxviii. [3] *Bonum Nuncium,* loc. cit.

Introduction

The tract produced a profound impression throughout England. That an eminent Jewish Rabbi should bless the new Republican Government, and should bear testimony to its having "done great things valiantly," was peculiarly gratifying to the whole body of Puritans. To the Millenarians and other sectaries it was a source of still deeper satisfaction, for their wild faith now received the sanction of one of the Chosen People, a sage of Israel, of the Seed of the Messiah. Besides the Latin edition which Dury distributed among all the leading Puritans, and which was probably read in Parliament, two English editions issued anonymously by Moses Wall were rapidly sold. Nevertheless, its effect proved transitory. Sober politicians, who still recognised that the new-fledged Republic had, as Fairfax said, "more public affairs" to despatch than the Jewish question, had begun to fear lest their hands might be forced by Menasseh's *coup*. This feeling was strikingly reflected in a tract by Sir Edward Spencer, one of the members of Parliament for Middlesex. Addressing himself with feline affection "to my deare brother, Menasseh ben Israel, the Hebrewe Philosopher," he expressed his readiness to agree to the admission of the Jews on twelve conditions artfully designed to strengthen the hands of the sectaries who bebelieved that, besides the dispersion of the Jews, their conversion was also a necessary condition of the Millennium.[1] Spencer's tract was the signal for a revulsion of feeling. Sadler, afterwards one of Menasseh's firmest friends, threw doubts on the authenticity of Montezinos's story,[2] and Fuller

[1] This tract has been the source of a curious misunderstanding. Kayserling, who apparently never examined more of it than the title-page, on which the author is described as " E. S. Middlesex," ascribed it to " Lord Middlesex," and regarded it as favourable to Menasseh (*Misc. Heb. Lit.*, ii. p. 33). Had he looked at the Latin translation at the end he would have found the name of the author given in full. Moreover, the writer, so far from being philo-Semitic, expressly states that the object of his pamphlet was the " taking off the scandall of our too great desire of entertayning the unbeleeving Nation of the Jewes." Kayserling's errors have been adopted without inquiry by Graetz, Adler, and other writers.

[2] " Rights of the Kingdom," p. 39.

did not scruple to criticise the Zionist theory on practical grounds.[1] Even the faithful Jessey held his peace in tacit sympathy with Spencer's scheme. As for Menasseh, he showed no disposition to acquiesce in Spencer's proposals. The result was that the sensation gradually died away, though a few stalwart Tolerationists like Hugh Peters still clamoured for unconditional Readmission.[2]

Thus both the Toleration and Messianic movements proved unavailing for the purposes of the Jewish Restoration. There remained a third view of the question which made less noise in the world, but which was destined to bring about gradually and silently a real and lasting solution—the view of Political Expediency.

III. Cromwell's Policy

The statesmen of the Commonwealth, who knew so well how to conjure with human enthusiasm, were essentially practical men. To imagine that they were the slaves of the great religious revival which had enabled them to overcome the loyalist inspiration of the cavaliers is entirely to misconceive their character and aims. The logical outcome of that revival, and of the triumph of the Puritan arms, would have been the Kingdom of Saints, but Cromwell's ambition aimed at something much more conventional. Imperial expansion and trade ascendency filled a larger place in his mind than the Other-worldly inspirations which had carried him to power.

With the unrestricted Toleration principles of the Baptists he had no sympathy, and still less with the Messianic phantasies of the Fifth Monarchy Men which Menasseh ben Israel had virtually embraced. His ideas on Religious Liberty were certainly large and far in advance of his

[1] "Pisgah-sight of Palestine," Book V. pp. 194 *et seq.*
[2] "Good Work," &c., *loc. cit.*

times,[1] but they were essentially the ideas of a churchman. Their limits are illustrated by his ostentatious patronage in 1652 of Owens' scheme of a Toleration confined to Christians.[2] Still he was not the slave of these limits. The ingenious distinction he drew between the Papistry of France and that of Spain, when it became necessary for him to choose between them, and his complete disregard of the same principles in the case of the Portuguese alliance, show how readily he subordinated his strongest religious prejudices to political exigencies. As for the mystics and ultra-democrats, his views were set forth very clearly in his speech to the new Parliament in September 1651, when he opposed the Millenarians, the Judaisers, and the Levellers by name.[3] It is impossible for any one reading this speech side by side with Menasseh ben Israel's tracts to believe that the author of it had any sympathy with the wilder motives actuating the Jewish Rabbi.

What was it, then, that brought these two different characters so closely together? That the Readmission of the Jews to England was one of Cromwell's own schemes —part and parcel of that dream of Imperial expansion which filled his latter days with its stupendous adumbration and vanished so tragically with his early death—it is impossible to doubt. We have no record of his views on the subject, beyond a short and ambiguous abstract of his speech at the Whitehall Conferences, but there is ample evidence that he was the mainspring of the whole movement, and that Menasseh was but a puppet in his hands. His main motives are not difficult to guess. Cromwell's statecraft was, as I have said, not entirely or even essentially governed by religious policy. He desired to make England

---

[1] Writing to Crawford in 1643, he says : "The State, in choosing men to serve it, takes no notice of their opinions ; if they be willing faithfully to serve it—that satisfies. . . . Bear with men of different minds from yourself." Carlyle, "Cromwell's Letters and Speeches," i. p. 148.

[2] Gardiner, "History of the Commonwealth," vol. ii.

[3] Carlyle, "Cromwell's Letters and Speeches," vol. iii. pp. 23, 25, 26.

great and prosperous, as well as pious and free, and for these purposes he had to consider the utility of his subjects even before he weighed their orthodoxy. Now the Jews could not but appeal to him as very desirable instruments of his colonial and commercial policy. They controlled the Spanish and Portuguese trade; they had the Levant trade largely in their hands; they had helped to found the Hamburg Bank, and they were deeply interested in the Dutch East and West Indian companies. Their command of bullion, too, was enormous, and their interest in shipping was considerable.[1] Moreover, he knew something personally of the Jews, for he was acquainted with some of the members of the community of Marranos then established in London, and they had proved exceedingly useful to him as contractors and intelligencers.[2] There is, indeed, reason to believe that some of these Marranos had been brought into the country by the Parliamentary Government as early as 1643 with the specific object of supplying the pecuniary necessities of the new administration.[3]

Until the end of 1651 the Readmission question presented no elements of urgency, because there was a chance of its favourable solution without its being made the object of a special effort on the part of the Government or the legislature. By the treaty of coalition proposed to the Netherlands by the St. John mission early in 1651, the Jewish question would have solved itself, for the Hebrew merchants of Amsterdam would have *ipso facto* acquired in England the same rights as they enjoyed in Holland. That proposal, however, broke down, and as a result the famous Navigation Act was passed. The object of that measure was to exclude foreign nations from the colonial trade, and to dethrone the Dutch from their supremacy in the carrying

---

[1] *Trans. Jew. Hist. Soc.*, vol. i. pp. 73–74; vol. ii. pp. 17–18; Wolf, "Jewish Emancipation in the City" (*Jewish Chronicle*, Nov. 30, 1894); Graetz, *Geschichte*, vol. x. p. 19.

[2] Wolf, "Cromwell's Jewish Intelligencers" (Lond., 1891).

[3] S. R. Gardiner in the *Academy*, March 4, 1882.

and distributing traffic of Europe. Consequently it supplied a strong inducement to Jewish merchants—especially those of Amsterdam who were then trading with Jamaica and Barbados—to transfer their counting-houses to London. As such an immigration would have well served the policy embodied in the Navigation Act, it became desirable that some means of legalising Jewish residence in England should be found, and hence the question of Readmission was brought within the field of practical politics. This was the new form in which it presented itself. It was no longer a question of Religious Toleration or of the hastening of the Millennium, but purely a question of political expediency.

It appears that the St. John mission, when its failure became probable, was instructed to study the Jewish question, and probably to enter into negotiations with leading Jews in Amsterdam. Certain it is that its members saw a great deal of Menasseh ben Israel during their sojourn in Holland, and that Cromwell's benevolent intentions were conveyed to him. Thurloe, who was secretary to the mission, had several conferences with the Rabbi, and the Synagogue entertained the members of the mission, notwithstanding that public opinion ran high against them.[1] Strickland, the colleague of St. John, and formerly ambassador at the Hague, was ever afterwards regarded as an authority on the Jewish question, for he served on most of the Committees appointed to consider Menasseh's petitions. Still more significant is the fact that within a few weeks of the return of the Embassy a letter, the text of which has not been preserved, was received from Menasseh by the Council of State, and an influential committee, on which Cromwell himself served, was at once appointed to peruse and answer it.[2] Towards the end of the following year two passes couched

[1] *Vindiciæ Judæorum*, p. 5 ; *infra*, p. 111 ; "Humble Addresses," *infra*, p. 77.
[2] Cal. State Papers, Dom. (1651), p. 472.

in flattering terms were issued to the Rabbi to enable him to come to England.[1]

Meanwhile, the long-feared war broke out, and negotiations were perforce suspended. From 1652 to 1654 the popular agitation for the Readmission of the Jews spluttered weakly in pamphlets and broadsheets. In 1653 there was a debate in Parliament on the subject, but no conclusion was arrived at.[2] In the following year, shortly after the conclusion of peace, a new element was introduced into the question by the appearance on the scene of a fresh petitioner from Holland, one Manuel Martinez Dormido, a brother-in-law of Menasseh ben Israel, and afterwards well known in England as David Abarbanel Dormido.

The mission of Dormido was clearly a continuation of Menasseh's enterprise, and it was probably undertaken on the direct invitation of the Protector. With the restoration of peace on terms which rendered persistence in the policy of the Navigation Act indispensable, Cromwell must have been anxious to take the Jewish question seriously in hand. The negotiations opened by Thurloe with Menasseh in 1651 were probably resumed, and an intimation was conveyed to the Jewish Rabbi that the time was ripe for him to come to England and lay his long-contemplated prayer before the Government of the Commonwealth. Menasseh's reasons for not accepting the invitation in person are not difficult to understand. He doubtless refers to them in the passage from the *Vindiciæ* I have already quoted, where he says he was entreated by his kindred and friends, "considering the chequered and interwoven vicissitudes and turns of things here below, not to part from them."[3] His kindred and friends were wise. Owing to his quarrels with his colleagues in the Amsterdam Rabbinate his situation had become precarious, and it might have

[1] Cal. State Papers, Dom. (1651-52), p. 577 ; (1652-53), p. 38.
[2] Thurloe State Papers, vol. i. p. 387 ; Clarendon State Papers, vol. ii. p. 233.
[3] *Supra*, p. xvii.

become hopelessly and disastrously compromised had he, in the then incensed state of Dutch feeling against England—a feeling in which the leading Jews of the Netherlands participated—undertaken a mission to the Protector. Hence the delegation of the work to his brother-in-law. An indication of Menasseh's interest in the new mission is afforded by the fact that his only surviving son, Samuel ben Israel, was associated with Dormido, and accompanied him to London.

Unlike his distinguished relative, Dormido had nothing to lose by approaching Cromwell. A Marrano by birth, a native of Andalusia, where he had enjoyed great wealth and held high public office, he had been persecuted by the Inquisition, and compelled to fly to Holland. There he had made a fortune in the Brazil trade, and had become a leading merchant of Amsterdam, and one of the chiefs of the Synagogue. The conquest of Pernambuco by the Portuguese early in 1654 had ruined him, and he found himself compelled to begin life afresh.[1] He saw his opportunity in the mission confided to him by Menasseh. It opened to him the chance of a new career under the powerful protection of the greatest personality in Christendom. Unlike his brother-in-law, he had no Millenarian delusions. The Jewish question appealed to him in something of the same practical fashion that it appealed to Cromwell. While the Protector was seeking the commercial interests of the Commonwealth, Dormido was anxious to repair his own shattered fortunes.

On the 1st September he arrived in London, and at once set about drafting two petitions to Cromwell.[2] In the first of these documents he recited his personal history, the story of his sufferings at the hands of the Inquisition, and of the confiscation of his property by the Portuguese in Pernambuco. He expressed his desire to become a resident

---

[1] Wolf, "Resettlement of the Jews in England" (1888), p. 9.
[2] For text of these petitions see *Trans. Jew. Hist. Soc.*, vol. iii. pp. 88–93.

in England and a subject of the Commonwealth, and wound up by praying the Protector to use his good offices with the King of Portugal for the restitution of his fortune. The second petition was a prayer for the Readmission of the Jewish people to England, "graunting them libertie to come with theire famillies and estates, to bee dwellers here with the same eaquallnese and conveniences wch yr inland borne subjects doe enjoy." The petition, after a violent tirade against the Inquisition and the intolerance of the Apostolical Roman Church, pointed out that the Readmission of the Jews would be to the advantage of trade and industry, and would vastly increase the public revenues. These adroit appeals to the chief motives of the Protector's statecraft were followed by a suggestion that in the event of the prayer being granted the petitioner might be appointed to the control and management of the new community, with, of course, appropriate compensation for his services.

Despite their obviously selfish motives, Cromwell received these petitions with significant graciousness. They were at once sent to the Council, with an endorsement, stating that "His Highnes is pleased in an especiall manner to recommend these two annexed papers to the speedy consideracion of the Councell, that the Peticion may receive all due satisfacion and withall convenient speed." It is impossible not to be struck by the pressing nature of this recommendation, when it is considered that the chief petition dealt with a very large and important political question, and that its signatory was a man wholly unknown in England. Cromwell's action can only be explained by the theory that he was, as I have suggested, the instigator of the whole movement. Whether the Council were aware of this or not is impossible to say. They had as yet no decided opinions on the subject, but they saw that it was a large and difficult question, that its bearings were imperfectly known, and that its decision, either one way or the other, involved a very serious responsibility at a time when the religious element wielded so much power in the country, and withal so capriciously. At the personal instigation of the Protector, however, they consented to appoint a committee to consider the petitions. A month later, taking advantage of a meeting at which Cromwell was not present, the committee verbally reported, and the Council resolved, that it "saw no excuse to make any order."[1]

That Cromwell was disappointed by this result he speedily made clear. In regard to the Resettlement petition, he did not care to take the responsibility of giving a decision; but on the other petition he took immediate steps to afford satisfaction to Dormido, in spite of the refusal of the Council to have anything to do with it. He addressed an autograph letter to the King of Portugal, asking him as a personal favour to restore Dormido's property, or to make him full compensation for his losses.[2] Seeing that Dormido was an alien, and had absolutely no claim on the British Government, this personal intervention by Cromwell on his behalf affords a further strong presumption of his privity to the Jewish mission. It is also not a little significant that a few months later the Protector granted a patent of denization to Antonio Fernandez Carvajal, the chief of the little Marrano community in London, and his two sons.[3]

The question was, however, not allowed to rest here. Cromwell wanted an authoritative decision, which would enable him to do more than merely protect individual Jews, and it was clear that this could not be obtained unless a more important person than Dormido were induced to take the matter in hand. The question had to be raised to a higher level, and for this purpose it was necessary that it should make some noise in the country. Only one European Jew had sufficient influence in England to stimulate the popular

---

[1] State Papers, Dom. Interregnum, i. 75 (1654), pp. 596, 620.
[2] Rawl. MSS., A 260, fol. 57.   Text of this letter is given in *Trans. Jew. Hist. Soc.*, vol. iii. p. 93.
[3] *Trans. Jew. Hist. Soc.*, vol. ii. pp. 18, 45–46.

imagination, and to justify the Government in taking serious steps for the solution of the question. That man was the author of the "Hope of Israel." In May 1655 it was decided to send Samuel ben Israel back to Amsterdam to lay the case before his father, and persuade him to come to London.[1] There is no mystery as to who suggested this step. Menasseh in his diplomatic way merely tells us he was informed that his "coming over would not be altogether unwelcome to His Highness the Lord Protector."[2] There is, however, a letter extant from John Sadler to Richard Cromwell, written shortly after Oliver's death, in which it is definitely stated that Menasseh was invited "by some letters of your late royall father."[3] Sadler no doubt spoke from personal knowledge, for in 1654 he was acting as private secretary to the Protector, and the endorsement on Dormido's petitions recommending them to the Council bears his signature.[4] Under these circumstances we can well understand that Menasseh was induced, as he says, to "conceive great hopes," and that he resolved to undertake the journey. In October he arrived in London with the MS. of his famous "Humble Addresses" in his pocket.

During the five months that Menasseh was preparing for his journey, Cromwell was not idle. Colonial questions were occupying his mind very largely, and on these questions he was in the habit of receiving advice from one at least of the London Marranos, Simon de Caceres, a relative of Spinoza, and an eminent merchant who had large interests in the West Indies, and had enjoyed the special favour of the King of Denmark and the Queen of Sweden.[5] It was no doubt at the instigation of De Caceres that in April 1655 Cromwell sent a Jewish physician, Abraham de

---

[1] Cal. of State Papers, Dom., 1655, p. 585.
[2] *Supra*, p. xvii.   [3] *Infra*, p. lxxxvii.
[4] *Trans. Jew. Hist. Soc.*, vol. iii. p. 90.
[5] Wolf, "American Elements in the Resettlement" (*Trans. Jew. Hist. Soc.*, vol. iii. pp. 95–100); Wolf, "Cromwell's Jewish Intelligencers," 1891, pp. 11–12.

Introduction

Mercado, with his son Raphael to Barbados.[1] Later in the year he was deep in consultation with De Caceres in regard to the defences of the newly acquired island of Jamaica, and a plan for the conquest of Chili.[2] The most important result of these confabulations was a scheme for colonising Surinam (which since 1650 had been a British colony) with the Jewish fugitives from Brazil, who had been obliged to leave Pernambuco and Recife through the Portuguese reoccupation of those towns. The idea was, no doubt, suggested by Dormido, himself one of the victims of the Portuguese conquest. In order to attract the Jews, they were granted a charter in which full liberty of conscience was secured to them, together with civil rights, a large measure of communal autonomy, and important land grants.[3]

Thus a beginning was made in the solution of the Jewish question by their admission as citizens to one of the colonial dependencies of Great Britain. This was the first important step achieved by Cromwell, and it illustrates at once his deep interest in the Jewish question, and the practical considerations which actuated him in seeking its solution.

IV. The Appeal to the Nation

On his arrival in London, Menasseh, with his retinue of three Rabbis,[4] was lodged with much ceremony in one of the houses opposite the New Exchange, in the then

[1] Cal. of State Papers, Dom., 1655, p. 583.
[2] "Cromwell's Jewish Intelligencers," *loc. cit.*
[3] *Trans. Jew. Hist. Soc.*, vol. iii. pp. 82–86.
[4] Jacob Sasportas, who had acted as a "corrector" in Menasseh's printing-office in Amsterdam, and was afterwards elected Chief Rabbi in London, was a member of the mission (Graetz, vol. x. notes, p. xix). Raguenet states (*Histoire d'Oliver Cromwell,* p. 290) that two other Rabbis accompanied it, "Rabbi Jacob ben Azahel" and "David ben Eliezer of Prague." I have not been able to identify these persons, but tentatively I am disposed to think that "Azahel" is a corruption of "Heschel," and that the person referred to is Rabbi Josua ben Jacob Heschel of Lublin. Menasseh's elder son lived for some time in Lublin, and it is quite possible that Heschel came to London to lay the case of the persecuted Polish Jews before Cromwell.

fashionable Strand, the Piccadilly of its day. These houses were frequented by distinguished strangers who desired to be near the centre of official life at Whitehall, and the fact that Menasseh with his slender purse took up his abode in one of them, instead of seeking hospitality with his brother-in-law or his Marrano co-religionists in the city, shows at once the importance with which his mission was invested.[1] He was the guest of the Protector, bidden to London to discuss high affairs of state, and as such it was obviously inadmissible that he should be hidden away in some obscure address in an East-End Alsatia.

His first task after he had settled down in his "study" in the Strand was to print his "Humble Addresses," in which he appealed to the Protector and the Commonwealth to readmit the Jews, and stated the grounds of his petition. This tract was written and translated into English long before he left Amsterdam. It had probably been prepared three years before, when he first received his passes for England. That it was in existence at a time when his final mission was uncontemplated is proved by its mention in a list of his works he sent to Felgenhauer in February 1655 (N.S.).[2] The title is there given as *De Fidelitate et Utilitate Judaicæ Gentis*, and it is described as *Libellus Anglicus*. This was nine months before he arrived in London, and three and a half months before his brother-in-law sent for him. My impression is that the tract was prepared at the time of the St. John mission in 1651, and that Menasseh had drafted it in accordance with the advice of Thurloe, who had pointed out that the faithfulness and profitableness of the Jewish people were likely to weigh more with Cromwell than the relation of their dispersion to the Messianic Age.

At any rate, the style and matter of the pamphlet

---

[1] Wolf, "Menasseh ben Israel's Study in London," *Trans. Jew. Hist. Soc.*, vol. iii. pp. 144 *et seq.*
[2] Felgenhauer, *Bonum Nuncium Israeli*, p. 110.

are in welcome contrast to the fantastical theories of the
" Hope of Israel," resembling more the matter-of-fact
petition of Dormido. The Danielic prophecy is, it is true,
still asserted, but only as an aside, the case for the Readmission being argued almost exclusively on grounds of
political expediency. Incidentally certain floating calumnies
against the Jews—such as their alleged usury, the slaying
of infants for the Passover, and their conversion of Christians—are discussed and refuted. In regard to the conversion of Christians, Menasseh had completely changed
his attitude since writing the " Hope of Israel," for in that
work he had boasted of the conversions made by the Jews
in Spain.[1] The prudent restraints Menasseh had imposed
upon himself in the composition of this pamphlet are the
more marked, since we know that he had in no way
modified his original views as expounded in the " Hope
of Israel." This is shown by a letter he wrote to Felgenhauer early in the year, thanking him for dedicating to him
the *Bonum Nuncium Israeli,* one of the maddest rhapsodies
ever written.[2] In this letter he reiterated all his former
views, with the exception of his belief in the imminence
of the Millennium. Nor had he adopted any idea of com-
promising the question of the Readmission to meet the
prejudices or fears of the various political and religious
factions in England. His demand was for absolute freedom
of ingress and settlement for all Jews and the unfettered
exercise of their religion, " whiles we expect with you the
Hope of Israel to be revealed." The necessity of such a
privilege had been the more impressed upon him by the
renewal of the persecutions of his co-religionists in Poland,
which had sent a great wave of destitute Jews westward.
It was primarily for them and for the Marranos of Spain
and Portugal that he hoped to find an unrestricted asylum
in England.[3]

[1] *Infra,* p. 47.   [2] *Infra,* p. lxxix.
[3] Graetz, *Geschichte,* vol. x. pp. 52–82 ; *Mercurius Politicus,* Dec. 17,
1655 ; Thurloe State Papers, vol. iv. p. 333.

Introduction

Until the publication of the "Humble Addresses," there are but scanty clues in the printed literature of the time to the frame of mind in which Menasseh's mission found the English public. It would seem, from the silence of the printing-presses, that the nearer the people approached the Readmission question as a problem of practical politics, the less enthusiastic they became for its solution. This is not difficult to understand. The secular Tolerationists were unable to make headway against the dangers of unlimited sectarianism, to which their doctrines seemed calculated to open the door. Of their chief exponents, Roger Williams was in America, John Sadler was muzzled by the responsibilities of office, and Hugh Peters was without an influential following. Moreover, the prosecutions of James Naylor and Biddle were then prominently before the public as a lesson that Toleration had yet to triumph within the Christian pale. The Conversionists and Millenarians, who formed the great majority of the Judeophils, and who included all Menasseh's own friends except Sadler, attached no importance to the terms on which the Jews might be admitted, and were quite willing to acquiesce in legislative restrictions provided only they were admitted. The Economists and Political Opportunists, represented by Cromwell, Thurloe, Blake, and Monk,[1] did not dare to confess their true motives, since their worldly aims would on the one hand have been condemned by all the religious partisans of the Readmission, and on the other, would have alarmed the merchants of London, who had no desire for the commercial competition of a privileged colony of Hebrew traders.

This discouraging state of affairs was aggravated by foreign and Royalist intrigues. From the moment Menasseh's mission was thought of, the Embassies in London and the Royalist agents set to work to defeat it. The Embassies, especially that of Holland, opposed it on its true grounds,

[1] "Annals of England" (1655), vol. iii. p. 31.

Introduction

as a development of the policy of the Navigation Act.[1]
The Royalists were anxious to defeat it because, as Whitelock says, "it was a business of much importance to the
Commonwealth, and the Protector was earnestly set upon
it."[2] Moreover, they had hoped to attract the Jews to
their own cause, and they had been encouraged in this
hope by the substantial assistance already rendered to them
by wealthy Hebrews, like the Da Costas and Coronels.[3]
An intercepted letter from Sir Edward Nicholas, Secretary
to the exiled King, shows that the highest Royalist circles
took a profound interest in the Jewish question, and made
it their business to be well informed as to its progress.
Nicholas, indeed, seems to have known all about the negotiations which preceded Menasseh's journey to England.[4]

As soon as Menasseh reached London, he found himself the object of a host of calumnious legends, clearly
designed by the Royalists and foreign agents to disturb the
public mind. The story that the Jews had offered to buy
St. Paul's Cathedral and the Bodleian Library, which had
been circulated unheeded in 1649, was revived.[5] One of
Menasseh's retinue was accused of wishing to identify
Cromwell as the Jewish Messiah, and it was circumstantially
stated that he had investigated the Protector's pedigree in
order to prove his Davidic descent.[6] It was declared that
Cromwell harboured a design to hand over to the Jews the

[1] The interest of the Embassies in the question is illustrated by the frequent reference made to it in the despatches of Chanut (Thurloe, vol. ii. p.
652), Nieupoort (*Ibid.*, vol. iv. pp. 333, 338; "New York Colonial MSS.,"
vol. i. pp. 579, 583), Sagredo and Salvetti (*Revue des Études Juives*, No. 11,
pp. 103-104). Nieupoort's view is shown by the assurance he extracted
from Menasseh that there was no intention to invite Dutch Jews to England (Thurloe, vol. iv. p. 333).
[2] "Memorials," p. 618.
[3] *Trans. Jew. Hist. Soc.*, vol. i. pp. 70-71, 75.
[4] *Ibid.*, p. 44.
[5] *Infra*, p. 118. *London News Letter*, April 2, 1649 (Cartes Letters, vol. i.
p. 275).
[6] Jesse, "England under the Stuarts," vol. ii. p. 297; Tovey, *Anglia
Judaica*, p. 275.

farming of the customs.[1] At the same time their character
was painted in the darkest colours.[2] One of the most insi-
dious forms that this campaign took was an attempt to show
that the hope of converting the Jews, by which the larger
number of the friends of the Readmission were actuated, was
illusory, and that so far from becoming Christians, the Jews
would "stone Christ to death." For this purpose the pen
of a converted Jew, named Paul Isaiah, who had served as
a trooper in Rupert's Horse, was requisitioned.[3] It was a
hazardous experiment to employ Isaiah, for he might easily
have been hailed by the Conversionists as a proof of the
convertibility of the Jews. It was, however, notorious that
he had learnt the ethics of the wilder Cavalier swashbucklers
only too well,[4] and he was consequently regarded rather
as an "awful example" of the sort of Jew who might be
expected to listen to the Gospel than as an encouragement
to hope for the salvation of the whole people.

The publication of the "Humble Addresses" only
aggravated these popular misgivings. While the clerical
and commercial Anti-Semites disputed all the propositions
of Menasseh's pamphlet, the visionaries and friends of
Israel strongly resented the "sinfulness" of its insistence
on the profitableness of the Jews. The bias of public
feeling, as revealed by the tracts to which the "Humble
Addresses" gave rise, was distinctly less favourable than
in 1649, and was overwhelmingly hostile to an unre-
served acquiescence in the terms of the Jewish petition.
In 1649 an honest attempt to understand Judaism was
made, as we may see by the publication of Chilmead's
translation of Leo de Modena's *Historia dei riti ebraici*.
There is no trace of an appeal to this or any similarly

[1] Violet, "Petition against the Jews," p. 2.
[2] The violence of such tracts as Prynne's "Demurrer," Ross's "View of
the Jewish Religion," and the anonymous "Case of the Jews Stated," has
no parallel in the literature of the time.
[3] Paul Isaiah, "The Messias of the Christians and the Jews."
[4] Prynne, "Demurrer," Part I. p. 73.

Introduction

authoritative work in 1655–56, except in a stray passage
of an isolated protest against the calumnies heaped on the
Jews.[1]   On the contrary, the efforts of the new students
of Judaism, like Alexander Ross, were devoted to proving
that the Jews had nothing in common with Christians,
and that their religion " is not founded on Moses and the
Law, but on idle and foolish traditions of the Rabbins "—
that it was, in fact, a sort of Paganism.[2]   The historical
attacks on the Jews were the most powerful that had yet
been made, while the replies to them were few and by
obscure writers.[3]   What is most significant, however, is that
the chief friends of the Jews—the men who had encouraged
Menasseh six years before—were now either silent or openly
in favour of restrictions which would have rendered the
Readmission a barren privilege.   Sadler did not reiterate
the Judeophil teachings of his " Rights of the Kingdom ";
there was no echo of Hugh Peters's " Good Work for a
Good Magistrate," with its uncompromising demand for
liberty of conscience; and the pseudonymous author of
" An Apology for the Honourable Nation of Jews," which
had so strongly impressed the public in 1648, was dumb.
John Dury, who had practically started the first agitation
in favour of the Jews, was now studying Jewish disabilities
at Cassel, with a view to their introduction into England;[4]
and Henry Jessey, the author of " The Glory of Judah and
Israel," to the testimonies of which Menasseh confidently
appealed in the closing paragraph of his " Humble Addresses," had been won over to the necessity of restrictions.[5]
Not a single influential voice was raised in England in
support of Menasseh's proposals, either on the ground of

[1] Copley, "Case of the Jews is Altered," p. 4.
[2] "View of the Jewish Religion."
[3] See especially Prynne's "Demurrers," and "Anglo-Judæus," by W. H.
Only three ungrudging defences of the Jews were published—Copley's
"Case of the Jews," D. L.'s "Israel's Condition and Cause Pleaded" (a
very feeble reply to Prynne), and Collier's "Brief Answer."
[4] Dury, "A Case of Conscience." Harl. Misc., vol. vii. p. 256.
[5] "Life of Henry Jessey," pp. 67–68.

love for the Jews or religious liberty. The temper of the unlettered people, especially the mercantile classes, is sufficiently illustrated by the fact that only a few months before a Jewish beggar had been mobbed in the city, owing to the inflammatory conduct of a merchant, who had followed the poor stranger about the Poultry shouting, " Give him nothing ; he is a cursed Jew." [1]

Undeterred by the inhospitable attitude of the public, Menasseh formally opened his negotiations with the Government of the Commonwealth. His first step was to pay a visit to Whitehall, and present copies of his " Humble Addresses " to the Council of State. He was unfortunate in the day he selected for this visit, for it happened to be one of the rare occasions when Cromwell was not present at the Council's deliberations. The result was that, as on the similar occasion of the consideration of the report on Dormido's petition, the Council felt itself free to take no action. It contented itself with instructing its clerk, Mr. Jessop, " to go forth and receive the said books," and then proceeded with other business. [2]

That the Council had no desire to assume the responsibility of deciding the thorny Jewish question soon became manifest. A fortnight after Menasseh's abortive visit to Whitehall, Cromwell brought down to the Council a petition which had been handed to him by the Jewish Rabbi, in which were set forth categorically the several " graces and favours " by which it was proposed that the Readmission of the Jews should be effected. [3] The Protector evidently felt none of the misgivings of his advisers. It is probable, indeed, that in his masterful way he misunderstood the trend of public feeling. He had convinced himself that, as an act of policy, some concession to the Jews was desirable. His strong instinct for religious liberty

[1] Philo-Judæus, "The Resurrection of Dead Bones,' p. 102.
[2] State Papers, Domestic. Interregnum, vol. i. 76, p. 353.
[3] *Ibid.*, p. 374. For text of petition, see *infra*, pp. lxxxii–lxxxiv.

Introduction

inclined him favourably to the more academic aspects of
the question, and his profound sympathy with persecuted
peoples had been stirred by the accounts Menasseh had
personally given him of the dire straits of the Jews in
Poland, Sweden, and the Holy Land, and of the cruelties
inflicted on them in Spain and Portugal.[1] Moreover, his
patriotism revolted at the idea that Protestant England
should be *particeps criminis* in a policy of oppression which
was so peculiarly identified with Papistical error. Thus
impressed, he cared little for the outcries of the pamphleteers
or the nervous scruples of his councillors, and he set himself to force on a prompt solution. At his instance a
motion was made " That the Jews deserving it may be
admitted into this nation to trade and traffic and dwell
amongst us as Providence shall give occasion," [2] and this,
together with the petition of Menasseh and his " Humble
Addresses," was at once referred to a Committee. At the
same time it was made clear to that body that the Protector expected an early report.[3]

So much is evident from the fact that the Committee
met the same afternoon and reported the next morning.
Its task was not an easy one. The feeling of the Council
was by no means hostile to the Jews, but it had no
enthusiasm for their cause, and it probably felt that an extension of official toleration beyond the limits of Christianity was a hazardous experiment. On the other hand,
it was no longer possible for it to express this feeling in
the same unceremonious fashion as had been done in the
case of Dormido. The Jewish question had become the
question of the day owing to Menasseh's visit. Public
feeling had been deeply stirred by it, and Cromwell had
placed it in the forefront of his personal solicitude. Some
action was necessary. The Committee seems to have dis-
creetly resolved that the wisest course to pursue was one

[1] Harl. Miscellany, vol. vii. p. 618.
[2] *Infra*, p. lxxxiv.   [3] State Papers, Dom. Inter., i. 76, p. 374.

which would absolve it of responsibility, and leave Cromwell and the outside public to fight it out between them. Accordingly it reported that it felt itself incompetent to offer any advice to the Council, and it suggested that the views of the nation should be ascertained by the summoning of a Conference of representative Englishmen who might assist it in framing a report.

This resolution was duly reported to the Council on the following day, when Cromwell was again present. How little the Protector estimated the difficulties in his path is shown by the fact that the Committee's recommendation was at once acted upon. John Lisle, Sir Charles Wolseley, and Sir Gilbert Pickering, three members of the Committee notoriously devoted to Cromwell, were instructed to meet the Lord President the same afternoon, and draw up a list of the personages to be summoned to the proposed Conference.[1] The list was duly presented to the Council on the following morning, and, under the vigilant eye of the Protector, approved. At the same time the terms of a circular convening the Conference were agreed upon, and the 4th December was fixed for the meeting.[2]

Nothing is more significant than the rapidity with which these steps were taken. On Tuesday the 13th November Menasseh's petition was sprung on the reluctant Council. On the following Thursday summonses to a National Conference were being sent out from Whitehall, the Council having meanwhile held three meetings, at all of which the Jewish question was discussed, and a Committee specially charged with the question having held two further meetings. In all this we may clearly trace the personal insistence of the Protector.

Bruited abroad through the congregations of the divines and the constituents of the politicians and merchants to whom the summonses to the Conference had been addressed, the question of the Readmission of the Jews now came to

[1] State Papers, Dom. Inter., i. 76, p. 375.
[2] *Ibid.*, pp. 378–379. For text of Circular see *infra*, p. lxxxiv.

Introduction

the forefront of national politics. Amid considerable
popular excitement, the Conference met in the Council
Chamber at Whitehall[1] on the first Tuesday in December.

It was a notable gathering—one of the most notable in
the whole history of the Commonwealth. The statesmen
present were the most eminent on the active list of the
moment. There was Henry Lawrence, the Lord President,
with four of his civilian colleagues on the Council, Sir
Gilbert Pickering, Sir Charles Wolseley, Lisle the regicide,
and Francis Rous. Close by was Walter Strickland, the
diplomatist, who had represented the Commonwealth at
the Hague, and had shared with Oliver St. John the
honours and mortifications of the famous mission of 1651.
In the same inner circle were John Lambert, "the army's
darling," and one of the most brilliant of Cromwell's
veterans, and William Sydenham, one of the founders of
the Protectorate. The law was represented by Sir John
Glynne, Chief Justice of the Upper Bench, and William
Steele, Chief Baron of the Exchequer. Lord Chief Justice
St. John had also been invited, but he astutely stayed away.
Those who knew St. John must have regarded his absence
as ominous. On behalf of the mercantile community there
appeared Alderman Dethick, the Lord Mayor of London,
Alderman Cressett of the Charterhouse, Alderman Riccards,
and Sheriff Thompson. These men were official nonen-
tities, for the real representatives of Commerce were Sir
Christopher Pack, the late Lord Mayor and the leading
mercantile authority in the country, William Kiffen, the
wealthy merchant-parson, and the regicide Owen Rowe,
now deputy-governor of the Bermuda Company.

It was, however, on the religious side that the Conference
was strongest. Sixteen theologians and divines, the flower
of Puritan piety and learning, responded to Cromwell's
invitation. There was Dr. Cudworth, Regius Professor
of Hebrew, the philosophic opponent of atheism, whose

[1] *Publick Intelligencer*, December 10, 1655.

xlvii

"Intellectual System" is an English classic. There, too, were Dr. Owen, most famous of Independent divines and most fearless of the champions of religious liberty, and John Caryll, the great Puritan Bible commentator. Oxford University sent Dr. Goodwin, President of Magdalen College, and Henry Wilkinson, Canon of Christ Church. Cambridge appeared in the person of the learned Dr. Whitchcote, Provost of King's. Among the preachers were William Bridge of Yarmouth; Daniel Dyke, one of Cromwell's chaplains in ordinary; Henry Jessey, the Baptist Judeophil and friend of Menasseh; Thomas Manton, mildest and most genial of Presbyterians, "the prelate of the Commonwealth," as Wood calls him; Dr. Newcomen, one of the authors of "Smectymnuus"; Philip Nye, the sturdy Independent and champion of toleration; Anthony Tuckney, one of the most prominent divines of the Westminster Assembly, and three lesser lights, William Benn of Dorchester, Walter Craddock of All Hallows the Great, London, and Samuel Fairclough. John Carter, the vehement enemy of Presbyterianism and monarchy, could not attend, for he was on his deathbed at Norwich when the invitation reached him.[1]

It is not difficult to see that the Conference had been carefully organised with a view to a decision favourable to the Jews. The great majority of the members were conspicuous for their attachment to the cause of religious toleration, while not a few of the laymen were equally notorious for their devotion—some for their subservience —to Cromwell. And yet its upshot proved very different from what the Protector anticipated.[2]

The first meeting was chiefly concerned with the legal problem. After the proposals of Menasseh ben Israel had been read, Cromwell himself laid down the programme of the proceedings in two questions.

[1] The list of members is given in State Papers, Dom. Inter., i. 76, p. 378.
[2] *Publick Intelligencer*, loc. cit.

Introduction

(1) Whether it be lawful to receive the Jews?

(2) If it be lawful, then upon what terms is it meet to receive them?[1]

The first question was purely technical, and only the lawyers were competent to pronounce an opinion on it. Accordingly, the two Judges present, Glynne and Steele, were called upon to speak. After an elaborate review of the status of the Jews in the pre-expulsion period, and the circumstances under which they were banished in 1290, both expressed the opinion that "there was no law which forbad the Jews' return into England."[2] The grounds of this decision are nowhere stated. It was probably based on the fact that the banishment in 1290 was an exercise of the royal prerogative in regard to the personal "chattels" of the King and not an Act of Parliament, and that the force of the decree expired with the death of Edward I. At any rate, Cromwell had gained his first point,[3] and he joyfully adjourned the Conference to the following Friday, adjuring the divines meanwhile to ponder well the second question.[4]

What happened at the two following meetings, which were held on the 7th and 12th December,[5] we do not know in detail. The records of the time only afford us scanty glimpses of the opinions expressed, without any indication of the days on which they were respectively uttered. It is clear, however, that the feeling of the clergy turned out to be on the whole unfavourable to Menasseh's petition. The calumnies of the pamphleteers had done their work. The idea of public religious services at which Christ might be blasphemed stayed the hands of the most tolerant. Others

---

[1] [Henry Jessey.] "A Narrative of the late Proceedings at Whitehall Concerning the Jews, &c.," Harl. Misc., vii. p. 623. See also Burton (*pseud. i.e.* Nathaniel Crouch), *Judæorum Memorabilia.*   [2] *Ibid.*
[3] That the Judges' decision was given at the first meeting of the Conference is clear from a statement made by Nye to Prynne on the morning of the second meeting ("Short Demurrer," p. 4).
[4] *Publick Intelligencer,* loc. cit.   [5] *Ibid.*

xlix   *g*

feared that unrestricted liberty of Jewish worship would create in the Synagogue a nucleus round which the Judaical sectaries would rally. Dr. Newcomen drew a harrowing picture of English converts to Judaism joining the immigrants in offering children to Moloch.[1] The moderate majority, impressed, probably, by a weighty and elaborate opinion drawn up by Dr. Barlow, librarian of the Bodleian, and presented to the Conference by Dr. Goodwin,[2] were strongly in favour of an admission under severe restrictions. Even the level-headed Nye, who was ready to tolerate all religious follies so long as they were peaceable, asked for "due cautions warranted by Holy Scripture."[3] It was in vain that Lawrence and Lambert, supported by the learned commentator Caryll, combated these opinions.[4]

On the eve of the third meeting Cromwell sought to strengthen the Judeophils by adding to the Conference Hugh Peters, the oldest of the advocates of unrestricted Readmission, together with his favourite chaplain, Peter Sterry, and Mr. Bulkeley, the Provost of Eton.[5] This, however, did not improve matters, for Peters had meanwhile heard something of the Marranos in London and their papistical dissimulation of their religion, and he vigorously denounced the Jews as "a self-seeking generation" who "made but little conscience of their own principles."[6] This discourse seems to have produced a con-

---

[1] *Judæorum Memorabilia*, p. 170.

[2] Barlow, "Several Miscellaneous and Weighty Cases of Conscience" (1692), Fifth Treatise. See also p. 1 of the Bookseller's Preface. Rev. S. Levy believes (*Trans. Jew. Hist. Soc.*, iii. p. 152) that this opinion was drawn up at the request of Robert Boyle. This is improbable, as it is clear from the resemblances between Barlow's recommendations and the report ultimately drawn up by the Committee of the Council (*infra*, p. lxxxiv), that the opinion was submitted to the Whitehall Conference, and Boyle was not a member of that body. Goodwin, who was President of Magdalen College, is much more likely to have asked Barlow for the opinion, especially as we know that he was in favour of "due cautions" (*Jud. Mem.*, p. 174).

[3] *Jud. Mem.*, p. 174.   [4] *Ibid.*, pp. 170, 175.

[5] State Papers, Dom. Inter., i. 76 (1655), p. 412.

[6] This is shown by two letters in the Domestic State Papers (see *Trans. Jew. Hist. Soc.*, vol. i. p. 46).

siderable impression on the Conference, for Thurloe, writing to Henry Cromwell on the 17th, expressed the shrewd opinion that "nothing will be done."[1]

So far, however, the essential point for which Cromwell had been striving had not been jeopardised. He was desirous of securing the admission of the Jews on liberal terms, but at a pinch he would no doubt have agreed to religious and civil restrictions, provided the commercial activity of the immigrants was not unduly fettered. Hence the terms favoured by the majority of the clergy did not trouble him very seriously.

At the final meeting, which was held on the 18th December,[2] the commercial question was broached. On this occasion the doors of the Council Chamber were, for some sinister reason, thrown open to the public,[3] and an excited crowd, armed with copies of Prynne's newly published tract on the Jewish question,[4] collected to hear the debate. The proceedings were tempestuous from the beginning, and gradually they took the form of a vehement demonstration against the Jews. Merchant after merchant rose and violently protested against any concessions, declaring that the Hebrews were a mean and vicious people, and that their admission would enrich foreigners and impoverish the natives.[5] Even strangers took part in these tirades, and a Mr. Lloyd, who was not a member of the Conference, distinguished himself by a "fierce" harangue.[6] The climax was reached when Sir Christopher Pack, the most eminent citizen of his day, and a devoted adherent of the Protector, ranged himself with the opponents of Menasseh, in an

---

[1] Thurloe State Papers, vol. iv. p. 321.
[2] *Publick Intelligencer*, loc. cit.
[3] Spence's "Anecdotes," p. 77.
[4] "A Short Demurrer," Part I. The publication of the pamphlet was hurried to be in time for the Conference. It was written in seven days, and the preface is dated December 14, four days before the last meeting (*cf.* Preface to "Second Demurrer," 1656).
[5] *Jud. Memor.*, p. 175 ; Burton, "Diary," p. 309.
[6] Burton, *loc. cit.*

li

address which is said to have been the most impressive
delivered during the whole course of the Conference.[1]

The advocates of out-and-out exclusion were, however,
as little likely to carry the day as the champions of unrestricted admission, for the majority of the members of the
Conference were divines who were anxious that the Jews
should be converted, and for that reason desired that they
should be somehow or other brought into the country.
Moreover, since the decision of the Judges, the question was
no longer whether exclusion should be persisted in, but
only on what terms admission should be sanctioned. This
was probably pointed out to the merchants, and an attempt
to arrive at a compromise was made. After some private
confabulations, Henry Jessey rose to announce the terms
that had been agreed upon. The appearance of Jessey, the
profound Rabbinical student, the friend of Menasseh, and
one of the veterans of the Readmission cause, seemed to
betoken a Jewish victory. What must have been the
astonishment of his friends when he stated, with naïve
satisfaction, that the basis of the compromise was that the
Jews should only be admitted to decayed ports and towns,
and that they should pay double customs duties on their
imports and exports![2]

Cromwell now saw his whole scheme crumbling to
pieces. That, if put to the vote, Jessey's compromise
would be adopted by an overwhelming majority was patent
to everybody. In that case not only would the commercial
design which Cromwell had at heart be defeated, but the
Marranos in London, who had served him so well, would be
practically banished. At all hazards a vote had to be prevented.[3] Cromwell acted with characteristic promptness
and audacity. Rising from the chair of state, he addressed

---

[1] Burton, *loc. cit.*
[2] "Life of Henry Jessey," pp. 67–68.
[3] That Cromwell's interposition took place under these circumstances is
an inference of the present writer's. The statements in Jessey's "Life"
clearly point to this conclusion.

Introduction

the Assembly. Ingeniously ignoring the proposed compromise, he began his speech with a review of the differences of opinion revealed by the various speakers. They were, he scornfully declared, a babel of discordances. He had hoped that the Preachers would have given him some clear and practical advice, but they had only multiplied his doubts. Protesting that he had no engagements to the Jews but what the Scriptures held forth, he insisted that "since there was a promise of their conversion, means must be used to that end, which was the preaching of the Gospel, and that could not be done unless they were permitted to dwell where the Gospel was preached." Then, turning to the merchants, he harped sarcastically on the accusations they had brought against the Jews. "You say they are the meanest and most despised of all people. So be it. But in that case what becomes of your fears? Can you really be afraid that this contemptible and despised people should be able to prevail in trade and credit over the merchants of England, the noblest and most esteemed merchants of the whole world?" It was clear, he added sharply, that no help was to be expected from the Conference, and that he and the Council would have to take their own course. He hoped he should do nothing foolishly or rashly, and he asked now only that the Conference would give him the benefit of their prayers, so that he might be directed to act for the glory of God and the good of the nation.[1] So saying, he vacated the chair in token that the proceedings were at an end.

The speech was a fighting speech, delivered with great animation, and is said to have been one of the best Cromwell ever made.[2] It achieved its object, for the Conference broke up without a word of protest, and the crowds dis-

[1] These fragments of Cromwell's speech are gathered from Jessey's "Narrative," Crouch's *Judæorum Memorabilia*, pp. 175-176, and Spence's "Anecdotes," p. 77.
[2] Testimony by Rycaut, who was present in the crowd (Spence's "Anecdotes," p. 77).

persed in cowed silence. Cromwell left the Council Chamber in a towering passion, and it was some days before he recovered his equanimity.[1]

The battle was, however, not yet over. Cromwell had dismissed the Conference, but the Committee of the Council of State had yet to report. It could not well, in sober writing, take the view of the Protector's strategic speech, nor could it ignore the instruction of the Council to which it owed its existence. Accordingly it set itself to the drafting of a report which should express the obvious views of the Conference without conflicting too violently with Cromwell's equally obvious design. The report accepted the view of the Judges that there was no law against the Readmission, and then proceeded to set forth under six heads the views urged by the Conference, including the view of the merchants, that "great prejudice is likely to arise to the natives of this Commonwealth in matters of trade." Finally, it laid down seven conditions, apparently borrowed from Barlow's opinion,[2] by which the Readmission should be governed. The Jews should have no autonomous jurisdiction; they should be forbidden from blaspheming Christ; they should not profane the Christian Sabbath; they should have no Christian servants; they should be ineligible for public office; they should print nothing against Christianity, and they should not discourage those who might attempt to convert them, while the making of converts by them should be prohibited. No restriction on their trading was suggested.[3]

What became of this document is not clear. A clean copy of it, undated and unendorsed, is preserved in the

[1] Writing to Henry Cromwell about the Conference a week later, Thurloe says, "I doe assure you that his highness is put to exercise every day with the peevishness and wroth of some persons heere" (State Papers, vol. iv. p. 343).
[2] *Cf.* Conditions, ii., iii., iv., v., ix., xi., and xvii., in Barlow, "The Care of the Jews," pp. 67, 68, 70, 71, and 73.
[3] *Infra*, p. lxxxiv–lxxxv.

State Papers, but there is no reference to it in the Order Book of the Council of State.[1]   And yet it is certain that the Committee presented it to the Council, for the Conference was only a means of enlightening the Committee, and the Council still looked to it for advice.   It is probable that it was never formally accepted by the Council.   When it was in due course brought up, Cromwell most likely objected to its presentation.   After his experience of the Conference, it was clear to him that whatever was done would have to be done more or less unofficially.   The acceptance of the report would have involved legislation, in which case the proceedings of the Conference would have been repeated in a form far more difficult to control, and perhaps impossible to defeat.   Gratified by the omission of trade restrictions from the report, and feeling the necessity of retaining the support of the Council in the further steps he might take, the Protector probably assured them that he was in agreement with them on most points, and that he would do nothing unwarranted by the views they had expressed.   At the same time he doubtless pointed out that many other important questions claimed the attention of Parliament, and that it would be well if men's minds were not further disturbed by the Jewish question. Accordingly he advised that the report should be ignored and the matter allowed to drop.[2]

Here the question rested at the end of 1655.   The result was not encouraging, but at any rate one important point had been gained.   The prevailing idea that the incoming of Jews and their sojourn in the land were illegal

[1] In the Calendar of State Papers, Dom. (1655–1656), p. 15, it is hypothetically dated November 13, the day on which Menasseh's proposals were referred to the Committee.   This date is absolutely impossible, as the Committee could not have ascertained the views it reported to the Council in the course of a single afternoon.   If it was not drawn up on the 15th, it could not have been drawn up until the Conference was over, as the Conference was specifically summoned to advise the Committee.

[2] I have to thank Dr. Gardiner for this ingenious conjecture.   It entirely accords with all the known facts.

had been completely and finally shattered. This was the thin end of the wedge, and it had been so securely driven in, that John Evelyn entered in his Diary under date of December 14th: "Now were the Jews admitted."[1]

V. CROMWELL'S ACTION

Had the Diarist waited until the close of the Whitehall Conferences he would probably have modified his opinion. Although the technical question of the right of incoming had been decided, the cause of the Readmission had not been materially advanced. The universal demand for restrictions rendered it impossible for the Jews to avail themselves of their legal right without an assurance of protection from the Government. As late as the following April no complete settlement on this point had been reached, for in the passage from the *Vindiciæ* already quoted, Menasseh wrote on the 10th of that month, "As yet we have had no finall determination from his most Serene Highnesse."[2]

What happened after the Conferences is somewhat obscure, owing to the reticence of the public records on the Jewish question. It is certain, however, that before Cromwell's death a favourable decision was arrived at, and that an organised Jewish community came into the light of day in London, protected by definite rights of residence, worship, and trade. This is proved by the petitions for the re-expulsion of the Jews presented to Charles II. on his arrival in London in 1660, and especially by a statement in a petition of the Lord Mayor and Aldermen of the City of London, that "in that grand Complicacon of mischeifs brought on yor Maties good subjects by ye corrupt interest of the late usurper *ye admission of Jews to a free cohabition and trade in these dominions* was found to be a most heavy pressure on yor Peticon^{rs.}"[3]

---

[1] Edit. Bohn, vol. i. p. 327.   [2] *Supra*, p. xvii.
[3] Guildhall Archives. Remembrancia, vol. ix. No. 44, pp. 1-18. I printed the text of this petition in full in the *Jewish Chronicle*, November 15, 1899.

Introduction

How had this free settlement been brought about? It is not altogether impossible to reconstruct the story, although the materials are scanty and vague.

Cromwell's parting speech to the Whitehall Assembly, and the continued residence of Menasseh in London, must have excited apprehension among the extreme Judeophobes. The decision of the Judges and the Protector's threat that he and the Council would take their own course rendered a formal proclamation of Readmission by no means improbable. On the other hand, the great bulk of the nation had shown itself unfavourable to the scheme, and there was just a chance that this might stay Cromwell's hand. This popular ill-feeling the anti-Semitic pamphleteers now set themselves to inflame. It was probably hoped by this means, if not to intimidate the Protector, at any rate to strengthen the Council in their resistance to his original programme.

The new year had scarcely dawned when the indefatigable pen of Prynne was again at work on an enlarged edition of his "Demurrer." In this work he especially devoted himself to the legal question, amplifying by some twenty pages his argument that the expulsion by Edward I. remained valid, and could only be reversed by an Act of Parliament. In February he published Part II. of the "Demurrer," containing a further instalment of documents relating to the history of the Jews in England in the twelfth and thirteenth centuries. The object of this work, which is a monument of research, and which until a generation ago was the chief printed source of our knowledge of the mediæval history of the English Jews, was to show that the Jews had never lived in England except under severe disabilities, and that they were a people of phenomenal viciousness, clippers of coin, crucifiers of children, and the blaspheming devotees of a ghastly blood cultus. Less learned, but not less virulent, was Alexander Ross, whose calumnious " View of the Jewish Religion " was published

about the same time. Several anonymous pamphleteers
followed suit. The campaign does not seem to have excited much agitation, but it probably had the effect of
deciding Cromwell not to attempt a public solution of
the question in the sense of his own private wishes and
of Menasseh's petition.

All that was urgent he had, indeed, already done.
Shortly after the termination of the Whitehall Conferences
he had verbally assured the London Marranos of his personal protection, and had given them permission to celebrate divine worship after the Jewish fashion, on condition
that the services were held in private houses.[1] These
favours were conveyed through John Sadler, no doubt in
order to avoid any further apprehensions of a reopening of
the Jewish question that might be aroused by granting an
audience to Menasseh. The restriction in regard to the
privacy of the services shows that Cromwell had definitely
resolved to adhere to his compromise with the Council and
to respect the spirit of their report. Legally the Jews were
entitled to celebrate divine worship in public, for, by the
repeal of the Recusancy Acts by the Long Parliament in
1650, the practice of every kind of religious duty, "either
of prayer, preaching, reading or expounding the Scriptures,"
had been legalised, the celebration of mass being alone excepted.[2] It would, however, have been dangerous for the
Jews to claim this right, and Cromwell no doubt pointed
out to them that, in that case, it would be necessary to
apply to Parliament for legislation, which could only have
taken the form of enacting the oppressive recommendations
of the Whitehall Conferences. Under these circumstances
the Marranos could not but acquiesce. That their desire
for synagogue services was entirely due to their Jewish
piety, or was animated by a craving for martyrdom, is,

[1] These grants are mentioned in a Jewish petition subsequently presented to Cromwell (*infra*, pp. lxxxv-lxxxvi).
[2] Gardiner, "Hist. of the Commonwealth," vol. i. pp. 396-97.

moreover, very unlikely. The outbreak of war with Spain had rendered it impossible for them to continue, in their guise of *Nuevos Cristianos*, to attend the services in the Spanish Ambassador's chapel, and as they were bound by the Act of 1650 to resort to some place "where the service or worship of God is exercised," they were confronted by the necessity of either posing as pseudo-Protestants or frankly practising Judaism. The former course was out of the question, especially after Hugh Peters's condemnation of their hypocrisy at Whitehall. Hence their request to be permitted to worship as Jews. By Cromwell's acquiescence in this request and his promise of protection a secret beginning in the way of Readmission had been informally accomplished.

This arrangement was, however, not destined to endure. It was an evasion of the will of the Whitehall Conferences —an attempt, as Graetz has well said, to readmit the Jews "nicht durch das grosse Portal sondern durch eine Hinterthür."[1] It was condemned to failure, too, because its secret could not be kept. Even before the end of 1655 Cromwell's intentions were known. In a scrap of a Royalist letter of intelligence, dated December 31, and preserved in the State Papers, the writer says, "The Jews, we hear, will be admitted by way of connivancy, though the generality oppose."[2] The secret arrangement with regard to divine worship was also soon bruited abroad. In a despatch dated January 28, 1656, Salvetti, the diplomatic agent of the Grand Duke of Tuscany, informed his master that "the affair of the Jews continues in the state I have already described; meanwhile they may meet privately in their houses, but they have not yet established a synagogue."[3] In a later despatch (February 4) he confirms

[1] Graetz, *Geschichte der Juden*, vol. x. p. 122.
[2] Cal. State Papers, Dom., 1655–56, p. 82.
[3] Brit. Mus. Add. MSS. 27962. In a despatch dated January 14, Salvetti refers to the Jewish question, but makes no mention of the arrangement respecting divine worship. On the same date, too, the well-informed Dutch

this information and amplifies it. "It is thought," he writes, " that the Protector will not make any declaration in their favour, but tacitly he will connive at their holding private conventicles, which they already do, in their houses in order to avoid public scandal." [1]

From the Royalist spies and the diplomatists the news was quickly conveyed to the anti-Semites in the City. Although the dangers of a Jewish immigration *en masse* and the scandal of a public synagogue had been averted, the enemies of the Jews—especially their competitors in trade—were not inclined to acquiesce without a struggle in the tacit toleration of even a small community of Hebrew merchants. But what could be done? As Jews the position of the intruders was legal, and any attempt to persecute them in that capacity would probably be resented in a disagreeable fashion by the masterful Protector. Moreover, as the most serious evils of the Jewish problem had been provided against, and the public mind was preoccupied with the war with Spain, it might be difficult to enlist a large measure of support in an agitation against the strangers. An opportunity for showing their teeth soon presented itself to the City merchants, and they were not slow to avail themselves of it.

Early in March 1656 a proclamation was issued by the Privy Council declaring all Spanish monies, merchandise, and shipping to be lawful prize. The ink of this document was scarcely dry—indeed it had not been formally published—when, on the denunciation of an informer, the house of Don Antonio Rodrigues Robles, a wealthy Spanish merchant and Marrano of Duke's Place, City, was entered by bailiffs armed with a Privy Council warrant instructing them to "seize, secure, and keep under safe

ambassador, Nieupoort, informed the States-General that it was generally understood that the Lord Protector would take no further steps (Thurloe State Papers, vol. iv. p. 328). It would seem, then, that the transaction took place between the 14th and the 28th January.

[1] *Ibid.*

custody all the goods and papers therein found." On the same day the Commissioners of Customs, acting under a similar warrant, took possession of two ships in the Thames, the *Two Brothers* and the *Tobias*, which were believed to be Robles's property.[1] On the face of it, this action seemed to have no connection with the Jewish question. The fact that the information on which the warrants were based was presented to the Council by so staunch a friend of the Jews as Thurloe suffices to show that its Jewish bearing was at first quite unsuspected. It was apparently the private enterprise of a perfidious scrivener named Francis Knevett, who, after obtaining the confidence of several members of the Marrano community in his professional capacity, had discovered that under the new proclamation he might betray them with advantage to himself.[2] This seems also to have been the view of Robles, for in a petition he immediately addressed to the Protector he disputed the validity of the seizures on the purely legal ground that he was a Portuguese and not a Spaniard, and that his rights as a Merchant Stranger, which were consequently unaffected by the war with Spain, had been unjustly invaded.[3] On this point the Council, to whom the petition was referred, ordered an inquiry, and one of its members, Colonel Jones, was deputed to take evidence.

Meanwhile some suspicion that the case was aimed at the newly acquired privileges of the Marranos seems to have got abroad. Many of the Jews in London were of Spanish birth, and others, though natives of Portugal, were probably endenizened Spaniards, since in their guise of *Nuevos Cristianos* they had held high office under the King of Spain.[4] It was clear, then, that if the case against Robles was established other prosecutions would follow, and in that way the

[1] State Papers, Domestic. Interregnum, cxxv., No. 38, i. 76, p. 604; i. 112, p. 289; cxxvi., No. 105.
[2] *Ibid.*, cxxvi., No. 105, iv.
[3] *Ibid.*, cxxvi., No. 105.
[4] *Trans. Jew. Hist. Soc.*, vol. i. p. 63.

small Jewish community would be broken up. The danger was all the greater since the protection and privileges so recently acquired by the Jews had only been granted verbally, and might easily be repudiated if public opinion proved too strong for the Protector. There was, however, no immediate reason why the leading Marranos, who had hitherto been in negotiation with Cromwell, should take up Robles's cudgels, for he belonged to a party in the Synagogue which had imbibed strong Royalist sympathies in Holland and France, and which, consequently, had kept itself aloof from Menasseh's Readmission campaign. They accordingly confined themselves to the presentation of a petition to the Protector, in which they asked that the "favours and protection" accorded to them, including the right of worship, might be confirmed in writing. At the same time they prayed for a license to acquire ground for a Jewish cemetery. This document was signed by Menasseh ben Israel, Antonio Fernandez Carvajal, and five other Marranos, but Robles was not among it signatories.[1]

Cromwell at once referred this petition to the Council, but the Lord President, apparently recognising that the Jewish question was coming up in a new form, held it back until the Robles case had been dealt with.[2] The fact that Robles was a Jew had, indeed, already been ascertained, and the belief that the prosecution was aimed at all his co-religionists was gaining ground owing to a new outburst of activity on the part of the anti-Semites. The anxiety of the Marranos at the shelving of their petition became accentuated by this agitation, and especially by the doubts which it seemed to be producing in the minds of some of their best friends. The wavering feeling in high places was made disagreeably manifest to them by a letter addressed to Menasseh ben Israel by John Sadler, in which that friend of the Jews

---

[1] State Papers, Dom. Interregnum, cxxv., 58. *Infra*, p. lxxxv.
[2] See endorsement of the petition. *Infra*, p. lxxxvi.

pointed out that the charges of ritual murder and *quasi* idolatry preferred by Prynne and Ross were being widely discussed, and that a public answer to them was urgently necessary.[1]   Before Menasseh's reply was written Colonel Jones presented an interim report to the Council, from which it appeared *inter alia* that Knevett had filed a further information denouncing other Marranos as Spanish subjects.[2]

It was now no longer possible to ignore the existence of an anti-Jewish conspiracy.   The first action of the Jews was to hurry forward the publication of Menasseh's reply to Prynne and Ross.   This took the form of the famous *Vindiciæ Judæorum*—the third tract printed in the present volume.   It was described merely as "A Letter in Answer to certain Questions propounded by a Noble and Learned Gentleman touching the reproaches cast on the Nation of the Jewes."   The date of its appearance, however, fixes its relation to the Robles crisis, for it was published ten days after Colonel Jones's report, while the seriousness of that crisis is strikingly illustrated by the urgent and earnest tone of the pamphlet.   Menasseh evidently felt that not only his own grandiose idea of a new asylum for Israel was at stake, but that even the small progress that had been achieved towards that end was threatened by a more rigid exclusion of the Hebrew nation.   He threw his whole soul into this fresh vindication of his people and their claims.   Nothing, indeed, that had come from his facile pen had been more dignified, more impressive, more convincing.   The vanity, the superficiality, the pretentious mysticism of his former works had gone.   He was no longer playing a part even to himself.   He was merely

[1] *Infra*, p. 107.   The hypothesis that John Sadler was the author of the letter which gave rise to the *Vindiciæ Judæorum* is based on the facts that he was at the time the go-between in the negotiations with Cromwell, that he was an intimate friend of Menasseh, and that he had already given some thought to the blood accusation and other charges against the Jews ("Rights of the Kingdom," p. 74).
[2] State Papers, Dom.   Inter., i. 77, April 1, 1656 ; cxxvi., No. 105, xi.

the champion of his people in a moment of their sore trial, writing from a heart whose every throb was for their welfare and their honour. The simple eloquence of this essay, its naïve garrulousness, the glimpses it yields of a pious, gentle, self-denying character, made it one of the most effective vindications of the Jews ever written. The best tribute to its value is afforded by the fact that it has since been frequently reprinted in all parts of Europe when the calumnies it denounced have been revived.

The *Vindiciæ Judæorum* was a fitting prelude to the dénouement that followed. With this certificate in their hands the Marranos felt that they might risk claiming their legal rights as Jews, and thus at once repudiate their Spanish nationality and challenge a settlement of their status in the country. The decision was a bold one, but there was shrewd method in its apparent rashness. If the Marranos were technically Spanish subjects, they were in reality testimonies to the intolerance of Spain which made that country, in Cromwell's words, "the natural, the providential enemy of England,"[1] and which was one of the grounds of the war. Like the Protestant traders whose liberty of conscience had been trampled on in Spain they also had been persecuted, though in a worse form. They were fugitives from the Inquisition, and consequently had a peculiar claim on the indulgence and consistency of the English people, who at that moment were filled with righteous horror at the religious policy of the "Popish enemy."

In pursuance of this idea Robles now addressed a fresh petition to the Protector, which reached the Council of State on the 15th April,[2] five days after the publication of the *Vindiciæ*. In this document the purely legal question of nationality was dropped, and Robles confined himself to reciting how he and his kindred had been persecuted by the Inquisition in Portugal and Spain, how his father had died

---

[1] Carlyle, "Cromwell's Letters and Speeches," vol. ii. p. 161.
[2] State Papers, Dom. Inter., cxxvi., No. 105, i. ; i. 77, No. 11.

Introduction

under torture, how his mother had been crippled for life, and other members of his family burnt or sent to the galleys because they were Jews. He related that he had sought refuge in England, "intending therein to shelter himselfe from those tiranicall Proceedings and injoy those Beneffitts and Kindnesse which this Comonwth ever aforded to aflicted strangers." He appealed to Cromwell's notorious sympathy for "afflicted ones," and especially "owr nation the Jews," and skilfully suggested that a continuance of his prosecution would be tantamount to the introduction of the Inquisition into England. A week later affidavits confirming the statements in this petition were signed by all the leading Marranos and handed to Colonel Jones.[1] Thus the Crypto-Jews threw off their disguise. In the investigations which followed, the existence of over twenty Jewish families in London was revealed, and it was given in evidence that many of them had resided for years in the country.

These tactics produced dismay in the ranks of the anti-Semites. Knevett made a last despairing effort to construct a fresh case against the Jews by trying to bribe Robles's servants to assist him in framing a new information. In this he failed.[2] The case was now quickly disposed of. On April 25th the Council of State, still anxious to avoid responsibility for a decision, sent all the papers to the Admiralty Commissioners, with a request for a prompt report. On May 11th the Commissioners summoned the witnesses before them, but extracted little else from them than that Robles was believed to be Portuguese, and that they were all victims of the Inquisition. On May 14th the Commissioners reported that they were unable to give a definite opinion on the question of nationality. Two days later the Council screwed up their courage to a decision,

[1] State Papers, Dom. Inter., cxxvi., No. 105, ii. and iii. Most of the documents in the Robles case have been printed as an appendix to my paper on "Crypto-Jews under the Commonwealth" (*Trans. Jew. Hist. Soc.*, vol. i. pp. 76-86). [2] *Ibid.*, cxxvi., No. 105, vi.

lxv

and, without giving any reasons, ordered all the warrants to be discharged, and reinstated Robles in the possession of his goods, premises, and ships.[1]

The Jewish battle was won, and nothing now remained but to secure the fruits of victory in an inexpugnable form. What followed is, in detail, a matter of conjecture, but the broad lines of the settlement we know from the petition of the Corporation of the City of London, already quoted. Rights of "cohabitation and trade in these dominions" were formally accorded to the Jews in writing.[2] That this happened before the end of 1656 we may gather from a statement of Cromwell's intimate friend, Samuel Richardson, who, in his "Plain Dealing," published in that year, says of the Protector, "He hath owned the poor despised people of God, and advanced many of them to a better way and means of living."[3] The first steps were probably taken on the 26th June, when the long-deferred petition of the Marranos for a license to acquire a burial-ground and for a confirmation in writing of their rights of residence and worship came up for consideration.[4] The Council, still reluctant to engage their responsibility, made no entry of the discussion in their Order Book, and it was probably arranged that Cromwell should personally confirm the Jewish right of residence, subject to an understanding that the spirit of the recommendations presented to the Council after the Whitehall Conferences should be

[1] State Papers, Dom. Inter., i. 77, pp. 44, 78; cxxvii., 21, 40; i. 77, No. 19.
[2] There is a tradition in the synagogues that written privileges were granted, and this conforms with all the other evidence relating to the campaign. The disappearance of these documents is not surprising, as many of the older documents belonging to the Sephardi congregation in London passed into private hands. Moreover, after the Restoration the congregations would naturally wish to destroy all evidence of their negotiations with the Protector. It is probable that these documents are referred to in the State Papers, where mention is made of "a Jew living in London who has produced great testimonies under the hand of the late Lord Protector." (Cal. State Papers, Dom., 1659-60, p. 291.)
[3] "Tracts on Liberty of Conscience" (Hanserd Knollys Soc.), p. 240.
[4] See Endorsement of Petition, *infra*, p. lxxxvi.

observed. The right to acquire a cemetery was certainly granted. Cromwell probably further engaged himself to instruct the London city authorities to place no impediments in the way of the Jews trading on an equality with other citizens.[1] On their side, the Marranos must have agreed not to assist in an indiscriminate immigration of their co-religionists, not to obtrude their worship and ceremonies on the public, not to engage in religious controversy, and not to make converts.[2] The restriction with regard to worshipping in private houses was also probably revised, and the maintenance of a synagogue, subject to the other conditions, sanctioned.[3] In February 1657 Antonio de Carvajal and another leading Marrano, Simon de Caceres, signed the lease for a Jewish cemetery in Mile End.[4] Shortly afterwards another result of the settlement was made public. Solomon Dormido, a son of David Abarbanel Dormido and nephew of Menasseh ben Israel, was admitted to the Royal Exchange as a duly licensed broker of the City of London, the authorities waiving in his favour the Christological oath essential to the induction of all brokers.[5] As wholesale trading in the City was

[1] A similar course had been taken with regard to Protestant refugees in the city on November 13, 1655. (Guildhall Archives : Rep. lxiv. fol. 8ᵇ.)

[2] Some of these restrictions are clearly indicated by Menasseh's disappointment at the settlement. The prohibition of proselytising has always been remembered as one of the conditions of the Readmission, and it was religiously observed until the Rabbinate of the present ecclesiastical chief of the Anglo-Jewish community. In 1752, when certain Ashkenazi Jews were making proselytes in London, the Parnassim of the Portuguese synagogue wrote to the authorities of the German congregation, calling their attention to this condition, and the proselytisers were ordered to desist from "pursuing such unlawful practices." In 1760 a Jew was expelled from the synagogue and deprived of his burial rights for this offence. (Minute Books of the Duke's Place Synagogue, 1752, 1760.)

[3] Violet, "The Petition Against the Jews" (1661), p. 2 : "Cromwell and his Council did give a toleration and dispensation to a great number of Jews to come and live here in London, and to this day they do keep *public worship* in the City of London, to the great dishonour of Christianity and public scandal of the true Protestant religion."

[4] Abstract of lease in *Jewish Chronicle*, November 26, 1880, communicated by Mr. Israel Davis.

[5] Guildhall Archives, Rep. lxxiii. fol. 213.

transacted exclusively through brokers, the admission of a Jew to that limited fraternity is a substantial proof of the acquisition of untrammelled trading rights by the new community.

The victory, it will be observed, secured to the local Marranos all they required, and in a measure realised the aims of Cromwell's own policy. To Menasseh ben Israel, however, it was no victory: it was a compromise of a purely selfish nature, which left his idea of a proclamation of a free asylum to the persecuted and scattered remnants of Israel as remote as ever. We may be certain that he did not hide his grief or his indignation. There is indeed abundant reason for believing that he quarrelled over it with the new Jewish community. His hopes of returning to his old position in Amsterdam were shattered, for the Dutch Jews, who had always shared the Stuart sympathies of their Christian compatriots, had formally abandoned him when they found they had nothing to gain from his mission, and had opened negotiations on their own behalf with the exiled king at Bruges.[1] He might, perhaps, have secured his future by becoming Rabbi of the London community had he been content to abide by the terms of the new settlement. This, however, he sturdily refused, and although he was deserted by all his friends, and his monetary resources were exhausted, he continued from his lodging in the Strand to urge on Cromwell the issue of the proclamation on which he had set his heart.

That he must have quarrelled with the London Marranos immediately after the settlement is shown by a letter he addressed to Cromwell towards the end of 1656, in which he asked for pecuniary help, and stated that he (the Protector) was "the alone succourer of my life in this land of strangers."[2] Cromwell responded with a gift of £25,

[1] Menasseh had assured Nieupoort that he did "not desire anything for the Jews in Holland" (Thurloe, iv. p. 333). The negotiations with Charles II. are recorded in Brit. Mus. Add. MSS. 4106, fol. 253.
[2] *Infra*, p. lxxxvi.

and in the following March granted him a pension of £100 a year, dating from February, and payable quarterly.[1] Unfortunately this pension was never paid, and Menasseh became overwhelmed with cares.[2] Nevertheless, for six months longer he doggedly pursued his mission. In September 1657 his only surviving son, Samuel ben Israel, who had remained with him in England, died.[3] Then his spirit broke. Begging a few pounds from the Protector[4] he turned his steps homewards, carrying with him the corpse of his son.

A broken and beggared man he met his family at Middelburg, in Zeeland. He was now bent with premature age. The comely, good-tempered face, with its quizzing eyes and dandyish moustache, so familiar to us in Rembrandt's etching, had become hollow-cheeked and hollow-eyed. From the crow's-feet under the temples the whiskers had grown wildly until they formed a white patriarchal beard.[5] It was the wintering touch of the hand of death. Two months later Menasseh died of a broken heart at the house of his brother-in-law, Ephraim Abarbanel, in the fifty-third year of his age.[6]

VI. The Real "Vindiciæ"

One more question remains to be elucidated. How did the seemingly precarious settlement of the London Jews manage to survive the wreck of the Commonwealth?

Both Menasseh and Cromwell had builded more solidly than they knew. If the solution of the Jewish question arrived at towards the end of 1656 was not wholly satis-

---

[1] Hist. MSS. Com. Rep., viii. pp. 94–95. Fifth Rep. of Dep. Keeper of Public Records, App. ii. p. 253.
[2] *Infra*, p. lxxxviii.
[3] *Ibid.*, p. lxxxvii.
[4] *Ibid.* Hist. MSS. Com. Rep., viii. p. 95.
[5] Compare frontispiece with portrait at p. 105.
[6] Kayserling, "Menasseh ben Israel." (Misc. of Hebrew Literature, Series ii. pp. 68, 93.)

factory, it was precisely in that fact that its real strength lay. Experimental compromise is the law of English political progress. From the strife of wills represented in its extremer forms by Cromwell's lofty conception of religious liberty on the one hand, and by the intolerance of the sectaries on the other, had emerged a compromise which conformed to this law, and which consequently made the final solution of the question an integral part of English political evolution. The great merit of the settlement was that while it disturbed little, it gave the Jews a future in the country on the condition that they were fitted to possess it.

The fact that in its initial stage it disturbed so little rendered it easy for Charles II. to connive at it. Had Menasseh ben Israel's idea been realised in its entirety, the task of the restored Monarchy would have been more difficult. London would have been overrun by destitute Polish and Bohemian Jews driven westward by persecution, some fanaticised by their sufferings, others plying the parasitic trades into which commercial and industrial disabilities had driven the denizens of the Central European Jewries.[1] Many of them would have become identified with the wild Judaical sectaries who were the bitterest enemies of the Stuarts, while the others would have given new life to the tradition of Jewish usury, which for nearly four hundred years had ·been only an historical reminiscence in the country. Under these circumstances, we can well conceive that a re-expulsion of the Jews might have been one of the first tasks of the Restoration.

From this calamity England and the Jews were saved by the restricted character of the compromise of 1656. When the Commonwealth fell to pieces the Jewish community of London consisted only of some forty or fifty families of wealthy and enterprising merchants, scarcely

[1] For the condition of the Ashkenazi Jews at this epoch see Graetz's *Geschichte*, vol. x. pp. 52–82.

Introduction

distinguishable in their bearing and mode of life from the best kinds of merchant-strangers hailing from Amsterdam, Bordeaux, Lisbon, Cadiz, and Leghorn.

Nevertheless, efforts to procure their expulsion were not wanting. Royalists who recognised in them a relic of the hated Commonwealth, merchants whose restricted economic science resented their activity and success, and informers who imagined that their toleration was a violation of English law, set to work early to denounce them. These manœuvres began, indeed, as soon as the breath was out of Cromwell's body. Only a few weeks after the Protector's death a petition was presented to Richard Cromwell demanding the expulsion of the Jews and the confiscation of their property.[1] At the same time, Thomas Violet, the notorious informer and pamphleteer, made a collection of documents bearing on the illegality of the Jewish settlement, which he submitted to Mr. Justice Tyril, together with an application that the law should be set in motion against the intrusive community. The worthy Justice shrewdly suggested to Mr. Violet that in the then confused political situation he would do well to take no action. It would, he opined, be only prudent to await the establishment of a stable Government before moving in so serious a matter.

A few months later Charles II. re-entered London, and the Commonwealth was at an end. Naturally, everybody looked to the new régime to redress the particular grievance or grievances he harboured against "the late execrable Usurper," and the anti-Jewish party was particularly prompt in its representations under this head. Scarcely had Charles arrived in the Metropolis when the Lord Mayor and Aldermen of the City of London presented to him a humble petition, bitterly complaining of the action of Cromwell in permitting the Jews to re-enter the land, and asking the

[1] [Richard Baker], "The Marchants Humble Petition and Remonstrance" (London, 1659), p. 17.

King "to cause the former laws made against the Jews to
be put in execution, and to recommend to your two Houses
of Parliament to enact such new ones for the expulsion of
all professed Jews out of your Majesty's dominions, and to
bar the door after them with such provisions and penalties,
as in your Majesty's wisdom should be found most agreeable to the benefits of religion, the honour of your Majesty,
and the good and welfare of your subjects."[1] The long
pent-up wrath of the City found full expression in this
petition, which must be read in its entirety to be appreci-
ated. Thomas Violet followed with another petition, which
was equally violent.[2] He declared that by law it was a
felony for any Jew to be found in England. He did not,
however, propose their expulsion, as he did not think that
would be the best way of turning them to profitable
account. His suggestion was in the first place that all
their estates and properties should be confiscated, and then
that they should be cast into prison and kept there until
ransomed by their wealthy brethren abroad. A third petition, dated November 30, 1660, is preserved among the
Domestic State Papers, but the names of the authors are
not given. It runs very much on the lines of the City
petition, but it admits the hypothesis of Jews residing in
England under license, provided they were heavily taxed.[3]

No direct reply to any of these petitions is recorded.
The views of the new Government are, however, no mystery.
In the first place, there was no real Jewish question in the
country, inasmuch as the Jews were very few, their character
was above reproach, and the practice of their religion was
conducted with so much tact and prudence that it was
impossible in sober truth to be moved by Violet's impas-
sioned complaint of "a great dishonour of Christianity and
public scandal of the true Protestant religion."[4] Conse-

[1] Guildhall Archives : Remembrancia, vol. ix. No. 44, pp. 1–18.
[2] Violet, "A Petition against the Jews" (London, 1661).
[3] State Papers, Dom., Charles II., vol. xxi. p. 140.
[4] "Petition," p. 2.

quently the Government were free to consider the question exclusively from the point of view of secular politics. Once regarded in this light the conclusion could not be long in doubt. Cromwell's maritime and commercial policy had been adopted by the statesmen of the Restoration, and the success of this policy—represented by the re-enacted Navigation Act—depended to no inconsiderable extent on toleration of the Jews.

Moreover, Charles was under personal obligations to the Jews, and had assured them of his protection even before he came by his own. The Jews of Amsterdam, and some of the wealthier Jews in London, had assisted him during his exile, especially the great family of Mendez da Costa and Augustin Coronel, the agent for Portugal and a personal friend of Monk.[1] Shortly after the mission of Menasseh ben Israel to Cromwell these Jews had approached Charles II. at Bruges and had assured him that they had neither assisted nor approved the Rabbi's negotiations. Thereupon General Middleton had been instructed to treat with them for their support to the Royalist cause, and Charles had promised that "they shall find when God shall restore his Majesty that he would extend that protection to them which they could reasonably expect, and abate that rigour of the law which was against them in his several dominions."[2] That these negotiations were not without practical result is beyond question, for the Da Costas and Coronels, as well as several other Jewish families, were exceedingly active on Charles's behalf during the last few years of the Commonwealth.

It must not be imagined that this Royalist activity represented any double-dealing on the part of the Jews. Those who, like Carvajal and De Caceres, had fled direct from the Inquisition to England, were faithful to Cromwell to the end. The Royalist Jews were men who had acquired their Cavalier sympathies in France and Holland, and shared

[1] *Trans. Jew. Hist. Soc.*, vol. i. pp. 71, 74-75.
[2] Brit. Mus. Add. MSS. 4106, f. 253.

them with their Christian fellow-citizens in those countries. None of them were parties to the negotiations with Cromwell in 1655-56, and none had ever affected Puritan sympathies. They probably had conscientious objections to Republicanism, for they were of the aristocratic Sephardi branch of Israel, with some of the bluest blood of Spain in their veins and immense wealth in their strong-boxes. Their dissent from their Puritan brethren was an early illustration of the falsity of the hypothesis of Jewish political solidarity, which is to this day a cherished delusion of the anti-Semites.

Charles II. did not confine himself to ignoring the anti-Semitic petitions. Having made up his mind that the Jews should be protected, he sought, like Cromwell, to throw the responsibility for his decision on the Constitutional Government. Before the end of 1660 an Order of the Lords in Council was sent to the House of Commons, recommending that measures should be taken for the protection of the Jews.[1] There is no record of any such measures having been adopted. It was probably felt that the most convenient course to pursue was to continue the policy of personal connivance inaugurated by Cromwell, as by that means men's minds would be least disturbed, and an experiment which was likely to produce good results would not be hampered. Moreover, should the experiment fail, it would be all the easier to deal with it if it had not received any legislative sanction.

Accordingly, the Jews passed from the personal protection of Cromwell to that of Charles. In 1664, when an attempt was made by the Earl of Berkshire and Mr. Ricaut to obtain their expulsion, the King in Council disavowed the scheme, and assured the Jews "that they may promise themselves the effects of the same favour as formerly they have had so long as they demean themselves peaceably and quietly with due obedience to his Majesty's laws and without scandal to his Government.[2] A similar course was

---

[1] Journal of the House of Commons, December 17, 1660.
[2] State Papers, Dom., Chas. II., Entry Book xviii. (1664), fol. 79.

Introduction

taken by the Privy Council in 1673 and 1685, when attempts were made by informers to prosecute the Jews for the exercise of their religion.[1]   Finally the King marked his personal gratitude to the Jews by knighting Coronel soon after the Restoration, and by a generous distribution of patents of denization among the members of the Synagogue.[2]

Thus the Cromwellian settlement was confirmed, and the path was definitely opened by which the Jews might win their way to the citizenship of the United Kingdom.

How that path was successfully trodden is a story which cannot be told in detail here.   Its main feature, how-ever, must be briefly referred to, for it supplies the justi-fication for the campaign which Menasseh ben Israel and Oliver Cromwell waged so gallantly on behalf of the Hebrew people in the first half of the seventeenth century.

The Jews won their way to English citizenship not because they remained the *servi cameræ*, which had been their status under the Norman and Angevin kings, and which they had practically resumed under the Protectorate and the Restoration, but because they literally realised the portraiture of the Hebrew citizen which Menasseh ben Israel vainly placed before the British nation in 1655 in his tract, *De Fidelitate et utilitate Judaicæ Gentis.*   In this way they gradually substituted for the personal protection of the Crown the sympathy and confidence of the nation.

Their old enemies in the City of London were their first converts.   The wealth they brought into the country, and their fruitful commercial activity, especially in the colonial trade, soon revealed them as an indispensable element of the prosperity of the City.[3]   As early as 1668 Sir Josiah Child, the millionaire governor of the East

[1] The text of these orders in Council has been printed by Webb, " The Question whether a Jew may hold Lands " (Lond., 1753), pp. 38-40.
[2] Some of these patents are printed by Webb in an appendix to " The Question," pp. 17-19.   For Coronel's knighthood see Le Neve's " Pedigrees of Knights," Harl. Soc. Pub. (1869).
[3] Wolf, " Jewish Emancipation in the City " (*Jew. Chron.*, November 30, 1894).

India Company, pleaded for their naturalisation on the score of their commercial utility.[1]   For the same reason the City found itself compelled at first to connive at their illegal representation on 'Change, and then to violate its own rules by permitting them to act as brokers without previously taking up the Freedom.[2]   At this period they controlled more of the foreign and colonial trade than all the other alien merchants in London put together.   The momentum of their commercial enterprise and stalwart patriotism proved irresistible.   From the Exchange to the City Council Chamber, thence to the Aldermanic Court, and eventually to the Mayoralty itself, were inevitable stages of an emancipation to which their large interests in the City and their high character entitled them.   Finally the City of London—not only as the converted champion of religious liberty but as the convinced apologist of the Jews—sent Baron Lionel de Rothschild to knock at the doors of the unconverted House of Commons as parliamentary representative of the first city in the world.

Jewish emancipation in England was, in short, the work of the English democracy—almost of the same democracy which in the thirteenth century had spued the Hebrews forth, when their kingly protectors had made their residence in the land conditional on their acting as the usurious instruments of the Royal Exchequer, and which in the seventeenth had resented their readmission under the influence of deeply rooted prejudices, inherited from that dark age.   It was no mere homage to the abstract principle of Religious Liberty like the emancipations on the Continent which, in the name of the Rights of Man, suddenly called forth the oppressed Jews from their Ghettos and bade them take up a new life, from which they were sundered by centuries of mediæval seclusion.   Religious Liberty in England broadened on more cautious lines.   Dissenters, Roman Catholics, and

---

[1] Child, "A New Discourse of Trade" (Lond., 1668), p. 5.
[2] Wolf, "Jewish Emancipation," *loc. cit.*

Introduction

Jews have each been taken into the bosom of the nation by separate legislative action, and as the result of practical demonstrations of the futility, nay, the disadvantage, of their exclusion. The gradual emancipation of the English Jews, first socially and then in the municipalities, enabled them to show that their civic qualities entitled them to the fullest rights of citizenship; and it was the realisation of this fact—not by statesmen or philosophers, but by their neighbours and fellow-citizens themselves—that eventually gave them the position they now enjoy.

The story of Jewish emancipation in England is the true *Vindiciæ Judæorum*—the avenging of Menasseh's broken heart and the vindication of his touching trust in his people. It is something more. It is one of many justifications of that fine conception of statecraft, deeply rooted in infinite sympathy with human freedom, which is the secret of Britain's greatness, and of which Oliver Cromwell must ever be regarded as the typical exponent in English history.

VII. DOCUMENTS

The following is a selection of the documents referred to in the foregoing narrative. They have been selected chiefly on account of their personal bearing on Menasseh's efforts :—

1. Fragment of a letter from Menasseh ben Israel to an unknown correspondent in London (Harl. Miscel., vol. vii. p. 623). The original was probably in French or Latin :—

" AMSTERDAM, *September* 5407 [1647].

" *Senhor, no pueda enar !* that is, sir, I cannot express the joy that I have when I read your letters, full of desires to see your country prosperous, which is heavily afflicted with civil wars, without doubt by the just judgment of God. And it should not be in vain to attribute it to the punishment of your predecessor's faults, committed against ours ; when ours being deprived of their liberty under deceitfulness, so many men were slain only because they kept close under the tenets of Moses, their legislator."

2. Abstract of a letter relating to the "Hope of Israel" from Menasseh ben Israel to John Dury (Thorowgood, "Jews in America," 1650, p. xvii). The original seems to have been in French :—

"AMSTERDAM, *November* 25, [1649].

"By the occasion of the questions you propose unto me concerning this adjoyned Narrative of Mr. Antonio Montezinos, I, to give you satisfaction, have written instead of a Letter a Treatise, which I shortly will publish & whereof you shall receive so many copies as you desire. In this Treatise I handle of the first inhabitants of America which I believe were of the ten Tribes; moreover that they are scattered also in other Countries, & that they keep their true Religion, as hoping to returne againe into the Holy Land in due time."

3. Portion of a letter on the same subject from Menasseh ben Israel to John Dury (Thorowgood, *ibid.*). Like the foregoing, the original was in French :—

"AMSTERDAM, *December* 23, 1649.

"[In my Treatise] I declare how that our Israelites were the first finders out of America; not regarding the opinions of other men, which I thought good to refute in few words onely; and I thinke that the ten Tribes live not onely there, but also in other lands scattered every where; these never did come backe to the second Temple, & they keep till this day still the Jewish Religion, seeing all the Prophecies which speake of their bringing backe unto their native soile must be fulfilled : So then at their appointed time, all the Tribes shall meet from all the parts of the world into two provinces, namely Assyria and Egypt, nor shall their kingdome be any more divided, but they shall have one Prince the Messiah the Sonne of David. I do also set forth the Inquisition of Spaine, and rehearse diuers of our Nation, & also of Christians, Martyrs, who in our times have suffered seuerall sorts of torments, & then having shewed with what great honours our Jews have been graced also by severall Princes who professe Christianity. I proue at large, that the day of the promised Messiah unto us doth draw neer, upon which occasion I explaine many Prophecies."

Introduction

4. Letter from Menasseh ben Israel to Paul Felgenhauer (*Bonum Nuncium Israeli*, pp. 87 *et seq.*) :—

" D. Paulo Felgenhauer,
     Salutem & Benedictionem, à
    Deo Israelis reprecatur,
     Menasseh Ben Israel.

"Bonum istud, in novissimis & afflictissimis hisce temporibus populo Israeli à te, Vir spectatissime, allatum Nuncium, tanto fuit animo meo gratius, quo, post tot seculorum aerumnas & tam diu protractas spes nostras, flagrantius idipsum exoptare non desino ; modò præ rei magnitudine verbis tuis fides constare possit. Siccine, Bonarum rerum Nuncie bone, in procinctune jam est, ut adveniat Deus noster, Miserator Nostrum, utque nobis Desiderium tot seculorum, Messiam caput nostrum, tam brevi sit missurus ? Siccine tempus illud imminere ais, quo Deus ; hactenus offensus & aversus à nobis, iterum Populum suum consolabitur, & redimet non solum â Captivitate hac plusquam Babylonicâ, à servitute plusquam Ægyptiacâ in qua jam elanguit præ morâ, sed & ab iniquitatibus suis, in quibus quasi consumptus est ! Vtinam tam Verum esset, quam Bonum Nuncium tuum, tibique, tam Credere possem quàm vellem ! Utcunque quæ ad gaudii nostri confirmationem ex scriptis Propheticis Signa adfers Adventus Messiæ (ut fatear quod res est) lubens amplector ; & quo plus animo meo volvuntur ea, hoc magis spes mihi inde aliqua affulgere videtur.

"Ad Primum quod attinet, apud nostros Rabbinos id signum in confesso est : quum enim necesse sit Imperia hujus mundi omnia corruere, antequam Regnum & Potestas & Magnitudo Regni detur Populo sanctorum Altissimi, cui omnes Reges servire & obedire oportet, inde non obscure sequitur, immediatè ante adventum illum Messiæ & Instaurationem Regni ipsius, magnas Conturbationes, Tumultus, seditiones, intestina & crudelissima Bella, Regnorum & Populorum hinc inde devastationes præcedere debere ; Quæres quod brevi sit effectum sortitura, ex præsenti Imperiorum Mundi facie vero haud dissimile videtur.

"De Elia, secundo Adventus Messiæ nostri signo, quod ais, non diffitemur, quin & gaudemus maxime, quod in eo nos Judæi cum selectissimis Christiani Nominis Viris, in unam eandemque sententiam concurrimus, fore illum ex nostrâ Gente oriundum. Verum enim vero Elias ille cum nondum comparuerit nobis, eo usque saltem suspendatur spes nostra necesse est : adeo ut, donec illum Deus nobis revelaverit, certi & indubitati quicquam de Messiæ Adventu statuere minus tuum videatur.

"De Tertio isto Adventus Messiæ signo quod ais, nempe de hac Regni Israelis per totum Terrarum orbem prædicatione, id mihi non solum verisimile videtur, sed & tale quid jam in lucem prorumpere & effectum sortiri haud obscurè videmus : quin & Prædicatorem istorum haud contemnendus numerus mihi ipsi per literas innotuit, qui ex diversis mundi partibus ad consolandum Sionem prodierunt; inter alios Viros Nobilitate & Doctrinâ insignes, qui ad manum jam sunt.   En ex Silesia habemus *Abrahamum à Frankenberg*, ex Borussiâ *Joh. Mochingerum*, ex Galliâ Autorem Libelli Gallico idiomate editi, *Du rappel des Juifs*.   Ex Angliâ quos non?   Nuper auctoritate publicâ *Nathanael Homerius*, SS. Theol. Doctor, librum in folio edidit anglico idiomate, de hac ipsa materiâ ; & *D. Henricus Jesse*, nobis librum Belgico idiomate de *Gloriâ Jehudæ & Israelis*; publicè dedicavit.   Plures allegare possem, qui instar Nubeculæ istius I Reg. 18 (quam Elias ascendentem de mari vidit, & subito in tantam molem excrevit ut totum Cœli expansum contegeret) Indies numero & virtute accrescunt, donec tandem totum Terrarum ambitum prædicatione suâ sint completuri : Vt autē aliquod hajus rei specimen, ad testimonium tuum confirmandum tibi, mi Paule prebeam ; selegi tibi aliquot Virorum istorum ad me literas, quæ jam præ manibus habebam, quas legere poteris, & mecum gaudere, de ijs qui dicunt nobis, *Ibimus in domum Domini, stabunt adhuc pedes nostri in atriis tuis Ierusalem ;* qui ad cor Ierusalem loquuntur, prædicantes salutem & dicentes Sioni, *Deus tuus Regnabit.*

"Sed præter hæc mitto quoque ad Te, Vir Doctissime, autographum Panegyrici cujusdam quem meo Nomini inscripsit D. *Immanuel Bocarus Frances y Rosales* alias *Jacobus Rosales Hebræus*, Mathematicus & Medicinæ Doctor eximius, quem Imperator Nobilitatis Insignibus & Comitis Palatini dignitate donavit; idque eâ potissimum intentione mitto, ut videat Dominus exstare adhuc & discerni ad hunc usque diem surculos ex stirpe Davidicâ ortum ducentes.   Denique ut desiderio tuo faciam satis, en quoque Catalogum librorum, quos vel in lucem edidi jam, vel edendos penes me in parato habeo, sive Latino sive Hispanico idiomate.   Hisce te Deo Patrum nostrorum ejusque gratiæ & benignitati animitus commendo, Datum Amsterodami An. 1655, die I Febr."

5. Enclosures in the foregoing, being a letter from Nathaniel Holmes, with a postscript by Henry Jessey (*Bonum Nuncium Israeli*, pp. 103–106):—

"Nunc sequitur Clarissimi Viri, Nathanaelis Homesii SS. Theol.

Introduction

Doctoris Anglici ad me Epistolium, datum 24 Decemb. An. 1649. cum Subscriptione Reverendi D. Henrici Jesse ei annexâ.

"Animus mihi fuit, citius adte scribendi, Vir egregie, otium non fuit, Nec hodie ita mihi vacat, ut menti meæ, tantisque tuis scriptis (quamvis expectatione paucioribus) satisfaciam. Nondum de loco decem Tribuum, ex tuis literis responsum accepi ; quod in meis desideratum fuit ; non astu, vel curiositate. Veritatem insequor, ne Impostores pro Ebræis nobis obstrudantur. Scripsit quidam nuperime, Innodos Novæ Angliæ decem Tribubus esse prognatos. Alii Tartyros esse contendunt. Alii alios. Discrucior animi, ne fallar, usque dum literas tuæ me fecerint certiorem. Delectari videris D. Nicolai Apologiâ. Spero (ne glorier) te plura (ne dicam majora) visurum, meo de Mille Annis prodeunte tractatu. Quod opus ita me tenet occupatum, ut meæ ad te ituræ morentur literæ. Martyres in tuis literis vox est ; quæ, ni fallor, veteri Testamento haud innotuit. Verum sub Novo, viri celebres, Christum, ejusque Evangelium, ad mortem asserentes, primi illud nomen obtinuerunt. Facilè tamen concedo, quoslibet veritatis alicujus testes, Martyres Græce dictos fuisse. Sed (parcatur nostræ libertati Conscientiæ, quam lubentissimè tibi inter scribendum indulsero) nec pontificii jam post Concilium Tridentinum ullatenus habeantur propriè Christiani : nec Martyrium esse mihi videatur, pro hodiernâ Legis Mosaicæ observatione animam deponere. Quippe Lex illa quoad usum, ex plurimis veteris Testamenti suffragiis, ante hoc abolenda esset. Deut. 18, v. 18, 19. Psal. 50. v. 6-15, 23. Iesaiæ 66, v. 1-3. Vt olim multis jam annis transactis, Iudei ubi maxima indulgetur libertas non sacrificantes, vosmetipsos tamen vere Deum colere arbitramini, Libet tamen, non obstanti hâc dicendi libertate nos edoceri, dedocerique, quâ in re â veritate subsidimus, vel hallucinamur. Tractatum itaque quem nominas *De debito Christianorum erga Ebræos affectu*, mittas ; ut quantum in me est, typis mandetur, & in publicum promoveamus. De tempore adventus Messiæ quod incertum pronuncias, idque incertum comprobares experientiâ ; in promptu est responsio ; Illud Danieli prius ignoranti, tandem revelatum est ; idque ex libris illius, nobis. Et quamvis nonnulli (quos nominas) computando hallucinantes, in errorum gyris, & labyrintho sunt involuti ; non tamen hâc ratione deponendæ sunt de eâ re (tanquam nullius usus) Prophetiæ. Quippe quod expectamus, Danielis more cap. 9. v. 2 & v. 21. ut jam Vesperi ætatem, quo propius accedunt

lxxxi   *l* liberationum periodi, eo clarius elucescant revelationes ad easdem spectantes. Ægyptii Ethnicorum barbariores (te teste Egregie Vir) nascendum Mosen præsentiscebant, nescientibus tunc Israelitis natum Liberatorem. Quidni etiam Christiani Scripturas amplexi, adventum vestræ Messiæ secundum præviderent? In cujus adventu, (pace eruditionis vestræ asserentis, quod stupens mirabar, *Vestram salutem in ejus Adventu non esse sitam*) fundatur nostra, præsertim vestra æterna salus. Si enim verum foret, eum nondum venisse, & posthæc illum venturum ambigitur, labitur omnis prophetiarum Compages, totumque veteris Testamenti Systema ruit. Et ita de Scripturarum veritate actum est; ut de salute tum nostrâ, tum vestrâ actum est. Quæ si quippiam asserere videantur, Christi Messiæ *passionem* (Psal. 22. Isa. 53) *resurrectionem* (Psal. 16) *ascensionem* (Psal. 68) *sessionem ad dextram Patris* (Psal. 110) *potestatem super omnia regnantem,* more Adami novissime creati (Psal. 2. Psal. 8) omnino asserunt. Quæ omnia acurate comparata, Messiæ Filii Davidis adventum, abitumque, reditumque, elenchicè satis demonstrant. Non novum urgeo Testamentum, quod æquis miraculorum portentis nobis commendatum fuit, ut vetus Israeli. Vobis tamen Hebræis libentissimè favemus, utinamque plus multò favere possemus; quamvis nec Meritum, nec pro merito (vox Bibliis ignota) quicquam expectamus. Merces ex gratiâ datur non merito. Malum possumus, qui perfecte peccamus, mereri; bonum in quo omnimodo deficimus. Malum itaque pro nostro, bonum pro Christi merito (si voce utar) nobis compensatur. Hominum (fateor) alter de altero mereri dicatur, ut egomet tibi (vir Candidissime) pro tuis literis me multum debere agnosco. Quin & universa vestræ Nationi, flexis genibus servire molior, ut sive Nos Vobis, Vosvè Nobis facti Proselytæ utrique juxta Isaiam, & Ezechielem, cæterosque Prophetas, in unam coeamus ecclesiam. Nec non (confido) dilectissimus noster Iesseus idem meditatur; cui literas communicavi tuas, ad me missas. Pudet multum me tamdiu siluisse, verum tibi rescribenti, duplâ quoad possim diligentiâ compensabitur.

"*A Tui Observantissimo,*

"Nathanaele Homesio.

"Tuis hisce ex animo attestatur, assentitur, negociis à scribendo jam detentus, qui Sionis pulverem commiseratur, qui hæc propriâ manu subscripsi   H. Iesse."

6. Original French text of Menasseh ben Israel's de-
lxxxii

mands on behalf of the Jews presented to Oliver Cromwell (S. P., Dom. Inter., ci. 115).

" Ce sont icy les graces et les faveurs qu'au nom de ma nation hebreue moy, Menasseh ben Israel, requiers a vostre serenissime altesse que dieu fasse prosperer et donne heureux succez en toutes ses entreprises comme son humble serviteur lui souhaitte et desire.

" I. La premiere chose que je demande a vostre Altesse est que nostre nation hebreue sont reçeue et admise en cestee puissant republique sous la protection et garde de vostre altesse comme les cittoiens mesmes et pour plus grande securité au temps advenir je supplie votre altesse de faire jurer (si elle l'a pour aggréable) à tous ses chefs et generaux d'armes de nous deffendre en toutes occasions.

" II. Quil plaise a vostre altesse nous permettre synagogues publiques non seulement en Angleterre, mais aussi en touts austres lieux de conqueste qui sont sous la puissance de Vostre Altesse et d'observer en tout nostre religion comme nous devons.

" III. Que nous puissions avoir un lieu ou cimetiere hors la ville pour enterrer nos morts sans estre molestes d'aucun.

" IV. Qu'il nos soit permis de trafiquer librement en toute sorte de marchandise comme les autres.

" V. Que (afin que ceux qui vendront soyent pour l'utilité des citoyens et viven san porter prejudice à aucun ni donner scandale) vostre serenissime Altesse elise un personne de qualité pour informer et recevoir passeport de ceux qui entreront, les quels estant arrivez le faira scavoir et les obligera de jurer et garder fidélité a vostre Altesse en ce peix.

" VI. Et pour n'estre point à charge aux juges du peix touchaut les contestations et differents qui peuvent arriver entre ceux de nostre nation que vostre serenissime Altesse donne licence aux chef de la synagogue de prendre avec soy deux ausmoniers de sa nation pour accorder et juger tous les differents de procez conforme à la loy Mosayque avec liberté toutefois d'appeler de leur sentence aux juges civils deposant premierement la somme à laquelle la partye aurait esté condamnée.

" VII. Que si paradventure il y avait quelques loix contraires à nostre nation juifve que premierement et avant toutes choses elles soient revoquées affin que par ce moien la nous puissions demeurer avec plus grande securité sous la sauvegarde et protection de vostre serenissime Altesse.

" Lesquelles choses nous concedant vostre serenissime Altesse nous demeurerons toujours les très affectionnés et obligez à prier Dieu pour la prospérité de vostre Altesse et de vostre illustre et très sage conseil. Qu'il luy plaise donner heureux succez à toutes lés enterprises de vostre Serenissime Altesse Amen."

7. Circular issued by Cromwell's Council convening the Whitehall Conference (S.P. Dom. Inter., i. 76, 1655, pp. 378–79).

"Sir,—His Highness the Lord Protector and the Council having determined of a certain number of persons (whereof yourself is one) to meet with a Committee of the Council on Tuesday the fourth of December next in ye afternoon neare the Council Chambers in Whitehall to the intent some proposalls made to his Highness in reference to the nation of the Jewes may be considered of you are therefore desired by his Highness & the Council to take notice thereof & so meet at the said time and place for the purpose aforesaid.

Signed in the name &
by order of the Council
He. Lawrence

Whitehall,   Presidt
   16 Novem. 1655."

8. Report of the Sub-Committee of the Council of State after the Conferences at Whitehall (S. P., Dom. Inter., ci. 118).

"*That the Jewes deservinge it may be admitted into this nation to trade and trafficke and dwel amongst us as providence shall give occasion.*[1]

"That as to poynt of conscience we judge lawfull for the magistrate to admit in case such materiall and weighty considerations as hereafter follow be provided for, about which till we are satisfyed we cannot but in conscience suspend our resolution in this case.

"1. That the motives and grounds upon which Menasseh ben Israel in behalfe of the rest of his nation in his booke lately printed in this English tongue desireth their admission in this commonwealth are such as we conceave to be very sinfull for this or any Christian state to receave them upon.

---

[1] Dr. Gardiner has suggested to me, and I agree, that this paragraph is not a recommendation, but the thesis of the report. It is the text of the "reference" to the Sub-Committee by the Council, and the succeeding paragraphs constitute the report upon it. See *supra*, p. xlv.

lxxxiv

"2. That the danger of seducinge the people of this nation by their admission in matters of religion is very great.

"3. That their havinge of synagogues or any publicke meetings for the exercise of their worship or religion is not only evill in itselfe, but likewise very scandalous to other Christian churches.

"4. That their customes and practices concerninge marriage and divorce are unlawfull and will be of very evill exemple amongst us.

"5. That principles of not makinge concience of oathes made and injuryes done to Christians in life, chastity, goods or good name have bin very notoriously charged upon them by valuable testimony.

"6. That great prejudice is like to arise to the natives of this commonwealth in matter of trade, which besides other dangers here mentioned we find very commonly suggested by the inhabitants of the city of London.

"7. We humbly represent.

"I. That they be not admitted to have any publicke Judicatoryes, whether civill or ecclesiasticall, which were to grant them terms beyond the condition of strangers.

"II. That they be not admitted eyther to speake or doe anything to the defamation or dishonour of the name of our Lord Jesus Christ or of the Christian religion.

"III. That they be not permitted to doe any worke or anything to the prophanation of the Lord's Day or Christian sabbath.

"IV. That they be not admitted to have Christians to dwell with them as their servants.

"V. That they bear no publicke office or trust in this commonwealth.

"VI. That they be not allowed to print anything which in the least opposeth the Christian religion in our language.

"VII. That so farre as may be not suffered to discourage any of their owne from uisnge or applyinge themselves to any which may tend to convince them of their error and turn them to Christianity. And that some severe penalty be imposed upon them who shall apostatize from Christianity to Judaisme."

9. Petition of the London Marranos to Oliver Cromwell (S. P., Dom. Inter., cxxv. 58) :—

"To His Highnesse Oliver Lord Protector of the Comonwelth of England, Scotland & Ireland & the Dominions thereof.

"The Humble Petition of The Hebrews at Present Residing in this citty of London whose names ar vnderwritten

" Humbly sheweth

" That Acknolledging The manyfold favours and Protection yor
Highnesse hath bin pleased to graunt vs in order that wee may with
security meete priuatley in owr particular houses to our Deuosions,
And being desirous to be favoured more by yor Highnesse wee pray
with all Humblenesse y^r by the best meanes which may be such
Protection may be graunted vs in Writting as that wee may therewth
meete at owr said priuate deuosions in owr Particular houses without
feere of Molestation either to owr persons famillys or estates, owr
desires Being to Liue Peacebly under yo Highnes Gouernement, And
being wee ar all mortall wee allsoe Humbly pray yor Highnesse to
graunt vs License that those which may dey of owr nation may be
buryed in such place out of the cittye as wee shall thineke conuenient
with the Proprietors Leaue in whose Land this place shall be, and
soe wee shall as well in owr Lifetyme, as at owr death be highly
fauoured by yor Highnesse for whose Long Lyfe and Prosperity wee
shall continually pray To the allmighty God.

MENASSEH BEN ISRAEL.
DAVID ABRABANEL.
ABRAHAM ISRAEL CARUAJAL.
ABRAHAM COEN GONZALES.
JAHACOB DE CACERES.
ABRAHAM ISRAEL DE BRITO.
ISAK LOPES CHILLON.

Oliver P.
    Wee doe referr this Peticon
            to the Consideracon of y^r Councill.
March y^e 24th
    16$\frac{55}{6}$.   (Endorsement)
                                                Hebrews

                                        y^e 25 March 1656
                                        dd by the Lord Presid^t
                                        Gentlemen ye 26
                                            June 1656."

10. Petition of Menasseh ben Israel to Oliver Cromwell, probably written at the end of 1656 (S. P., Dom.
Inter., cliii. 122):—

" To his Highness the Lord Protector.
" May it please your Highnesse, what modestie forbidds necessitie (that ingens telum) compells; that having bene long time very

Introduction

sickly (an expensive condition) I make my moan to your Highnesse, as the alone succourer of my life, in this land of strangers, to help in this present exigence. I shall not presume to prescribe to your Highnesse but haveing great experience of your greatnesse in compassions as well as in majestie, I lay myselfe at your feet, that am your infinit obliged supplicant & servant

"MENASSEH BEN ISRAEL."

11. Further petition from Menasseh ben Israel to Oliver Cromwell. It is endorsed "17 Sep. 1657" (S. P., Dom. Inter., clvi. 89):—

"To his Highnesse, the Lord Protector, the humble petition of Menasseh Ben Israel.

"May it please your Highnesse, my only sonne, being now dead in my house, who before his departure, engaged me to accompany his corps to Holland, & I indebted here, I know not which way to turn mee but (under God) to your Highnesse for help in this condition, emploring your bowells of compassion (which I know are great & tender) to supply me with three hundred pounds, & I shall surrender my pension seal & never trouble or charge your Highnesse any more, I am very sensible considering your great past kindnesse (which with all thankfullnesse I acknowledge) how highly-bold this my petition is, but the necessitie of my present exigence & my experience of your admirable graciousnesse to mee have layd mee prostrat at your feet, crying, Help, most noble prince, for God's sake, your most humble supplicant   MENASSEH BEN ISRAEL."

12. Petition on behalf of the widow of Menasseh ben Israel, addressed to Richard Cromwell by John Sadler (S. P., Dom. Inter., cc. 8):—

"To his Highness the Lord Protector the humble petition of John Sadler.

"Sheweth that although your petitioner being often pressed to present petitions in behalf of the Jewes did rather dissuade their comming hither, yet by some letters of your late royall father & others of note in this nation some of their synagogs were encouraged to send hither one of their cheife rabbines, Menasseh Ben Israel, for admittance & some freedome of trade in some of these ilands. And when he had stayed heere so long, that he was allmost ashamed to returne to those that sent him or to exact their maintenance heere where they found so little success after so many hopes, it pleased his Highnes & the councell to setle on the said Menasseh a pension of 100£ a yeare which ere long he offered to resigne for 300£ for present satisfaction of debts & other pressures which lay so heavy on him that at length he submitted to resigne his former pension for a new grant of 200£ to be presently paid as the councell ordered.

"But notwithstanding his stay & expense in procuring several seales, he never gott one penny of the said 200£ but at length with his heart ever broken with griefe on losing heer his only sonne and his presious time with all his hopes in this iland he got away with so much breath as lasted, till he came to Midleburg & then he dyed. Leaving a poore desolate widow (with other relations) who solemnly professed she had not money enough to lay him in the sepulchres of his fathers, but for the charity of some that lent or gave them money. It pleased allso your Highess late father to receive one or 2 of the same poore widowes letters to your petitioner (whom they both trusted in that business) & with his owne hands to commit them to the especiall care of Mr. secretary Thurloe who hath also divers times minded the same, but your Highness exchequer is so charged that there is little hope of obteining it there.

"May it please your Highnesse in compassion to the said poore widow & relations of a man so eminent & famous in his owne & meny other nations & for the honour of Christian religion with many other reasons, to order the said 200£ out of the contingencies for the councell or some other treasure where it may be speedily had and without fees allso if it may be according to former orders.

"And your petitioner shall desire to pray."

PEREGRINANDO QVÆRIMVS.

MENASSEH BEN ISRAEL THEOLOGVS ET PHILOSOPHVS HEBRÆVS.

נר רגלי
נר רגלי דנדיך

ÆTATIS SVÆ
ANNO XXXVIII

ANNO
MDCXLII

Salom Italia   Sculpsit

Doctrina hic voluit, voluitq̃ Modestia pingi
An poterit vúltús chartá referre dúos?
Hos ocúlos, hæc ora vide. Conuenit utrinque
Illa súos vúltús dixit, & illa súos.

D.I.

THE
HOPE OF ISRAEL

Written
By *MENASSEH BEN ISRAEL*,
An Hebrew Divine, and
Philofopher.

Newly extant, and Printed at *Am-*
ſterdam, and Dedicated by the Author, to
the High Court, the Parliament of *England*,
and to the Councell of State,

The ſecond Edition correḉed and amended.

Whereunto are added,
In this ſecond Edition, ſome Diſcourſes
upon the point of the Converſion of the
JEWES.

By MOSES WALL.

LONDON
Printed by *R. I.* for *Livewell Chapman* at the
Crowne in *Popes*-Head Alley, 1652.

TO THE
Parliament, The Supream Court of
ENGLAND,

And to the ***Right*** *Honourable the Coun-cell of State,* Menaffeh Ben Ifrael, *prayes God to give Health, and all Happineſſe :*

T is not one caufe alone (moft renowned Fathers) which ufeth to move thofe, who defire by their Meditations to benefit Mankind, and to make them come forth in publique, to dedicate their Books to great Men ; for fome, and thofe the moft, are incited by Covetoufneffe, that they may get money by fo doing, or fome peece of Plate of gold, or Silver ; fometimes alfo that they may obtaine their Votes, and fuffrages to get fome place for themfelves, or their friends. But fome are moved thereto by meere and pure friendfhip, that fo they may publickly teftifie that love and affection, which they bear them, whofe names they prefixe to their Books; let the one, and the other, pleafe themfelves, according as they delight in the reafon of the Dedication, whether it be good or bad; for my part, I beft like them, who do it upon this ground, that they may not commend themfelves, or theirs, but what is for publick good.

As for me (moft renowned Fathers) in my dedicating
A 2   this

(3)

this Difcourfe to you, I can truly affirm, that I am induced to it upon no other ground then this, that I may gain
your favour and good will to our Nation, now fcattered
almoft all over the earth; neither think that I do this, as if
I were ignorant how much you have hitherto favored our
Nation; for it is made known to me, and to others of our
Nation, by them who are fo happy as near at hand, to
obferve your apprehenfions, that you do vouchfafe to help
us, not onely by your prayers; yea, this hath compelled
me to fpeak to you publickly, and to give you thanks for
that your charitable affection towards us, and not fuch
thanks which come only from the tongue, but as are conceived by a grateful mind.

Give me leave therefore (moft renowned Fathers) to
fupplicate you, that you would ftil favor our good, and farther love us.   Truly, we men doe draw fo much the nearer to Divine nature, when by how much we increafe, by
fo much we cherifh, and defend the fmall, and weak ones;
and with how much diligence doe you performe this, moft
renowned Fathers? who though you feem to be arrived
to the higheft top of felicity, yet you do not only not defpife inferior men, but you fo wifh well to them, that you
feem fenfible of their calamity; you knowing how acceptable to God you are by fo doing, who loves to do good to
them who doe good.   And truly it is from hence, that of
late you have done fo great things valiantly, and by an un-
ufuall attempt, and things much to be obferved among
the Nations.   The whole world ftands amazed at thefe
things, and the eies of all are turned upon you, that they
may fee whither all thefe things do tend, which the great
Governour of all things feems to bring upon the world by
fo great changes, fo famoufly remarkable, of fo many Nations; and fo all thofe things which God is pleafed to
have

have fore-told by the Prophets, do, and ſhall obtain their
accompliſhment.   All which things of neceſſity muſt bee
fulfilled, that ſo *Iſrael* at laſt being brought back to his
owne place ; peace which is promiſed under the Meſſiah,
may be reſtored to the world ; and concord, which is the
only Mother of al good things.   Theſe things I handle more
largely in this Treatiſe, which I dedicate to you (moſt renowned Fathers) you cannot be ignorant, that it is not only not unprofitable, but very uſeful for States and Stateſ-
men, to fore-ſee the iſſue (which yet is ever in Gods
hand) of humaine Councells, that ſo they may obſerve,
and underſtand from Divine truth, the events of things to
come, which God hath determined by his Spirit in his
holy Prophets.   I know that this my labour will not be
unacceptable to you, how mean ſoever it be, which I truſt
you will chearfully receive, becauſe that you love our Nation, and as part of it, the Author of this Diſcourſe.   But
I intreat you be certain, that I pour out continual prayers
to God for your happineſſe.   Farewell, moſt renowned
Fathers, and flouriſh moſt proſperouſly.

Menaſſeh Ben Iſrael.

✠✠

Menaſſeh Ben Ifrael,
To the Courteous Reader.

Here are as many minds as men, about the originall of the people of America *and of the firſt Inhabitants of the new World, and of the* Weſt Indyes; *for how many men ſoever they were or are, they came of thoſe two,* Adam, *and* Eve; *and conſequently of* Noah, *after the Flood, but that new World doth ſeem wholly ſeparated from the old, therefore it muſt be that ſome did paſſe thither out of one (at leaſt) of the three parts of the world ſc.* Europe, Aſia, *and* Africa; *but the doubt is, what people were thoſe, and out of what place they went. Truly, the truth of that muſt be gathered, partly out of the ancient Hyſtories, and partly from conjeꝗures ; as their Habit, their Language, their Manners, which yet doe vary according to mens diſpoſitions ; ſo that it is hard to finde out the certainty. Almoſt all who have veiwed thoſe Countryes, with great diligence, have been of different judgements: Some would have the praiſe of finding out* America, *to be due to the* Carthaginians, *others to the* Phenicians, *or the* Canaanites ; *others to the* Indians, *or people of* China; *others to them of* Norway, *others to the Inhabitants of the* Atlantick Iſlands, *others to the* Tartarians, *others to the ten Tribes. Indeed, every one grounds his opinion not upon probable arguments, but high conjeꝗures, as will appeare farther by this Booke. But I having curiouſly examined what ever hath hitherto been writ upon this ſubjeꝗ doe finde no opinion more probable, nor agreeable to reaſon, then that of our* Montezinus, *who ſaith, that the firſt inhabitants of* America, *were the ten Tribes of the* Iſraelites, *whom the* Tartarians *conquered, and drove away; who after that (as God would have it) hid themſelves behind the Mountaines* Cordilleræ. *I alſo ſhew, that as they were not driven out at once from their Country, ſo alſo they were ſcattered into divers Provinces, ſc. into* America, *into* Tartary, *into* China, *into* Media, *to the Sabbaticall River, and into* Æthiopia. *I prove that the ten Tribes never returned to the ſecond Temple, that they yet keepe the Law of* Moſes, *and our ſa-*
cred

(6)

cred Rites; and at laſt ſhall return into their Land, with the two Tribes, Judah, *and* Benjamin; *and ſhall be governed by one Prince, who is* Meſſiah *the Son of* David; *and without doubt that time is near, which I make appear by divers things; where, Reader, thou ſhalt finde divers Hiſtories worthy of memory, and many Prophefies of the old Prophets opened with much ſtudy, and care. I willingly leave it to the judgement of the godly, and learned, what happy worth there is in this my Book, and what my own Nation owes me for my paines: It is called,* The Hope of Iſrael; *which name is taken from* Jerem. 14. 8. *O the hope of Iſrael, the Saviour thereof. For the ſcope of this Diſcourſe is, to ſhow, that the hope in which we live, of the comming of the Meſſiah is of a future, difficult, but infallible good, becauſe it is grounded upon the abſolute Promiſe of the bleſſed God.*

And becauſe I intend a continuation of Joſephus *his Hiſtory of the* Jewes, *our famous Hiſtorian; I intreat, and befeech all Learned men, in what part of the world foever they live (to whom I hope that ſhortly this Diſcourſe will come) that if they have any thing worthy of poſterity, that they would give me notice of it in time; for though I have collected many Acts of the* Jewes, *and many Hyſtories out of the* Hebrewes, *the* Arabians, *the* Grecians, *the* Latines, *and other Authors of other Nations; yet I want many things for this my enterprize, all which I am willing to performe, that I may pleaſe my Nation; but rather to the glory of the bleſſed God, whoſe Kingdome is everlaſting, and his Word infallible.*

The

The Tranflator to the Reader.

His difcourfe of a Jew comming to my hand, and having perufed it, I thought it not inconvenient to make it fpeake *Englifh*; for the benefit of my Country-men, who wait for the redemption of *Ifrael*; and at the fame time of the *Gentiles* alfo. That the Author is a *Jew*, ought to be no fcandall to us (though fome of us Chriftian *Gentiles* are ignorant of, and fcandalized at the notion of the converfion of the *Jewes*, as the *Jewes* of old were, concerning our being converted, and grafted into the true Stock, as in *Acts* 11. 3.) for though God hath rejected them, yet not for ever: *Rom.* 11. 25, 26. And alfo the many prophefies both in the Old, and New Teftament, which concern their being received againe to grace, gathered from their difperfion, and fettled in their own Land; and their flourifhing eftate under, now our, and then their and our Prince, Jefus Chrift the Meffiah, who will then triumph glorioufly, and all his people with him; thefe and many more Promifes would want a fulfilling (which the God of Truth wil never fuffer) if there fhould not be the revolution of a time, in which they fhall be converted, and grace and peace be poured out upon *Jewes* and *Gentiles*; though firft upon the *Jew*, then the *Gentile*. But befides this, the Author expreffeth fo much learning that he deferveth honour of all; fo much ingenuity, and (fo far as his light reacheth) fo great a meafure of the knowledge and fear of God, that he may wel be fet for a pattern to us Chriftians, who profefs much better than he, but live much worfe. One thing is very remarkable in him, that wheras many of us (like them who canot fee Wood for Trees) though inviorned with mercies in thefe late revolutions, (I fpeake not to them who meafure mercies only, or chiefly, by plentiful tables, ful purfes, rich accoutrements, and the like; that wretched Generation is unworthy of the name of *Men*, much more of *Chriftians*) yet will unthankfully cry out, What have we got by all thefe troubles? and what hath been done? furely

ly

(8)

ly this *Jew* fhall rife up in judgement againft fuch unchriftian Chriftians; for he in his Epiftle Dedicatory fays, *The whole world ftands amazed at what the Parliament hath done;* befides he cordially and openly owns the Parliament, who as far as I know never did him nor his Nation any further good then to pray for them; (*though we hope, and pray, that their favour may extend to realities, towards that people, to whom certainly God hath made many, and great Promifes, and fhortly will give anfwerable performances:*) but many among us who injoy peace under them, and many other bleffings, (too many for an unthankfull Generation) doe refufe to acknowledge them, doe curfe them whom God hath bleffed, and even in their prayers to that God who cannot be deceived, or impofed upon ; doe vent themfelves againft this prefent Government, in expreffions fo wilde and falfe, that fuch Language would be accounted moft unworthy, in our addreffe to any confiderable perfon, much more then to the great God. I fhall only adde this, *fc.* Do not think that I aime by this Tranflation, to propagate or commend *Iudaifme* (which its no wonder if the Author doth fo much favour, efpecially in his thirtieth Section) no, through Grace I have better learned the truth, as it is in Jefus, but to give fome difcovery of what apprehenfions, and workings there are at this day in the hearts of the *Jewes;* and to remove our finfull hatred from off that people, whofe are the Promifes, and who are beloved for their Fathers fakes; and who of *Jewes,* we fhall hear to be, ere long, reall Chriftians.

B   The

(9)

The Authors of other Nations, which are quoted in this Treatife.

A
ABrahamus Ortelius
Agathias
Auguftinus
Alexis Vanegas
Alfonfus Cemedro
Alonfus Auguftianus
Alonfus de Erzilla
Alonfus Venerus
Arias Montanus.

B
Baronius
Berofus
Boterus
Bozius.

C
Conftantinus

D
Diodorus Siculus
Dion
Duretus.

E
Efelius Geradus
Eufebius Cefarienfis.

F
Famianus Strada
Francifcus de Ribera
Francifcus lopez de Gomara.

G
Garcilaffus dela Vega

Genebrardus
Goropius
Guil. Poftellus
Guilielmus Blawius
Guil. Schilkardus.

H
Henricus Alangre
Hugo Grotius

J
Jacobus Verus
Joan. de caftillanos
Joan. de Bairos
Joan. Roman
Joan. de Laet
Joan. Huarte
Jofephus d' Acofta
Joan. Linfcboten.

L
Lefcarbotus
Lucanus.

M
Manuel Sa.
Marcilius Facinus
Marinus.

N
Nicolaus Trigautius.

O
Origines
Orofius
Oforius Lufitanus.

P
Petrus de Cleza
Plancius
Petrus Simon
Petrus Hernandes de Quiros
Petrus Teixera
Pineda
Plato
Plinius
Pomarius
Proclus.
Porphyrius
Poffevinus
Plutarchus
Picus Mirandulanus
Ptolomæus.

S
Semuel Bochardus
Solinus
Strabo
Suetonius Tranquillus.

T
Tacitus
Thomas Malvenda

X
Xenophon.

Z
Zarate.

The Hebrew Bookes, and Authors.

TAlmudHierofolymitanum
Talmud Babylonicum
Paraphrafis Chaldaica
R. Simhon ben Johay
Seder holam
Rabot
Jalkot
Tanhuma

Jofeph ben Gurion
R. Sehadia Gaon
R. Mofeh de Egypto
R. Abraham Aben Ezra
R. Selomoh Jarhi
Eldad Danita
R. David Kimhi
R. Benjamin Tudelenfis
R. Mofeh Gerundenfis

R. Abraham bar R. Hiya
Don Shac Abarbanel
R. Jofeph Coen.
R. Abraham Frifcoll
R. Mordechay Japhe
R. Mordechay reato
R. Hazarya a-Adomi.

The

(10)

THE
RELATION
OF
ANTONY MONTEZINVS.

N the 18th. *of the Month of* Elul: *the 5404 year from the Worlds creation, and according to common compute, in* 1644. Aaron Levi, *otherwife called* Antonius Montezinus *came into this City* Amfterdam, *and related to the Sieur* Menaffeh ben Ifrael, *and other cheifetains of the* Portugal *Nation, Inhabitants of the fame City, thefe things which follow.*

That it was two years and a halfe, fince that he going from the Port Honda *in the* Weft-Indies, *to the* Papian *jurifdiction, he conducted fome Mules of a certaine* Indian, *whofe name was* Francifcus Caftellanus, *into the Province of* Quity, *and that there was one in company with him and other* Indians, *whofe name was* Francis, *who was called by all* Cazicus. *That it happened that as they went over the Mountaines* Cordilleræ, *a great tempeft arofe, which threw the loaden Mules to the ground. The* Indians *being afflicted by the fore tempeft, every one began to count his loffes; yet confeffing that all that and more grievous punifhments were but juft, in regard of their many fins. But* Francis *bad them take it patiently, for that they fhould fhortly injoy reft: the others anfwered, that they were unworthy of it; yea that the notorious cruelty ufed by the* Spaniards *towards them, was fent of God, becaufe they had fo ill treated his holy people, who wer of al others the moft innocent: now then, they determined to ftay all night upon the top of the Mountain. And* Montezinus *tooke out of a Box fome Bread, and Cheefe, and Jonkets, and gave them to* Francis, *upbraiding him, that he had spoken difgracefully of the* Spaniards; *who anfwered, that he had not told one halfe of the miferies and calamities inflicted by a*

B 2   *cruell*

*cruell, and inhumane people; but they fhould not goe unrevenged,
looking for helpe from an unknown people.*

After this Conference, Montezinus *went to* Carthagenia, *a City
of the* Indians, *where he being examined, was put in Prifon; and
while he prayed to God, fuch words fell from him; Bleffed be the
name of the* Lord, *that hath not made me an Idolater, a* Barbarian,
a Black-a-Moore, *or an* Indian; *but as he named* Indian, *he was
angry with himfelfe, and faid, The* Hebrewes *are* Indians; *then he
comming to himfelfe againe, confeffed that he doted, and added,
Can the* Hebrewes *be* Indians? *which hee alfo repeated a fecond, and
a third time; and he thought that it was not by chance that he had
fo much miftaken himfelfe.*

He thinking farther, of what he had heard from the Indian, *and
hoping that he fhould find out the whole truth; therefore as foon as
he was let out of Prifon, he fought out* Francifcus *beleeving that hee
would repeat to him againe what he had fpoken; he therefore being fet at liberty, through Gods mercy went to the Port*
Honda, *and according to his defire, found him, who faid; He
remembred all that he had fpoken, when he was upon the Mountaine; whom* Montezinus *asked, that he would take a journy with
him, offering him all courtefies, giving him three peeces of Eight,
that he might buy himfelfe neceffaries.*

Now when they were got out of the City, Montezinus *confeffed
himfelfe to be an* Hebrew, *of the Tribe of* Levi, *and that the Lord
was his God; and he told the* Indian, *that all other gods were but
mockeries; the* Indian *being amazed, asked him the name of his
Parents; who anfwered* Abraham, Ifaac, *and* Jacob; *but faid he,
have you no other Father? who anfwered, yes, his Fathers name
was* Ludovicus Montezinus; *but he not being yet fatisfied, I am
glad (faith he) to heare you tell this, for I was in doubt to beleeve
you, while you feemed ignorant of your Parents:* Montezinus *fwea-
ring, that he fpoke the truth, the* Indian *asked him, if he were not
the Son of* Ifrael, *and thereupon began a long difcourfe; who when
he knew that he was fo, he defired him to profecute what he had
begun, and added, that he fhould more fully explaine himfelfe, for
that formerly he had left things fo doubtfull, that he did not feem
at all affured of any thing. After that both had fatè downe
together, and refrefhed themfelves, the* Indian *thus began: If you
have a minde to follow me your Leader, you fhall know what ever*
you

*you defire to know, only let me tell you this, whatfoever the journey
is, you muft foot it, and you muft eate nothing but parched* Mayz,
and you muft omit nothing that I tell you; Montezinus *anfwered
that he would doe all.*

The next day being Munday, Cazicus *came againe, and bid
him throw away what he had in his Knapfack to put on fhooes made
of linnen packthred, and to follow him, with his ftaffe ; whereupon*
Montezinus *leaving his Cloake, and his Sword, and other things
which he had about him, they began the journey, the* Indian *carrying upon his back three meafures of* Mayz, *two ropes, one of which
was full of knots, to climbe up the Mountaine, with an hooked fork ;
the other was fo loofe, for to paffe over Marfhes, and Rivers, with
a little Axe, and fhooes made of linnen pack-thred. They being
thus accoutred, travelled the whole weeke, unto the Sabbath Day ;
on which day they refting, the day after they went on, till Tuefday,
on which day about eight a clock in the morning, they came to a River as bigge as* Duerus; *then the* Indian *faid, Here you fhall fee your
Brethren, and making a figne with the fine linnen of* Xylus, *which
they had about them inftead of a Girdle; thereupon on the other
fide of the River they faw a great fmoke, and immediately after,
fuch another figne made as they had made before; a little after
that, three men, with a woman, in a little Boat came to them, which
being come neare, the woman went afhore, the reft ftaying in the
Boat; who talking a good while with the* Indian, *in a Language
which* Montezinus *underftood not; fhe returned to the Boat, and told
to the three men what fhe had learned of the* Indian ; *who alwayes
eying him, came prefently out of the Boat, and embraced* Montezinus, *the woman after their example doing the like; after which, one
of them went back to the Boat, and when the* Indian *bowed downe to
the feet of the other two, and of the woman, they embraced him
courteoufly, and talked a good while with him. After that, the*
Indian *bid* Montezinus *to be of good courage, and not to looke that
they fhould come a fecond time to him, till he had fully learned the
things which were told him at the firft time.*

Then thofe two men comming on each fide of Montezinus, *they
fpoke in Hebrew, the 4th. ver. of* Deut. 6. Semah Ifrael, adonai Elohenu
adonai ehad; *that is,* Heare O Ifrael, the Lord our God is one God.

Then the Indian *Interpreter being asked, how it was in* Spanifh,
they fpoke what followes to Montezinus, *making a fhort paufe between every particular.*   B 3   1 Our

1 Our Fathers are *Abraham, Iſaac, Jacob,* and *Iſrael,* and they ſignified theſe foure by the three fingers lifted up; then they joyned *Reuben,* adding another finger to the former three.

2 We will beſtow ſeverall places on them who have a minde to live with us.

3 *Joſeph* dwels in the midſt of the Sea, they making a ſigne by two fingers put together, and then parted them.

4 They ſaid (ſpeaking faſt) ſhortly ſome of us will goe forth to ſee, and to tread under foot; at which word they winked, and ſtamped with their feet.

5 One day we ſhall all of us talke together, they ſaying, Ba, ba, ba; and we ſhall come forth as iſſuing out of our Mother the earth.

6 A certaine Meſſenger ſhall goe forth.

7 *Franciſcus* ſhall tell you ſomewhat more of theſe things, they making a ſigne with their finger, that much muſt not be ſpoken.

8 Suffer us that we may prepare our ſelves; and they turning their hands and faces every way, thus prayed to God, DO NOT STAY LONG.

9 Send twelve men, they making a ſigne, that they would have men that had beards, and who are skilfull in writing.

The Conference being ended, which laſted a whole day, the ſame men returned on Wedneſday, and Thurſday, and ſpake the ſame things againe, without adding a word; at laſt Montezinus *being weary that they did not anſwer what he asked them, nor would ſuffer him to goe over the river, he caſt himſelfe into their Boat; but he being forced out againe, fell into the River, and was in danger to be drowned, for he could not ſwim; but being got out of the water, the reſt being angry, ſaid to him; attempt not to paſſe the River, nor to enquire after more then we tel you; which the* Indian *interpreted to him, the reſt declaring the ſame things both by ſigns, and words.*

You muſt obſerve, that all thoſe three dayes the Boat ſtayed not in the ſame place, but when thoſe foure who came went away, other foure came, who all as with one mouth, repeated all the fore-mentioned nine particulars, there came and went about three hundred.

Thoſe men are ſomewhat ſcorched by the Sun, ſome of them weare their haire long, downe to their knees, other of them ſhorter, and others of them much as we commonly cut it. They were comely of body, well accoutred, having ornaments on their feet, and

leggs,

leggs, and their heads were compaſſed about with a linnen cloath.

Montezinus *faith, that when he was about to be gone, on Thurſ-day evening, they ſhewed him very much courteſie, and brought him whatever they thought fit for him in his journey, and they ſaid, that themſelves were well provided with all ſuch things, (ſc. meats, garments, flocks, and other things) which the* Spaniards *in* India *call their owne.*

The ſame day, when they came to the place where they had reſted, the night before they came to the River, Montezinus *ſaid to the* Indian ; *You remember* Francis, *that my Brethren told me, that you ſhould tell me ſomething, therefore I entreat you, that you would not thinke much to relate it. The* Indian *anſwered, I will tell you what I know, only doe not trouble me, and you ſhall know the truth, as I have received it from my fore-fathers ; but if you preſſe me too much, as you ſeeme to doe, you will make me tell you lyes ; attend therefore I pray, to what I ſhall tell you.*

Thy Brethren are the Sons of Iſrael, *and brought thither by the providence of God, who for their ſake wrought many Miracles, which you will not beleeve, if I ſhould tell you what I have learned from my Fathers ; we* Indians *made war upon them in that place, and uſed them more hardly then we now are by the* Spaniards; *then by the inſtigation of our Magicians (whom we call* Mohanes) *we went armed to that place where you ſaw your Brethren, with an intent to deſtroy them ; but not one of all thoſe who went thither, came back againe ; whereupon we raiſed a great Army, and ſet upon them, but with the ſame ſucceſſe, for againe none eſcaped; which hapned alſo the third time, ſo that* India *was almoſt bereft of all inhabitants, but old men, and women, the old men therefore : and the reſt who ſurvived, beleeving that the Magicians uſed falſe dealing, conſulted to deſtroy them all, and many of them being killed thoſe who remained promiſed to diſcover ſomewhat that was not knowne ; upon that they deſiſted from cruelty, and they declared ſuch things as follow :*

That the God of thoſe Children of *Iſrael* is the true God, that all that which is engraven upon their ſtones is true; that about the end of the World they ſhall be Lords of the world; that ſome ſhall come who ſhall bring you much good, and after that they have enriched the earth with all good things, thoſe Children of *Iſrael* going forth out of their Country, ſhall ſubdue the whole World to them,

them, as it was fubject to them formerly ; you fhall be happy if you make a League with them.

Then five of the chiefe Indians (*whom they call* Cazici *who were my Anceftors, having underftood the Prophefie of the Magicians, which they had learned of the Wife men of the* Hebrewes, *went thither, and after much entreaty, obtained their defire, having firft made knowne their minde to that woman, whom you faw to be for an Interpreter, (for your Brethren will have no commerce with our* Indians) *and whofoever of ours doth enter the Country of your Brethren, they prefently kill him ; and none of your Brethren doe paffe into our Country. Now by the help of that Woman we made this agreement with them.*

1 That our five *Cazici* fhould come to them, and that alone at every feventy moneths end.

2 That he to whom fecrets fhould be imparted, fhould be above the age of three hundred Moones, or Months.

3 And that fuch things fhould be difcovered to none in any place where people are, but only in a Defart, and in the prefence of the *Cazici;* and fo (faid the *Indian*) we keep that fecret among our felves, becaufe that we promife our felves great favour from them, for the good offices which we have done to our Brethren, it is not lawfull for us to vifite them, unleffe at the feventy months end: Or if there happens any thing new, and this fell out but thrice in my time ; Firft, when the *Spaniards* came into this Land ; alfo, when Ships came into the Southerne Sea; and thirdly, when you came, whom they long wifhed for, and expected. They did much rejoyce for thofe three new things, becaufe that they faid, the Prophefies were fulfilled.

And Montezinus *alfo faid, that three other* Cazici *were fent to him by* Francifcus, *to* Honda, *yet not telling their names, till he had faid, you may fpeake to them freely, they are my fellowes in my Function of whom I have told you, the fifth could not come for age, but thofe three did heartily embrace him; and* Montezinus *being asked of what Nation he was, he anfwered, an* Hebrew, *of the Tribe of* Levi, *and that God was his God, &c. which when they had heard, they embraced him againe, and faid : Upon a time you fhall fee us, and fhall not know us; We are all your Brethren, by Gods fingular favour ; and againe, they both of them bidding farewell, departed, every one faying, I goe about my bufineffe ; therefore*

fore

fore none but Francifcus *being left, who faluting* Montezinus *as a Brother, then bade him farewell, faying, farewell my Brother, I have other things to doe, and I goe to vifite thy Brethren, with o-ther* Hebrew *Cazici. As for the Country, be fecure, for we rule all the* Indians; *after we have finifhed a bufineffe which we have with the wicked* Spaniards, *we will bring you out of your bondage, by Gods help; not doubting, but he who cannot lye, will help us; according to his Word; endeavour you in the meane while that thofe men may come.*

The Hope of Israel.

Sect. i.

 T is hard to fay what is certaine among the fo many, and fo uncertaine opinions concerning the originall of the *Indians* of the new World. If you aske, what is my opinion upon the relation of *Montezinus*, I muft fay, it is fcarce poffible to know it by any Art, fince there is no demon-ftration, which can manifeft the truth of it; much leffe can you gather it from Divine, or humane Writings; for the Scriptures doe not tell what people firft inhabited thofe Countries; neither was there mention of them by any, til *Chriftop. Columbus, Americus, Vefpacius, Ferdinandus, Cortez,* the Marqueffe *Del Valle,* and *Francifcus Pizarrus* went thither; and though hitherto I have been of this minde, that I would fpeake only of folid, and infallible things, (as thofe things are which concerne our Law) and the obfcurity of the matter, making me doubt, whether it would be worth awhile for me to attempt it; yet at laft I was content to be perfwaded to it, not that I looke to get credit by it, but that my friends, and all who feeke for truth, that have put me upon this work, may fee how very defirous I am to pleafe them.

I fhall fpeake fomewhat in this Difcourfe, of the divers opinions which have been, and fhall declare in what Countries it is thought

C

the

(8)

the ten Tribes are; and I fhall clofe, after that I have brought them into their owne Country, which I fhall prove by good reafons, following the Revelations of the holy Prophets, who I beleeve cannot be expounded otherwife, whatever fome thinke; yet I intend not to difpute thefe things, but according to my cuftome, fhall lay down fairly, and faithfully, the opinions of the *Jewes* only.

SECT. 2.

YOu muft know therefore, that *Alexis Vanegas* faith, that the firft Colonies of the *West-Indies* were of the *Carthaginians*, who firft of all inhabited *New-Spaine*, and as they encreafed, fpread to the Ifland *Cuba*; from thence to the continent of *America*; and after that towards *Panama, New-Spaine*, and the Ifle of *Peru*. And he grounds himfelfe on that reafon, that as the *Carthaginians* (who of old did moft ufe the Seas) fo thofe of *Peru*, and the Inhabitants of *New-Spaine*, did make ufe of Pictures inftead of Letters.

But this opinion doth not satisfie, becaufe they anciently were white men, bearded, and civill in converfe; but contrarily thofe of *Panama*, St. *Martha*, and the Ifles in *Cuba*, and *Barlovent*, went naked. Further-more, who can thinke that the language which he faith, they firft fpoke, fhould be fo foone changed, that it fhould be wholly another; and there is no agreement between the one and the other. The learned *Arias Montanus* thinkes, that the *Indians* of *New-Spaine*, and *Peru*, are the Off-fpring of *Ophir* the fonne of *Jokton*, the nephew of *Heber*. And he backes his opinion, by the name *Ophir*, which by transpofition of letters, is the fame with *Peru*; and he adds, that the name *Parvaim* in the duall number, doth fignifie the *Ifmus* between *New-Spaine* and *Peru*, which firft was called *Ophir*, then *Peru*; and that thefe Countries are that *Peru*, from whence King *Solomon* brought Gold, precious Stones, &c. as in 1 *King. chap.* 9. *v.* 10. & 2 *Chron.* 9. 21. This opinion feems more probable than the other, and may be backed by another name of the River *Piru*, which according to *Gomoras*, lyes in the fecond degree from the Equinoctiall line, from *Panama* 222. miles; as alfo by the name of the Province *Jucatan*, which may be derived from *Joktan* the father of *Ophir*. But befides that this notation is fomewhat farre fetcht, it croffes what *Jofephus Acofta* affirmes in 1. *Hiftor.* of *Jud. c.* 13. who faith, that the name *Peru* was unknowne to the *Indians* themfelves before thofe *Spaniards* gave that name. Add

to

(18)

to this what *Garcillaſſo de la Vega* in the firſt part of his Commentary on *Peru, c.* 4. ſaith, that when a certaine *Spanyard, Baſco Nunnez de Balboa*, lived in that Country, and asked a Fiſher-man, what was the name of that Province, he anſwered *Beru*; (which was the Fiſher-mans owne name, he thinking that was the queſtion) and he farther ſaid, that the name of the River where he fiſhed, was called *Pelu.* Hence you may ſee, that *Peru* is made of both thoſe words; which also many *Spanyards* beſides him, we have mentioned, doe teſtifie. Beſides, who can thinke that *Solomon* neglecting the *Eaſt-Indies*, a place ſo rich, and abounding with all things, ſhould ſend a Fleet ſo farre off as to the *Weſt-Indies.* Alſo we read in 1 *King.* 9. that *Solomon* made ships in *Ezion-Geber* on the ſhoare of the red Sea, which alſo *Yehoſaphat* did, with *Ahaziah*, as *Ezra* ſaith, in 2 *Chron.* 20. and it is certaine that thoſe of thoſe Countries went that ordinary way to *India.* And it will not follow, that becauſe the holy Scripture ſometimes ſaith, that they went to *Tarſis*, and ſometimes; that they went to *Ophir*, that therefore both thoſe places are the ſame; ſince that *Tarſis* is not, as ſome thinke *Carthage*, or *Tunes* in *Africa* for that the Navie of *Solomon* did not ſet ſayle from *Yoppa*, a port of the Mediterranean, but from *Ezion-Geber*, a Port of the red Sea, from whence they could not ſayle to *Carthage*, but to the *East-Indies.* The anſwer of *Iſaac Abarbanel* to that argument, cannot be admitted, who ſaith, that an arme of *Nilus* did run into the red Sea, and another arme ran into the Mediterranean, by *Alexandria* in *Ægypt*; ſince it was never heard, that ſhips of great burden, did ſwim in thoſe rivers; and would not he then have built his Navie in the Port of *Alexandria?* It is more true that *Tarſis* is the Ocean, or *Indian* Sea; and becauſe they came into the Ocean, after that they had ſayled over the red Sea, which is but narrow, therefore the Scripture ſaith, *They Sayled to* Tarſis. *Rabbi Yonathan ben Uziel* followes this opinion, who in his Paraphraſe, for *Tarſis*, puts (the Sea.) The ſame ſaith *Franciſcus de Ribera*, in his Comment. on *Jonah*, and alſo *Rabbinus Yoſephus Coen*, in his *Chronology*; who aſcribe the word *Tarſis*, to the *Indian* Sea; becauſe that *Ophir* is the ſame Country, which of old is called, *The Golden Cherſoneſus*; and by *Joſephus, The Golden Land*; and at this day *Malacca*; from whence they brought Ivory, for the great number of Elephants which are there; none of which are in the *Weſt-Indies*, and *Solomons* Navie ſtayed in thoſe Ports of *India* three yeares, becauſe they traded with the Inhabi-

C 2

tants!

tants! I know that learned *Grotius,* and famous *de Laet* thinke differently; as alfo thofe quoted by them; but I fhall not infift in confuting their opinions becaufe I ftudy brevity. I doe like of, in part, the opinion of the *Spaniards* who dwell in the *Indies,* who by common consent doe affirme that the *Indians* come of the ten Tribes. And truly they are not altogether miftaken, becaufe in my opinion, *they were the first planters of the Indies;* as also other people of the *East-Indies* came by that Streight which is between *India,* and the Kingdome of *Anian.* But that people, according to our *Montezinus,* made warre upon thofe Inhabitants the *Ifraelites,* whom they forced up unto the mountaines, and the in-land Countries, as formerly the *Brittaines* were driven by the *Saxons* into *Wales.*

SECT. 3.

THe firft ground of that opinion is taken from 2 *Efdra.* 13. *v.* 40. &c. (which we quote as ancient, though it be Apocryphall) where it's faid, that the ten Tribes which *Salmanafter* carried captive in the reigne of *Hofeas,* beyond *Euphrates,* determined to goe into Countries farre remote, in which none dwelt, whereby they might the better obferve their Law. And as they paffed over fome branches of *Euphrates,* God wrought Miracles, ftopping the course of the Floud, till they had paffed over; and that Country is called *Arfareth.* From whence we may gather, that the ten Tribes went to *New-Spaine,* and *Peru,* and poffeffed thofe two Kingdoms, till then without Inhabitants. *Genebrardus,* quoting *Efdras* concerning that wandring of the ten Tribes, faith, that *Arfareth* is *Tartaria* the greater, and from thence they went to *Greenland,* for that *America* is lately found to be on that fide farther from Sea, than it is upon other fides, being almoft an Ifland, and they might paffe from *Greenland* by the ftreight of *Davis* into the Country *Labrador,* which is now called *India,* being fifty miles diftant from thence, as *Gomoras* faith in his Hiftory. The fame journying of the ten Tribes into *India,* is confirmed by that which *P. Malvenda* reports, That *Arfareth* is that Promontory which is neare to *Scythia,* or *Tartary,* neare the Sea, called by *Pliny, Tabis,* where *America* is parted from the Country of *Anian* by a narrow Sea; which alfo on that fide parts *China,* or *Tartary* from *America;* fo that there might be an eafie paffage for the ten Tribes through *Arfareth,* or *Tartary* into the

the Kingdomes of *Anian*, and *Quivira*; which in time might plant the new world, and firme land; which in bigneſſe equals *Europe*, *Aſia*, and *Africa* put together; *Alonſus Auguſtinianus* counting from the ſhoare of the North Sea, from the Country of *Labrador* 3928 miles, and from *Sur* 3000. miles; but *Gomaras* counts from *India* by the South, and *Sur*, 9300. miles; which ſpace is bigge e- nough for the ten Tribes, that they may there ſpread in places hitherto unknowne.

S E C T. 4.

HE ſtrengthens this opinion, that in the Iſle St. *Michael*, which belongs to the *Azores*, the *Spaniards* found Sepulchres under ground, with very ancient Hebrew letters, which *Genebrardus* hath Printed, *in lib. 1. chro. p. 159.* From whence we gather, that in that inſcription there is a miſtake of the letter (T.) ſo that the ſenſe of it is, *How perfect is God. Sehalbin is dead. Know God.* Unleſſe you will have them to be proper Names, and to ſignifie him that is dead, and his Father, in which ſenſe for (M) you muſt read (B) and then the ſenſe will be, *Meetabel ſeal, the Son of Matadel*; such names ending in (el) are common in Scripture, as *Raphael, Immanuel,* and the like. Let it ſuffice him who is pleaſed with neither of thoſe con- jectures, that *Hebrew* Letters were found there. And though that Iſland is remote from the *Weſt-Indies*, yet it might be by accident that they might put in thither.

S E C T. 5.

THat ſeemes to be to the purpoſe which *Garcillaſſos de la Voga* ſaith in his Comment. on *Peru, lib. 3. c. 1. That in* Tiahuanacu *a Province of* Collai, *among other Antiquities, this is worthy of memory, (being ſcituated at the Lake which the* Spaniards *call* Chutuytu*) That among the great buildings which are there, one was to be ſeene of a very great pile, which hath a Court* 15. *fa- thoms broad; a wall that compaſſeth it, 2 furlongs high; on one ſide of the Court is a Chamber* 45 *foot long, and* 22 *broad; and the Court, the Wall, the Pavement, the Chamber, the Roofe of it, the entrance, the poſts of the 2 gates of the Chamber, and of the en- trance, are made only of one ſtone; the three ſides of the Wall are an ell thick; the* Indians *ſay, that that House is dedicated to the Maker of the World.* I conjecture that building to be a Synagogue,

C 3   built

built by the *Ifraelites*; for the Authors who writ about the *Indies*, tell us, that the *Indians* never ufe Iron, or Iron weapons. Alfo the *Indians* were Idolaters, and therefore it could not be that they fhould build an house to God. *P. Acofta in lib. 6. Ind. hiftor. c.* 14. mentions fuch buildings as are in that place; and he reports that he measured a ftone which was 38. foot long, 18 foot broad, and fixe foot thick. *Petrus Cieza* in his firft part of his Chronicles of *Peru, c.* 87. relates, That in the City *Guamanga,* which is fcituated by the river *Vinaque,* there is a vaft building, which becaufe then it feemed almoft ruined by time, it therefore had lafted many yeares. He asking the neighbouring *Indians,* Who built that great Pile? He learnt, that it was made by a people (who were bearded, and white as the *Spaniards*) who came thither a long time before (and ftaid fome time after) the *Indians* raigned there ; and the *Indians* faid, that they had received it from their Fathers by Tradition. The fame *Cieza, cap.* 10. 5. of the Antiquity of *Tiguanac,* faith, that what the *Indians* boaft to be very ancient, can by no meanes be compared with that Ancient building, and other things. From all which you may well gather, that the firft Inhabitants of that place were the *Ifraelites* of the ten Tribes, becaufe they were white, and bearded.

S E C T. 6.

TO this opinion adde an argument taken from what Logicians call *a fimili*; for he that will compare the Lawes and Cuftomes of the *Indians* and *Hebrewes* together, fhall finde them agree in many things; whence you may eafily gather, That the *Indians* borrowed thofe of the *Hebrewes* (who lived among them) before, or after they went to the unknowne Mountaines. The *Indians* of *Jucatan,* and the *Acuzainitenfes* doe circumcife themselves. The *Totones* of *New Spaine,* and *Mexicans* (as *Roman* and *Gomaza* in the generall Hiftory of the *Indians* teftifie) rend their garments, if there happen any fudden misfortune or the death of any. *Gregorius Gracias in Monarchia Ingafonum,* an Ifle of *Peru,* faith, that *Guainacapacus* hearing that his fonne *Atagualpa* fled for feare of the Army of his enemy, he rent his garments. The *Mexicans,* and *Totones,* or the *Totonacazenfes* kept continually fire upon their Altars, as God commands in *Leviticus.* Thofe of *Peru* doe the fame, in their Temples dedicated to the Sun. The *Nicaraguazenfes* doe forbid their women who were lately brought a bed, to enter their

Tem-

Temples, till they are purified. The inhabitants of *Hispaniola* thinke those doe fin, who lye with a woman a little after her childe-birth. And the *Indians* of *new Spaine* doe feverely punish Sodomie. Many of the *Indians* doe bury their dead on the Mountaines; which alfo is the *Jewish* cuftome; and *Garcias* faith, the name *Chanan* is found in thofe Countries. You may wonder at this, that the *Indians* doe every fifty yeares celebrate a Jubilee, with great pomp, in *Mexico*, the Metropolis of the whole Province. Alfo that on the Sabbath day all are bound to be prefent in the Temple, to performe their Sacrifices, and Ceremonies. They alfo were divorced from their wives, if they were not honeft. The *Indians* of *Peru, New-Spaine,* and *Guatemala* did marry the Widdowes of their dead Brethren. May not you judge from thefe things, that the *Jewes* lived in thofe places, and that the *Gentiles* learned fuch things of them? Adde alfo to what hath been faid, that the knowledge which the *Indians* had, of the Creation of the world, and of the univerfall Flood, they borrowed from the *Ifraelites.*

S E C T. 7.

THe fourth ground of this opinion is, that the *Indians* are of a browne colour, and without beards; but in the new world, white, and bearded men were found, who had never commerce with the *Spaniards*; and whom you cannot affirme to be any other than *Ifraelites*; becaufe alfo as they could never be overcome, fo fhall they never be fully knowne, as appeares by what followes. *Petrus Simon* a *Francifcan*, in his Hiftory of finding out the firme Land, faith, that in the reigne of *Charles* the fifth, he commanded one called *Philippus de Utre* thither, to difcover, and plant thofe Countries; that he found them unknowne toward the North of *America* about five degrees, in the Province of *Omeguas*, which is neare the Province of *Venezuela*, and now is called *Garracas*. And he having learned of their neighbours, the greatneffe of that people both in wealth, and in war, he determined to war upon them. Who when they had marched a good way, at laft found a rich City, full of people, and faire buildings; and not farre off two Husband-men tilling the ground; whom they would have made Prifoners, that they might be their interpreters. But when they faw themfelves fet on, they fled apace towards the City; but *Philippus d'Utre* and his Souldiers followed them hard on Horse-back, and had almoft taken them;
where-

whereupon the Hufband-men ftood ftill, and with their Speares wounded *Philip* in the breaft, piercing through his Breft-plate made of wooll to keep off Arrowes. He wondering at the dexterity of that people, judged it a wifer courfe, not to make war upon that Province, and people fo expert in warre, and who dared to refift armed men. Therefore he retreated with his Company. And to this day none goe to that people, neither is it knowne which way to goe to them. It is probable that they are *Ifraelites* whom God preferves in that place againft the day of redemption. *Alonfus de Erzilla* teftifies the fame thing, in 2. part. *fua Araucaniæ. Cant.* 27. where defcribing thofe places, he thus fpeakes in Spanish.

> *Some Countries there, fo populous are seen,*
> *As one continued City; which have been*
> *Never as yet difcovered; but unknowne*
> *To other Nations; have laine hid alone;*
> *Not found by forreigne sword, nor forreigne trade*
> *Doe either feeke, nor fuffer to be made,*
> *But unacquainted live, till God fhall pleafe*
> *To manifeft his fecrets: shew us thefe.*

SECT. 8.

IOannes *Caftilianus Vicarius* living in the City *Pampelona* of *Nova Granada* in *Peru*, faith, that when *Gonzalus Pifarrus* had revolted from his people, he fent fome to fearch out new Countries of the *Indians* who lived East-ward, whofe number could never be knowne, becaufe that (as fome fay) their Country is above two thoufand miles in length, if you compute from the head of the river *Maragnon*, which runs neare *Andes* of *Cufco*, unto the place where it runs into the Sea, where therefore the River began to be navigable, *Petrus d' Orfna* being a Captaine, went by water, and his Souldiers with him, in Vessels called Canows; which when they were too fmall for the force of the ftreame, he built Brigandines, on the banke of the River *Guariaga*, which wafhing the Province *Chachapoyas*, runs into *Maragnon*. He was fcarce gone aboard his Brigandines, when one of his own Souldiers named *Aquirre*, a ftout man, killed him, who by common confent fucceeded the flaine. When they had gone a little way, they found a plaine without a mountaine, where many houfes ftood on each fide of the banke of *Maragnon*, being built by

the

the *Indians.* They ſtill went on for forty eight houres together, and
ſaw nothing but tall, and white houſes, which they feared to goe into,
becauſe the Inhabitants were numerous, and becauſe they heard the
noyſe of Hammers; for which cauſe they thought the Inhabitants to
be Gold-ſmiths. They went on ſtill, and now ſayled in the North
Sea, but alwayes neare to the ſhoare of the Province of *Margareta,*
where *Aquirre* was catcht by the Inhabitants and hanged; for they
heard that he had killed his Captaine *Petrus de Orſua.*

SECT. 9.

CAſpar *Bergarenſis* (whom I have oft ſpoke with) went from
the City *Laxa,* which is in the Province of *Quiti* in *Peru,* and
accompanied the Colonell *Don Diego Vaca de la Vega* going to ſeeke
a new Country.

In the yeare 1622. they came to the Province *Jarguaſongo,* which
had been diſcovered by Captaine *Salines;* and they paſſed the Mountaines *Cordilleræ,* where the River *Maragnon* is not above a ſtones
caſt over. In the Province of the *Inde Mainenſes* they built a City,
whoſe name was St. *Franciſcus de Borja,* at *Eſquilache.* In his company were one hundred *Spaniards* in Canows. Having conquered thoſe
Indians, and compelling them to ſweare fealty to the King of *Spaine;*
the Colonell being inſtructed by the *Mainenſes,* went to other places, after he had put a Garriſon into his new City. Having ſailed fifty
leagues in the River (he found ſome Cottages of the *Indians* which
there hid themſelves) by favour of many Rivers which there run into
Maragnon. When they had ſayled into the River *Guariaga,* where
Petrus de Orſua had built his Brigandines, and was killed by *A-
quirre;* they asked the *Indians* whom they had taken (who were
called *Guariaga,* from the Rivers name) what people doe live on the
Rivers side? they told the Colonell, that five dayes journey off, there
live men of tall ſtature, comely in preſence, and have as great beards
as the *Spaniards* have, valiant, and warlike, who are not ſkilled in
Canowes, though the reſt of the *Indians* uſe no other; he preſently
returned the ſame way he came.

SECT. 10.

IN *Farnambuc* about forty yeares ſince, eight *Tabaiares* had a
minde to looke out new Countries, and to ſee whether the Land
that was beyond, and unknowne, were inhabited. They having ſpent

D   foure

foure moneths in travelling Weftward, they came to mountaines, to whofe top they got with difficulty, and found a plaine which a plea-fant river doth compaffe, by whofe banke fide dwelt a people who loved commerce, they were white, and bearded; and this five of the *Tabaires* (for three perished by the way, and only five returned) told to the *Brafilians* after nine moneths.

S E C T. ii.

IN our time, under King *Philip* the third, Captaine *Ferdinades de Queiros* being returned out of *India* (where he had fpent moft of his life) to *Rome,* he fhewed a Table of Lands yet undifcovered. From thence he went to *Madrid,* and five fhips were given him by the Governour of *Panama* (to whom he was fent) to perfect his defigne. He began his journey, and was fcarcely entred the South Sea, but he found Land, which he called, *The Ifle of Solomon,* and *Hie-rufalem,* for reafons which he told me. He in his courfe of fayling al-wayes kept clofe to the fhoare of thofe Iflands; he faw thofe Iflan-ders of a browne colour, and took many; others dwelt in greater If-lands, and more fruitfull; thefe were white, and wore long garments of filk; and the Pilot being bid to bring his Ship neare the fhoare, he fplit his Ship upon a Rock, (and the Iflanders running greedily to the fight) which being funke, the Captaine went thence, looking for the firme Land, which he found to be forty degrees beyond; and he went three hundred miles neare the fhoare; aud when he perceived the Country to be inhabited by the fmoke which he faw, and would put into a Port on the fide of the River, there ran to him many white men, of yellow haire, tall like Giants, richly cloathed, and of long beards. But one of the Veffels being wracked in the Havens mouth, he was forced to put out to Sea; whereupon the Iflanders fent two Cha-loffi of a browne colour, (as the inhabitants were of the firft Ifland) with fheep, and other provifions, and fruits, but defiring, and threat-ning them, if they did not depart: The Captaine brought thofe Cha-loffi into *Spaine,* from whom the *Spaniards* could learne nothing but by fignes; and inftead of anfwers, (when they were asked) would fhew their beards, as if fuch thofe were, who were their Lords, and had fent them, and if they were asked about Religion, they would hold up their fingers to Heaven, implying, that they worfhipped but one God. A little while after, they dyed in *Spaine.* The Captaine re-turned to *Panama,* having left his two Ships which were wracked;
and

and when the Governour fued him, by meanes of the Senators, who are over the *Indian* affaires, he was difmiffed, and returned with his Ships into *Spaine*, where he abode two yeares before his matters were difpatched. But the King created him Marqueffe of the Countries found out by him, and commanded to give him a good Army, where-with to compaffe his defignes. But he scarce got to *Panama*, when he dyed, not without fufpition of being poyfoned by the Governour.

S E C T. 12.

THat which I am about to tell, fhall ferve for a proofe of that which I faid of the *Weft-Indians.* A Dutch Mariner told me, that not long fince he was with his fhip in *America*, feven degrees towards the North between *Maragnon*, and great *Para*, and he put into an Harbour in a pleafant River, where he found fome *Indians* who underftood *Spanifh*, of whom he bought Meats, and Dywood; after he had ftayed there fix moneths, he underftood that that River extended eighteen leagues towards the *Carybes Indians*, as far as the fhip could goe; and that the River is divided there into three branches, and they fayling two months on the left hand, there met them white men, and bearded, well bred, well cloathed, and abounding with gold and filver; they dwelt in Cities enclofed with wals, and full of people ; and that some *Indians* of *Oronoch* went thither, and brought home much gold, filver, and many precious ftones, Which he having underftood, fent thither fome Sea-men; but the *Indian* dyed by the way, who was their guide, and fo they did not proceed, but ftayed there two months, and trucked with the *Indians* who were fixty leagues from Sea. That Province is called *Fisbia*, and is subject to *Zealand*; they have no commerce with the *Spaniards*, and the inhabitants travell fecurely every way. I heard that ftory by accident from that *Dutch* Mafter of the Ship ; whence fome of us gueffing them to be *Ifraelites*, had purpofed to fend him againe to enquire more fully. But he dyed fuddenly the laft yeare, whence it feemes that God doth not permit that thofe purpofes fhould take any effect till the end of dayes.

S E C T. 13.

YEt I give more credit to our *Montezinus*, being a *Portingal*, and a *Jew* of our Order; borne in a City of *Portingal*, called
D 2 *Ville-*

Villefleur, of honeſt and known Parents, a man about forty yeares old, honeſt, and not ambitious. He went to the *Indies*, where he was put into the Inquiſition, as the ſucceſſor of many who were borne in *Portingal*, and deſcended from them, whom the King of *Portingal*, *Don Manuel* forced to turne Chriſtians: (*O wicked, and unjuſt action*, ſaith *Oſorius*; and a little after, *This was done neither according to Law, nor Religion*,) and yet to this day they privately keep their Religion, which they had changed, being forced thereto. He being freed from the Inquiſition, very diligently ſought out theſe things, and oft ſpoke with thoſe men, and then was not quiet till he came hither, and had told us that good newes. He endured much in that journey, and was driven to great want, ſo that no houſe would give him food, or give him money for his worke. I my ſelfe was well acquainted with him for ſix months together that he lived here; and ſometimes I made him take an Oath in the preſence of honeſt men, that what he had told, was true. Then he went to *Farnambuc*, where two yeares after he dyed, taking the ſame Oath at his death. Which if it be ſo, why ſhould not I beleeve a man that was vertuous, and having all that which men call gaine. And who knowes but that ſhortly the truth of that Prognoſtick may appeare, which our *Montezinus* learned from the *Mohanes*; anſwerable to that which *Jacobus Verus* an Aſtrologer of *Prague* writ after the apparition of the Comet in *Ann.* 1618. and dedicated to his Highneſſe the Prince *Palatine*, where he thus diſcourſeth: The Comet going towards the South, doth intimate that the Cities and Provinces which God doth threaten, are thoſe of the *Weſt-Indies*, which ſhall revolt from the King of *Spaine*, who will finde that loſſe greater then he imagined, not that the *Indians* rebell againſt him of themſelves, but that they are provoked to it being ſtirred up by others. Neither did the Comet only fore-tell that, but the eclipſe of the Sun, which was in that Country the yeare before. Thus far the Aſtrologer. Our ancient Rabbins ſay, though we doe not beleeve the Aſtrologers in all things, yet we doe not wholly reject them, who ſometimes tell truth.

SECT. 14.

THus farre of the *Weſt-Indies*, of which *Iſaiah* may be underſtood (becauſe it lyes in the midſt of the Sea, and alſo hath many Iſlands) in *Iſa.* 60. 9. *The iſles ſhall waite for me, and the ſhips of Tarſhiſh firſt, to bring their Sons from far, their ſilver and*

and their gold with them, Jer. 31. 10. *Heare the Word of the Lord O ye Nations, and declare it in the isles afar off, and say, He that scattereth Israel will gather him,* Psal. 97. 1. *The Lord reigneth, let the earth rejoyce, and the multitude of isles be glad.* Where part of the ten Tribes doe dwell unknown to this day.

S E C T. 15.

YOu must know that all the ten Tribes were not carried away at the same time. *Pul* the King of *Assyria* (as I shew in the second part of my Reconciler) conquered, and carried away the Tribes of *Reuben, Gad,* and halfe *Manasseh,* in the reigne of *Peka,* as vou may see in 1 *Chron.* 5. 26. and *Josephus in li.* 9. *c.* 11. *Tiglahpilefer* eight yeares after took *Ijon, Abel-beth-maachah, Hazor-Gilead, Galilee,* all the land of *Naphtali,* and he carryed away all the Captives into *Assyria,* in 2 *King.* 15. 29. At last *Shalmaneser* King of *Assyria,* nine yeares after, in the reign of *Hoshea* the Son of *Elah,* besieged *Samaria* three yeares; which being taken, he carried away. *Hoshea,* with the rest of the Tribes, in 2 *King.* 17. 6. Of those three times the Prophet *Isaiah* speakes, *Isa.* 9. 1. saying, the first captivity was gentle, if you compare it with the last, which was grievous, and unsufferable, when the Kingdome and Monarchy of *Israel* ceased.

S E C T. 16.

THe ten Tribes being conquered at severall times, we must thinke they were carried into severall places. As we beleeve they went to the *West-Indies* by the strait of *Anian,* so we thinke that out of *Tartary* they went to *China,* by that famous wall in the confines of both. Our argument to prove it, is taken from the authority of two Jesuites, who erected their Colledges in those Countries. *Nicholaus Trigantius* a Dutch-man in his discourse of the Christian expedition under-taken by the Jesuites to *Sina,* saith, We finde that in former time the *Jewes* came into these Kingdomes. And when that society had for some yeares seated it selfe in the Court of the *Pequinenses,* a certaine *Jew* came to *P. Matthæus Riccius;* he was borne in *Chamfamfu* the metropolis of the Province *Honan,* and was surnamed *Ogay;* and now being licensed to the degree of a Doctor, he went to *Pequin.* But when he read in a certaine Booke writ by a Doctor of *China,* concerning the *European* affaires, That our

D 3 fathers

fathers are not *Sarazens,* and know no God but the Lord of Heaven and Earth ; and would perfwade himfelfe that ours did profeffe the Law of *Mofes,* he went into the Church with *P. Matthœas Riccius.* On an Altar there was the effigies of the Virgin *Mary,* and the childe Jefus, whom St. *John* his fore-runner worfhipped with bended knees; now that day was the Holy-day of *John* the Baptift. The *Jew* thinking it was the effigies of *Rebecca,* and her two Sons, *Jacob* and *Efau,* he bowed also to the Image, but with this Apology, that he worfhipped no Images, but that he could not but honour thefe who were the Parents of our Nation. And he afking if the foure E-vangelifts on both fides of the Altar, were not foure of the twelve fons of *Jacob*; the Jefuite anfwered, Yes, thinking he had afked of the twelve Apoftles. But afterward the *Jew* acknowledged to the Jefuite that he was an *Ifraelite*; and he found the Kings Bible, and acknowledged the *Hebrew* Letters, though he could not read them. By this occafion our people learnt, that ten or twelve families of *Ifraelites* were there, and had built a very neat Synagogue which coft ten thoufand Crownes, in which they have kept the five Bookes of *Mofes* with great veneration for fix hundred yeares. He alfo affirmed, that in *Hamcheu* the Metropolis of the Province *Chequiona,* there are farre more Families, with a Synagogue; and elfe-where that many Families live without a Synagogue, becaufe that by little and little they are extinguifhed. He relating many things out of the Old Teftament, he differed but little in pronouncing thofe names. He faid, that fome among them were not ignorant of the *Hebrew* Tongue, but that himfelfe had neglected it, having ftudied the *China* Tongue from a Childe. For which caufe he was counted almoft un-worthy of their fociety, by the Ruler of the Synagogue. But he chiefly looked after this, that he might get to be Doctor. Three yeares after *P. Matthæus Riccius* fent one of our brethren to that Metropolis, who found all thofe things true. He compared the beginnings, and endings of the Bookes which the *Jewes* keep in their Synagogue, with our Pentateuch, and faw no difference, this only, that thofe had no pricks. The other Jefuite is *Alfonfus Cimedro,* who likewife faith, that there is a great number of *Jewes* in the Province of *Oroenfis,* on the Weft part of *China,* who know nothing of the comming, and fuffering of Jefus. And he from thence gathers, that they are of the ten Tribes, (which opinion I alfo am of) becaufe thofe *Chinefes* obferve many *Jewifh* Rites, which you may fee in a manufcript, which
the

the noble *Jaochimus Wicofortius* hath. And why might not some of them saile from *China* to *New-Spaine*, through the streight between *China*, and *Anian*, and *Quivira*, which doe border upon *New-Spaine*; and from thence they went to the Isles of *Panama*, *Peru*, and those thereabouts. These in my judgement are those *Chinefes* of whom *Ifaiah* speakes, Chap. 49. verf. 12. (treating about *Ifraels* returne to his Country.) *Behold, these shall come from afarre, and these from the North, and from the West, and these from the Land of Sinim.* And so *Ptolomy* in *lib. 7. c. 3. tab.* 11. cals it The country of *Sinim*, or *Sina*; and this is the true fenfe of the words; *Aben Ezra* therefore is miftaken, who derives it of Sene, a bush or wood, which he placeth in *Ægypt*.

SECT. 17.

I Could eafily beleeve, that the ten Tribes as they increafed in number, fo they fpread into more Provinces before-mentioned, and into *Tartary*. For *Abraham Ortelius* in his Geography of the World, and Map of *Tartary*, he notes the place of the *Danites* which he cals the Hord, which is the fame which the Hebrew *Jerida*, fignifying *A defcent*. And lower, he mentions the Hord of *Naphtali*, poffeffed by *Peroza* in the yeare 476. *Schikhardus* in his Tarich or feries of the Kings of *Perfia*, amplifies the Hiftory of this War, where *ex lib. 4. of Agathias*, he thus faith, *A little after, when they were eafed of that Plague*, (*fc.* 7. yeares drought) *in the time of the Emperour* Zeno, Firuz *made a double warre with* Naphtali, *in which at laft he was deftroyed. For first of all he was brought to the ftreights of places unknowne; who then fought for peace upon this condition (and obtained it) that he fhould fweare that he would never after provoke them; and that he fhould doe reverence to this Conquerour in token of fubjection: which afterward by the counfell of the Magicians he performed craftily, for he bowed towards the Eaftern Sun, that his owne people might thinke that he bowed rather to the Sun (after his Country cuftom) then to honour his Enemy. But he did not truly performe that firft agreement, though confirmed by Letters Patents; who becaufe he could not digeft the difgrace of bowing to his Enemy, he prepared a new Army and went againft them; but a fecond time he being entrapped by the badneffe of the Country, he loft his life; and many with him, in a Gulf which the* Naphthalites *had prepared for him, having dreffed it*

*it over with reeds, and some earth throwne a top; they having left
in the middle some high grounds, and trees where their Scouts
were, that their stratagem might not be found, and that the* Perfi-
ans *might more confidently attempt the ditch. Thus a rash King
paid for his perfidy, he excelling more in daring, then in counsell,
as* Agathias *saith. The patent by which peace had been agreed, was
hung upon a speare, and might be seene of him at distance, that he
might remember his Oath, repent, and desist from his enterprise;
but he cared little for that. But when by his unexpected fall he
saw he should dye, it is said that he pulled off from his right eare a
pearle of huge bigneffe, and whiteneffe, and least any after him
should finde it (more likely that his corps should not be knowne) he
threw it a great way off.* The same Author askes, who those *Naphthalites* were, and by many arguments he proves that they are the relicks of the *Jewes;* saith he, *I doe wholly thinke that they are the
relicks of the* Jewes *of the Tribe of* Naphtali, *whom* Triglath Pileffer
the Affyrian *carried into those places, in* 2 King. 15. 29. *For* 1. *The
name, in the best copies of* Agathias, *which* Lewenclavius *hath
mended, is the same fully; in other Bookes it wants nothing but an
(h) now it is scarce poffible that in a word of many syllables that
should fall out by chance.* 2. *Their countenance discovers it, for
as* Procopious I. C. *saith, they are not blacke, or foule in their
countenance, as the* Auns *are among whom they live, but the only
white men of that Country; that it may evidently appeare that
they came from some other place thither.* 3. *Their manners a-
gree, for the same Author saith, that they are not* Nomades, *as
the* Huns *who are unconstant in their dwelling, and eate up one place
after another; but they inhabite one certaine place. Befides, they
obferve Law and equity, as the* Romans; *and have pollicy, being
well governed by their Prince: both which is rare among their
neighbour Nations. Alfo they doe not lay abroad their dead, as
the* Barbarians *doe, but they decently cover them with earth. Laftly, their jornalls doe teftifie that many* Jewes *live there, especially
in the mountaines, who have fearched to the mid-land countries of*
Eaft-Afia, R. Benjamin, f. 23. *From thence (the coaft of* Perfia)
is 28. dayes journey to the mountaines* Nifebor, *which are neare the
river* Gozan. *The Ifraelites which come from thence into* Perfia,
say, that there in the Cities of Nifebor, *are four Tribes (fc.* Dan,
Zebulon, Afor, Naphtali,) *of the firft captivity, which* Shalmanefer
the

the Aſſyrian *carried thither, as in* 2 King. 17. 6. *he brought them
to* Habor, *and* Halah, *the river* Gozan *and the Mountaines of*
Media. *The compaſſe of that Country is twenty dayes journey; and
they poſſeſſe Cities, and Caſtles upon the Mountaines, by one ſide
of which, runs the river* Gozan ; *neither are they ſubjeɛt to the
Nations, but have a Governour over them, by name* R. Joſeph
Amarkela *a Levite, and there are among them ſome who ſtudy
wiſdome. They ſow, and reap ; yea they wage war to the Country of* Cuth. *In* the ſame place *Ortelius* adds, in the Country *Tabor,* or *Tibur* (which *Solinus* commends, in *c.* 49.) they dwell a
people, who though they have loſt the holy writings, they obey
one King, who came into *France,* in Ann. 1530. and ſpoke with
Francis the firſt, was burnt at *Mantua* by the command of the
Emperour *Charles* the fifth, because that he did privately teach
Judaiſm to Chriſtian Princes,and to theEmperour himſelfe. *Boterus* ſaith the ſame in his relations of the fartheſt part of *Tartary.*
But both these were deceived ; for *Rabbinus Joſephus Cohon,* a
man worthy to be beleeved, relates this more truly in his Chronology, ſaying, that the *Jew* who came out of that Country, was the
brother of the King of the *Iſraelites,* was called *David* the *Reubenite ;* and having ſeene *India* in his paſſage, he came to *Portugal,*
where he converted the Kings Secretary to Judaiſm, who fled from
thence with him, taking the name of *Selomoh Molho ;* he in
ſhort time was ſo well verſed in the Law, yea in the *Cabala* it ſelfe,
that he made all *Italy* admire him. The Secretary together with the
Reubenite, endevoured to draw the Pope, *Charles* the fifth, and
Francis the firſt to Judaiſm. *Selomoh Molho* was taken at *Mantua,* and burnt alive, in the yeare 1540. He yet was offered his life,if
he would turne Chriſtian. The *Reubenite* was by *Charles* the fifth
carried priſoner into *Spaine,* where he ſhortly after dyed. *Abraham
Friſol Orchotolam* remembers the *Reubenite,* ſaying, Forty five years
agone *David Reubenita,* a Prince of the *Iſraelites,* came from *Tabor,* a Province of *Tartary,* into *Europe,* who ſaid that two Tribes
are there; and other Tribes a little farther, under their Kings, and
Princes,and alſo an unſpeakable number of people. Perhaps the Province *Tabor* is the ſame that *Habor;* which is mentioned in 2 King.
17. 6. that the ten Tribes were brought by *Salmaneſer* to *Habor,*
and *Halah ;* now the Hebrew letters (*h*) and (*t*) are neere in fa-
ſhion. *Eldad Danita* of the Tribe of *Dan,* came out of thoſe Coun-

E   tries

tries five hundred yeares agone (a letter from whom, which we call *Sephar Eldad Danita,* is kept to this day) and being examined by the Rabbins, was found an approved man. The learned Rabbi *David Kimhi,* who lived 450. yeares since, in *etymol. suo* in the word *Segiah,* he saith, *Rabbi Jonah* writes of the name of *Rabbi Juda Aben Karis,* that he heard *Eldad Danita* say, &c. And so what I said is true, as appeares by the testimonies produced.

S E C T. 18.

PArt of the ten Tribes also live in *Ethiopia,* in the *Habyssin* Kingdome; as divers *Habyssins* reported at *Rome. Boterus* in his relations speakes the same thing, that two potent Nations doe live neare *Nilus,* and that one of them is that of the *Israelites,* who are governed by a mighty King. A Cosmographer who hath added notes to *Ptolomyes* tables, saith thus in his table of *New Africa;* that part of *New Africk* was unknowne of old, the head of *Nilus* not being knowne, which is in the Mountaines of the Moone, as the Ancients call them ; where there dwels a great number of *Israelites,* paying tribute to *Prester John. Rabbi Abraham Frisol* in the Book already quoted, saith, that in his time some who had been in those Countries, reported the same to *Hercules* the Duke of *Ferraria.* And without question from hence the *Habyssins* learned Circumcision, the observation of the Sabbath, and many more *Jewish* rites. Of these *Isaiah* seemes to speake, in *Isa.* 18. 1, 2. *Woe to the Land which under the shadow of sails doth saile beyond the rivers of* Ethiopia, *by whom* (the Prophet saith) *are sent Ambassadors in ships of Bulrushes,* (such as the *Æthiopians* use, commonly called *Almadiæ.*) *Bring back a people driven out of their Country, and torn, and more miserable then any among us. Gifts shal be brought to the Lord of Sebaoth, in the place where the name of the Lord of Sebaoth is worshipped, in the mount Sion.* The Prophet *Zephany* saith the same, in *Zeph.* 3. 9, 10. *Then will I give to the people that they speaking a pure language, may all call upon the name of God, whom they shall serve with reverence ; from beyond the rivers of* Ethiopia *they shall bring to me for a gift,* Hatray *the daughter of my dispersed ones,* (that is, the Nations of *Æthiopia.*) Which agrees with that of *Isa. And your Brethren,* (which are the ten Tribes) *shall bring gifts to the Lord.*

S E C T.

SECT. 19.

ANd without doubt they alfo dwell in *Media*; from thence they paffed *Euphrates*, whither they were firft brought, as in 2 *King.* 17. 24 and in the book of *Tobit*. *Josephus* alfo fpeakes of them in the Preface of his Book of the War of the *Jewes*, that the *Jewes* did think that their brethren, who dwelt beyond *Euphrates*, and farther, would rebell againft the Romans. *Agrippa* in his Oration to the people of *Jerufalem*, that they would not rebell againft the *Romans*, fpeakes thus; *What affociates doe ye expect to joyne with you in your rebellion, and war? doth not all the knowne world pay tribute to the* Romans? *Perhaps fome of ye hope to have help from them beyond* Euphrates. And in *lib. 2. Antiquit. c. 5.* fpeaking of thofe who in the time of *Ezra* returned from *Babylon* to *Jerufalem*, he faith, *All Ifrael dwelt in* Media ; *for two Tribes only dwelt in* Afia, *and* Europe, *and lived fubject to the* Romans ; *as the other ten on the other fide* Euphrates, *where they are fo many, that they cannot be counted.* It is not therefore to be doubted, the people encreafing after their firft tranfportation, they fought out new places, which we have formerly mentioned.

SECT. 20.

LAftly, all thinke, that part of the ten Tribes dwell beyond the river *Sabbathian*, or fabbaticall. *Rabbi Johanan* the Author of the *Jerufalem Talmud*, who lived 160. yeares after the deftruction of the fecond Temple, faith in his treatife of the *Sanhedrim, cap. 17.* That the ten Tribes were carryed into three places, *fc.* to the Sabbaticall river, to *Daphne* the suburbs of *Antioch*, and thither where a cloud comes downe and covers them: And that they fhall be redeemed from thofe three places; for fo he opens that place of *Ifa. Cha.* 49. 9. *That they may fay to the Captives, Goe forth,* (*fc.* to them who are at the Sabbaticall river) *to them that are in darkneffe, fhew your felves,* (*fc.* to them who are compaffed with the cloud) *and to all, they fhall be refrefhed in the wayes,* (*fc.* to them who live in *Daphne* of *Antioch* which is in *Syria.*) Whence you may obferve, that the learned man *l' Empereur* tranflated it ill, *at the fides of Antioch*, whereas *Daphne* is the proper name of a pleafant Grove near *Antioch*. *Sedar olam* makes mention of that cloud, and calls them *mountaines of obfcurity*, And in *Talmud tractat. Sanhedr. c. 11.*

E 2

R Jonathan

R. Jonathan ben Uziel, who lived a hundred yeares before the deftruction of the fecond Temple, in *Exod.* 34. 10. where the Lord faith, *I will doe wonders before all thy people, fuch as was never done in the whole earth, or in any Nation,* &c. and he refers all thofe things to the tranfportation of the people. *He fhall draw them to the rivers of Babylon : and fhall carry them to the Sabbaticall river, and fhall teach them, that thofe miracles were never performed to any Nation of the known world.*

Our ancient Rabins in *Berefit Rabba* (no mean book) in *Perafach,* do fay that *Tornunfus* asking how it fhould appeare that the day which we keep, is the feventh day, on which God refted after the creation of the world; *Rabbi Aquebah* (who lived 52 yeares after the deftruction of the fecond Temple) anfwered by an argument taken from the ftones of the Sabbatical River, which in the fix dayes are toffed up and down with a continuall motion, but do reft on the Sabbath day and move not. The fame is faid in the *Babylonian Talmud, tractat. Sanhed.* c. 7. *& in Tanuh Perafach.* c. 9. *In eodem Berefit Raba, in Perafach* 37. *Rabbi Simon* faith, *The ten Tribes were carried to the Sabbaticall river but Juda and Benjamin are difperfed into all Countrys.* In *Afirim Raba,* the laft verfe of the Song, its faid, *Our bed is flourifhing*; that it is meant the ten Tribes, which were carried to the Sabbaticall river; and that river running all the week, doth caufe the ten Tribes there remaining to be fhut up; for though on the feventh day the river doth reft, yet it is forbidden by our Law to take a journey then; and for that reafon they remained there miraculoufly, as loft, and concealed from us. So that of *Ifa.* 49. *That they fay to the prifoners, go forth,* is interpreted of them in *Jalcut.* *R. Aquebah* after the fame manner explains that of *Levit.* 36. 38. *And ye fhal perifh among the heathen.* And that of *Ifa.* 27. *ult. And they fhall come, who were ready to perifh in Affyria.* Becaufe they are remote from the reft, therefore another Rabbi in Bamibar *Raba Parafa* 16. applyes to them that of *Ifaiah* 49. 12. *Behold them who come from farre*: that fo all thofe Authors mention that River.

The teftimony of *Jofephus* is famous, *lib.* 7. *de Bel. Jud. cap.* 24. faying, *The Emperour Titus paffing between Arca, and Raphanea, Cities of King Agrippa, he faw the wonderfull river, which though it be fwift, yet it is dry on every feventh day ; and that day being paft, it refumes its ordinary courfe, as if it had no change ; and it*

always

*always obſerves this order. It is called Sabbaticall; from the
ſolemne feaſt of the Jews, becauſe it imitates their reſt every
ſeventh day.* I know ſome do otherwiſe expound thoſe words of *Joſephus,* but they hit not his meaning, as appears by this, that he calls
the River, Sabbathio, or ſabbaticall: which word cannot be derived
but from Sabbath; and who doth not ſee that it ceaſeth to flow, or
move, on the Sabbath day; and ſo *Joſephus* muſt be underſtood according to my ſenſe. *Pliny* alſo confirms this opinion, *lib. 1. Nat. hiſt.
c. 2.* he ſaith, *In Judea a River lies dry every Sabbath;* yet I think
Pliny is deceived and ill informed, when he ſaith it is a River in Judea;
neither is to be found in Judea, but in another place, where many
Jewes live. R. *Selomoh Jarchi* who lived 540. years ſince mentions
that River in *Comment. Talm.* ſaying, The ſtones, and ſand of
that River do continually move all the ſix dayes of the week, until the
ſeventh. R. *Mardochus Japhe* in his learned book *Jephe Thoar*
ſaith, The *Arabians* derive Sabbathion from the Sabbath, who uſe
to adde the paticle (ion) to adjectives. The ſame ſaith, that it was
told him of an hour-glaſſe filled with the ſand of Sabbathion, which
ranne all the weeke till the Sabbath. And I heard the ſame from
my father; which teſtimony I account as good, as if I ſaw it my ſelfe;
(for fathers do not uſe to impoſe upon their ſons.) He told me that
there was an Arabian at *Lisborn,* who had ſuch an hour-glaſſe; and
that every Friday at evening he would walk in the ſtreet called the new
ſtreet, and ſhew this glaſſe to Jewes who counterfeited Chriſtianity,
and ſay, *Ye Jewes, ſhut up your ſhops, for now the Sabbath comes.*
Another worthy of credit, told me of another hour-glaſſe, which he
had ſome years before, before the Port *Myſketa.* The Cadi, or Judge
of that place, ſaw him by chance paſſing that way, and asked him,
what it was? he commanded it to be taken away; rebuking the Ma-
homitans, that by this, they did confirme the Jewiſh Sabbath. I
ſhould not ſpeak of theſe glaſſes, if the authority of ſuch a man whom
I have alledged, did not move me; though I beleeve that God did
not only work that miracle, that he might keep part of the ten Tribes
there, but other alſo, as you may ſee in *Eſdras.* R. *Moſes Gerunden-
ſis* a learned Cabaliſt, and Interpreter of the Law in *Paraſa Aazinu,*
thinks the River Sabbathion to be the ſame with Gozan, of *Guz,* which
ſignifies to ſnatch away, becauſe except the ſeventh day, on all the
other, it carryes with it, by its ſwiftneſſe, the very ſtones. Of this
there is mention in 2 *King.* whither the King of *Aſſyria* led his cap-

E 3   tives

tives; and fo relates *Benjamin Tudelenfis* in his journall, that part
of the ten Tribes dwelt at the bank of that River. But I know not
where the River Gozan is. In the year 5394, that is, 15 years agon in
the City *Lubin*, two *Polonians* after they had travelled long, they wrot
in Dutch a book of the originiall of the Sabbaticall River, but the Senate commanded it to be burnt at the Mart of Breflaw, by the perfwafion of the Jefuites. *Abraham Frifal* in his Orchot Olam. *c. 26.*
will have this river to be in *India,* he faith, *The head of the Sabbaticall river is in the country of Upper India, among the rivers
of Ganges.* And a little after, *The Sabbaticall river hath its originall from the other fide of Kalikout* (which lyes far above the bound
of *Lamik,* which he placeth beyond the *finus Barbaricus*) *and it parts
the Indians from the Kingdome of the Jewes, which river you may
certainly find there,* Though he takes *Gozan* for *Ganges,* for fome
nearneffe of writing; yet its not to be doubted that in that place there
are many Jewes, witneffe *Johannes de Bairos* in his Decads. *Eldad
Danita* fpeaking of the four Tribes: which he placeth at *Gozan* faith,
The Sabbaticall river is among them. *Jofephus* faith, that *Titus*
faw the Sabbathion between *Arca* and *Raphanea.* Which teftimony
feems the truer, becaufe its not to be thought that *Jofephus* would tel a
lie of him, by whom he might be rebuked. I think that ye muft look
for it not far from the Cafpian Sea: and I am not alone in this opinion. What ever it be it appeares that this river is fomewhere, and
that part of the ten Tribes are hid there; and I may fay with *Mofes*
in *Deut.* 29. 28, 29. *And the Lord caft them out of their Land in
anger, and in wrath; Secret things belong to the Lord our God.*
For it is not known when they fhall return to their Countrey; neither
can it perfectly be fhewed where they are, God fuffering it, as its faid
in *Deut.* 32. 26. *I determined to caft them forth unto the ends of
the earth, and to make their remembrance ceafe from among men.*
As if he fhould fay, I wil caft them unto the furtheft places of the world
that none may remember them; and therefore they are truly in Scripture called *imprifoned,* and *loft.*

SECT. 21.

NEither is there weight in the Argument which fome have
brought to me, if they be in the world, why doe we not know
them better? There are many things which we know, and yet know not
their original; are we not to this day ignorant of the heads of the four

Rivers

Rivers, *Nilus, Ganges, Euphrates,* and *Tegris?* alfo there are many
unknown Countryes. Befides, though fome live in knowne and neighbour Countrys, yet they are unknown by being behind Mountains;
fo it happened under the reign of *Ferdinand,* and *Ifabel,* that fome
Spaniards were found out by accident, at *Batueca,* belonging to the
Duke of *Alva,* which place is diftant but ten miles from *Salamanca,*
and near to *Placentia,* whither fome Spaniards fled, when the *Moors*
poffeffed *Spaine,* and dwelt there 800 years. If therefore a people
could lie hid fo long in the middle of *Spaine,* why may we not fay
that thofe are hid, whom God will not have any perfe&ly to know,
before the end of days?

And thefe things we have gathered concerning the habitations of
the ten Tribes, who, we beleeve, do ftill keep the Jewifh Rites, as in
2 *King.* 17. 26. when the Ifraelites were carryed captive by *Salmanefer,* and thofe of *Cuthah* came in their ftead, an Ifraelitifh Prieft
was fent by the King, to teach them, becaufe Lyons infefted them, for
that they were ignorant that there was another worfhip ufed in the
land: but when the Prieft faw that it was impoffible to take that people
wholly off from Idolatry, he permitted them to worfhip divers gods, fo
that they would acknowledge one, to be the mover of all things. The
fame is alfo fufficiently proved out of all the Hiftories which we have
alledged. And our brethren do keep the law more zealoufly out of their
land, then in it, as being neither ambitious, nor contentious (which
hath fometimes happened with the family of *David*) by which means
they might eafily erre in the true Religion, not acknowledge *Jerufalem,* and withdraw that obedience, which is due to the Lord, and
to his Temple.

SECT. 22.

WEE learne out of the firft of *Ezra,* that none of the ten Tribes
entred the fecond Temple; for it is faid that only fome of the
Tribe of *Judah,* and fome of *Benjamin* did returne. *Ezra* alfo faith
the fame in the first of *Chronicles,* that *Salmanefer* carryed the ten
Tribes to *Hala, Habor,* and *Hara,* and to the river *Gozan* to this day:
fo that you may gather that at that time they were there. So likewife
Jofephus in Antiq; Ind. lib. 11. *c.* 5.

Perhaps fome will fay, fince *Media* and *Perfia,* are near to *Babylon,* why did they not return to *Jerufalem* with the two Tribes? I
anfwer, becaufe fo few of the two neighbouring Tribes did return from
thence

thence to *Jerufalem*, for that they were wel feated in *Babylon*; or elfe becaufe they heard the Prophets fay, that they muft not look for any redemption but that which was to be at the end of dayes. How then can we thinke that they who were more remote, and alfo had learnt the fame things of the Prophets, fhould leave their place, perhaps to fuffer new miferies, and calamities? Befides, we doe not read that *Cyrus* gave leave to any to return, but only to the two Tribes of *Juda* and *Benjamin*. And alfo it is probable (as fome Authors affirme) that they could not goe up from thence, becaufe they had continually Wars with the neighbour people.

SECT. 23.

HItherto we have fhewed that the ten Tribes are in divers places, as in the *Weft-Indies*, in *Sina* ; in the confines of *Tartary*, beyond the river *Sabbathion*, and *Euphrates*, in *Media*, in the Kingdome of the *Habyffins* ; of all which the Prophet *Ifaiah* is to be underftood, in *Ifa.* 11. 11. *It fhall come to paffe in that day, that the Lord fhall fet his hand the fecond time to recover the remnant of his people, which fhall be left from* Affyria, *from* Egypt, *from* Pathros, *from* Ethiopia, *from* Elam, *from* Sinear, *from* Hamath, *and from the Iflands of the Sea.* From whence you may gather, that it is meant of thofe places where the ten Tribes dwell. *Syria* and *Ægypt* fhall be the two places of their generall meeting; as more fully hereafter.

Pathros, is not *Pelufium*, nor *Petra*, but *Parthia*, neare to the Cafpian Sea, where I thinke, with many others, the Sabbaticall river is. Although there is a *Pathros* in *Ægypt*, as the learned *Samuel Bochardus* faith in his holy Geography.

Chus, according to common opinion, is *Æthiopia*, as is proved out of *Jer.* 13. 23. and in this place of *Jeremy* are meant the *Ifrae-lites*, who live in the Country of the *Abyffins*.

Elam, is a Province in *Perfia*, as it appeares in *Dan.* 8. 2. where are defert places, in which, perhaps, the remnant of the ten Tribes is.

Shinar, is a Province about *Babylon*, as in *Gen.* 10. 10. where *Babel* is faid to be in *Shinar*; and *Dan.* 1. 2. it is faid, that *Nebuchadnezzar* carryed the holy Veffels to the Land of *Shinar*.

Hamath, there are many Hamaths mentioned in the Scripture, many underftand it of *Antioch*; but becaufe Geographers reckon up 12.

places

places named *Antioch,* therefore we can affirme nothing for certain; but I thinke, that that is meant, which is placed in *Sythia.* The feventy Interpreters by *Hamath,* underftand the Sun, from *Hamath* the Sun; and they tranflate it, From the rifing of the Sun; and I thinke it is no ill tranflation; for hereby all the *Ifraelites* who are in greater *Afia, India,* and *Sina,* may be underftood.

    The Iflands of the Sea; fo almoft all tranflate it; but I thinke it is to be rendred The Iflands of the Weft, for (*jam*) in holy Scripture fignifies *The Weft,* as in *Gen.* 28. 14. and in many other places; and upon this account thofe *Ifraelites* are implyed, who are Weftward from the Holy Land, among whom the *Americans* are.

S E C T. 24.

THe Prophet adds in *Ifa.* 11. 12. *And he fhall fet up a figne for the Nations, and he fhall affemble the out-cafts of* Ifrael, *and gather together the difperfed of* Judah *from the foure quarters of the earth.* Where he notes two things; 1. That he cals the *Ifraelites* out-cafts, but the *Iewes* fcattered; and the reafon is, becaufe the ten Tribes are not only farre off from the Holy Land, but alfo they live in the extremities and ends of Countries; from whence the Prophet cals them *caft-out.* But he doth not fay, that the *Ifraelites* are to be gathered from the foure quarters of the Earth, becaufe they are not fo difperfed through the World, as the Tribe of *Iudah* is, which now hath Synagogues, not only in three parts of the World, but alfo in *America.* The Prophet adds in *ver.* 13, *The envy alfo of* Ephraim *fhall depart, and the adverfaries of* Judah *fhall be cut off.* For then there fhall be no contention between *Iudah,* and the ten Tribes, which are comprehended under the name of *Ephraim,* becaufe their firft King *Feroboam* was of that Tribe. And then, as it is in *Ezek.* 37. 22. *One King fhall be King over them all, and they fhall be no more two Nations, neither fhall they be divided any more into two Kingdoms.* There fhall be one King to them both, of the family of *David.* Alfo the Lord at that redemption will dry up *Nilus,* and *Euphrates,* and will divide it into feven ftreames (anfwerable to his drying up the red Sea when they came out of *Ægypt*) perhaps that the feven Tribes, which are in thofe parts, may goe over it; as they paffe into their Country, as *Ifaiah* faith in ch. 27. 12, 13. *And it fhall be in that day, and he fhall fhake off from the bank of the river,* (fome underftand *Euphrates*) *unto the river of* Egypt (*Nilus*) *and ye, O children of* Ifrael, *fhall be gathered one by one.* Which was never done in the captivity of *Babylon.*   F   The

The Prophet *Isaiah* saith in chap. 11.11. *that he will return them the second time,* &c. Now the redemption from *Babilon,* cannot be called such an one, because all of them were not brought back to their Country. But the redemption shall be universall to all the Tribes, as it was when they went out of *Ægypt,* which redemption shall be like the first in many things, as I shewed in the third part of my *Reconciler;* and so it may be called the second, in reference to that first from *Ægypt.* Whence *Jeremiah* saith, Cha.23.7,8. *That then it shall not be said, He that brought Israel out of Egypt, but from the North, and from all Countries, whither he had driven them.* That they shall not mention their departure from *Ægypt,* for the cause fore-mentioned.

SECT. 25.

THe same Prophet, *sc. Isa.* 43. 5, 6. saith, *I will bring thy seed from the East, and will gather thee from the West: I will say to the North, Give up; and to the South, Keep not back; bring my Sons from farre, and my Daughters from the ends of the earth.* For *Media, Persia,* and *China,* lye on the East; *Tartary* and *Scythia* on the North; the Kingdome of the *Abyssins* on the South; *Europe* on the West, from the Holy Land. But when he saith, *Bring ye my sons from farre,* he understands *America;* so that in those verses he understands all those places, in which the Tribes are detained. Also in Chap. 49. from ver. 7. to the end of the Chapter, he saith, that that returne shall be most happy. And in ch. 56. verf. 8. God saith, *He that gathers the out-casts of Israel.* And the Prophet *Jeremiah,* in ch. 33. ver. 16. *In those dayes shall* Juda *be saved, and* Jerusalem *shall dwell safely.* It is certaine, and *Jerome* assents to all our Authors, that when *Judah* is joyned with *Israel,* by *Israel* the ten Tribes are meant. The same adds in *chap.* 31. *ver.* 15. in the comforting of *Rachel,* who wept for the carrying away her sons, *Joseph,* and *Benjamin,* the first by *Salmaneser* into *Assyria,* the last by *Nebuchadnezzar* into *Babilon,* he saith, in verf. 16. *Refraine thy voyce from weeping, and thine eyes from teares, for thy work shall be rewarded.* And it followes in Chap. 33. ver. 7. *And I will cause the captivity of* Judah, *and the captivity of* Israel *to returne, and I will build them up as at the first.* *Ezekiel* saith the same in Chap. 34. 13. and in Chap. 37. 16. under the figure of two sticks, on which were written the names of *Judah,* and *Ephraim,* by which he proves the gathering together of the twelve Tribes to be subject to

Messiah

Meſſiah the Son of *David*, in ver. 22. he faith, *And one King ſhall be King to them all*; according as *Hoſea* faith in Chap. 2. So alfo faith *Amos*, in chap. 9. verf. 14, 15. *And I will bring againe the captivity of my people* Ifrael, *and they ſhall build the waſt Cities, and inhabite them ; and they ſhall plant vine-yards, and drink the wine thereof: they ſhall make gardens,and eate the fruit of them. And they ſhall be no more pulled up out of their Land, which I have given them, faith the Lord thy God.* So alfo *Mica.* in cha. 2. 12. *I will ſurely aſſemble*, O Jacob, *all of thee, I will gather the remnant of* Ifrael, *I will alfo place him as the flock in the sheep-fold.* For that in the captivity of *Babilon* all were not gathered together. The Prophet *Zechariah* in chap. 8. 7. and in chap. 10. 6. and all the reft of the Prophets do witneffe the fame thing.

S E C T. 26.

BUt which way that redemption fhall be, no man can tell; but only fo farre as we may gather out of the Prophets. That at that time the ten Tribes fhall come to *Jeruſalem* under the leading of a Prince, whom fome Rabbins in the *Talmud,* and in some places of the Chaldy Paraphrafe, doe call *Meſſiah* the Son of *Joſeph*; and elfe-where *Meſſiah* the Son of *Ephraim* ; who being flaine in the laft War of *Gog* and *Magog,* fhall fhew himfelfe to be *Meſſiah* the fonne of *David,* who fhall be, as *Ekekiel,* and *Hoſea* fay, *The everlaſting Prince of all the twelve Tribes.* Our wife men doe, in many places, efpecially in the *Babilonian* Talmud, *in traſt. ſuca. c.* 5. make mention of that *Meſſiah* the fonne of *Ephraim*; where they fay, that he fhall dye in the laft war of *Gog,* and *Magog ;* and they fo expound that of *Zach.* 12. 10. *And they ſhall looke upon me whom they have pierced, and they ſhall mourne for him, as one mourneth for his only ſonne.* They adde alfo, that the foure Captaines, of whom the fame Prophet fpeakes in chap. 11. are, *Meſſiah* the fon of *David, Meſſiah* the fon of *Joſeph,* the Prophet *Elias,* and the high Prieft; which foure are thofe dignities,which fhall fhew their power in that bleffed age. Obferve, that fometime they call *Meſſiah* the fon of *Ephraim,* fometime of *Joſeph ;* for he fhall come out of the Tribe of *Ephraim,* and fhall be Captaine of all the ten Tribes, who gave their name to *Ephraim,* becaufe that their firft King *Jeroboam* was of that Tribe. Not without caufe doe they call him the fon of *Joſeph,* for he was the true type of the houfe of *Iſrael,* in his imprifonment, and future happineffe. Adde to this, that he was fo long hid from his brethren, that they did not know him: as in like manner the ten Tribes are at this day, who are led captive, but hereafter fhall come to the top of felicity, in the fame manner as *Jofeph* did. That *Meffiah* of *Jofeph* fhall dye in the battel of *Gog*, and *Magog*, and afterward fhall rife againe, that he may enjoy the dignity, not of a Kingly Scepter, but the office only of a Vice-roy, as *Jofeph* in *Ægypt*; for that the Empire of the houfe of *Ifrael* fell under the reigne of *Hofea* the fon of *Elah*; as the Prophet *Amos* faith in chap. 5. 2. Therefore the Kingdome of the ten Tribes fhall not be reftored, as *Ezekiel* faith in Chap. 37. under the reigne of *Meffiah* the fon of *David*, who fhall be everlafting; and by the death of *Meffiah* the fon of *Jofeph*, the ten Tribes fhall fee, that God will not that they fhould have more Kings then one. As its already fpoken.

SECT. 27.

THofe Tribes then fhall be gathered from all quarters of the earth, into Countries neare to the Holy Land; namely, into *Affyria*, and *Ægypt*; and from thence they fhall goe into their Country; of which *Ifaiah* fpeakes, in chap. 27. 13. *And it fhall be in that day, that the great trumpet fhall be blown, and they who were loft, fhall come into the Land of* Affyria; *and they who were caft out, into* Egypt; *and fhall worfhip the Lord in the holy mount at* Jerufalem. As if he fhould fay, as trumpets found, to call any army together: fo they fhall come together, who were dead (that is, difperfed through all *Afia*) into *Affyria*; and the out-cafts (that is, which are in *America*) fhall come by the *Mediterranean* Sea to *Alexandria* of *Ægypt*; and in the like manner thofe who are in *Africa*, when *Nilus* fhall be dried up, and *Euphrates* fhall be divided; as we have already faid. And becaufe the gathering together of the captivity, fhall begin at thofe who are in *America*, therefore *Ifaiah* faith, *The Iflands fhall truft in me, and the fhips of* Tarfis (that is of the Ocean) *firft of all, that they may bring thy fons from farre, and with them, their filver, and gold.* They fhall then come with fpeed from thofe Countries, proftrating themfelves at the mountaine of the Lord in *Jerufalem*, as the Prophet *Hofea* faith of that redemption in chap. 11. 11. *They fhall come as birds out of* Egypt, *and as Doves out of* Affyria; fo faith *Ifaiah* in Chap. 60. 8. *Who are thofe that fly as a cloud, and as Doves to their nefts?* They which

come

come firft, fhall alfo partake of this joy, to fee others to come to them every moment; for which caufe the fame Prophet faith, *Lift up thine eyes round about, aud behold them who gather themfelves to thee.* And because the two Countrys of *Affyria* and *Egypt,* fhall first of all kindly receive the people of *Ifrael,* and fhall know the truth, firft of all imbracing the Religion of the Jewes, facrificing and praying to God, therefore the prophet *Ifaiah* faith, in c. 19. 25. *Bleffed be Egypt my people, and Affyria the worke of my hands; but Ifrael is my inheritance.* For fo thofe words are to be underftood.

S E C T. 28.

ALL thofe are the fayings of the holy Prophets, from whence doth appeare the returne of Ifrael into their Country. It is given to none to know the time thereof, neither is it revealed to *Rabby Simeon ben Johay,* the Author of the Zoar; becaufe that God hath referved that myftery to himfelf, as *Mofes* faith. *It is hid with me.* And *Ifaiah* in ch. 63. 4. *For the day of vengeance is in my heart, and the year in which the redemption fhall come.* Which the Rabbins thus interpret, *I have reveiled it to my heart and not to Angells:* and elfewhere, *If any man tell you when Meffiah fhall come, beleeve him not.* So alfo the Angel faith to *Daniel* ch. 12. 9. *All things are clofed up and fealed to the time of the end.* Therefore all thofe, who fearch after that time, as *Rabbi Seadiah, Mofes Egyptius, Mofes Gerundenfis, Selomoh Jarchi; Abraham bar Ribi Hijah, Abraham Zacculo, Mordehai Reato, and Ifaac Abarbanel,* have been miftaken; for that they would go beyond humane capacity, and reveale that, which God concealed. And even to *Daniel* himfelfe (to whom was made knowne the fecret of the change of the four Monarchies) it was fo revealed to him, that hee confeffed he did not underftand it. Our Ancients did point at this from the Letter (m) in *Ifa.* 9. 7. where he faith, *Of the increase of his government:* which (m) in the Hebrew, being fuch an (m) which they write onely in the end of words, and a clofe letter, yet is put in the middle of the word, againft common practife: becaufe that the time of the fifth Monarchy fhall be hid, till the time when it fhall begin.

F 3   *S E C T.*

SECT. 29.

Y Et this I can affirm, that it shall be about the end of this age; and so the Prophet speaks of that age *about the end of dayes:* and that after many labours, and a long captivity. So *Balaam* prophesies, *Numb.* 24. 17. *I see, but not now; I behold, but not near; a Star shall come out of Jacob.* Isa. 24. 22. *They shall be cast into prison, and they shall be visited after many daies.* And Isa. 49. 14. *And Sion said, The Lord hath forsaken me, and my Lord hath forgotten me.* Hos. 3. 4, 5. *The children of Israel shall be many days without a King, and without a Prince: And after that they shall seek the Lord their God, and David their King.* The King and Prophet complains of that delay, in *Psa.* 44. *Psa.* 69. *Psa.* 74. *Psa.* 77. *Psal.* 83. And after that in *Psal.* 89. 50. 51. he thus concludes, *Remember, O God, the reproach of thy servants, who suffer so many injuries of so many people: wherewith they have reproached the steps of thy Messiah.* As yet at this day it is said, that ALTHOUGH THE MESSIAH WERE LAME, HE MIGHT HAVE COME BY THIS TIME. Though we cannot exactly shew the time of our redemption, yet we judge it to be near. For,

1 We see many prophesies fulfilled, and others also which are subfervient to a preparation for the same redemption; and it appears by this, that during that long and sore captivity, many calamities are fore-told us under the four Monarchies. *David* saith in *Psal.* 120. 7. *Lord when I speake of peace, they speake of war.* And elsewhere, *We are slaine all the day for thy name, and are accounted for sheep which are slain.* In Isa. 53. 7. *He shall be led as a sheep to the slaughter, and as a lamb before his shearers: he shall be dumb, and shall not open his mouth.* O how have we seen these things in the banishments of *England, France* and *Spaine!* and how have they proved those crimes, which most false men have said that ours did commit! Behold they have slaine them, not for wickednesses, which they did not commit, but for their riches which they had. O how have we seen all those things done by divine providence, for that those misfortunes for the most part happened on the ninth day of the month *Ab,* an ominous, and unhappy day, on which the first, and second Temple were burnt, and the spies wept without a cause.

SECT.

SECT. 30.

WHat fhall we fay of that horrible monfter, the Spanifh Inquifition, what cruelty hath not daily been ufed againft a company of miferable ones, innocents, old men, and children, of every
fex and age, who were flaine, becaufe they could not divine who was
their fecret accufer? But let us fee, why in al thofe places (in which that
Spanifh tyrannicall Empire rules,) they were flain, who would obferve
the law of *Mofes*; and by how many, and how great miracles hath
that law been confirmed; and what unrighteousneffe is there in it?
We daily fee examples of conftancy in ours, worthy of all praife, who
for the fanctifying of Gods name, have been burnt alive. Truly many who are ftill living, can witneffe all thofe things. In the year 1603.
At *Lisbone, Diogo d'Affumean*, a Monk of 24 years, was burnt
alive, who defended himfelfe in the Inquifition againft fome, who
would have reduced him to Chriftianity, who was born a Chriftian,
and made a Jew; which all wonder at; the Inquifitors being grieved
that they had publifhed the reafons which he had alledged, would
have recalled their fentence; but it was then too late; for it was di-
vulged through the world, which I my felfe have by me. Alfo the
Lord *Lope de Veray Alacron* deferves the praife of Martyrdome, who
being born of a noble, and eminent Family, and very learned in the
Hebrew, and Latine tongues, did imbrace our Religion; neither
thought it fufficient to be fuch himfelfe, but difcovered himfelfe to
many others; thereupon in *Ann.* 1644 in the twentieth of this age,
he being imprifoned at *Valladolid*, though he lived in the darke, yet
he difcovered light to many; neither could the great number of Do-
ctors, nor the greater affliction of his parents, move him from his
enterprife, either by tears or by promifes. He circumcifed himfelf
in prifon (O ftrange act, and worthy of all praife!) and named himfelfe *beleeving Judas*; and at laft, as a fecond *Ifaac*, offered himfelfe to the flames, contemning life, goods, and honours, that hee
might obtain immortall life, and good things that cannot perifh; in
the 25th yeer of his age. Now though thofe were not of the family
of Ifrael, yet they obtained an immortall glory, which is better then
this life.

Alfo we have many examples of our own, which did equalize them,
of which that is one, which is done in our time, and is worthy to be
remembred; *Ifaac Caftrenfis Tartas* (whom I knew, and fpoke
with)

with) a learned young man, and verſed in the Greek, and Latine; he being but newly come to *Fernambuc*, was taken by the *Portugeſe*, and carryed to *Lisbone*, and burnt alive; he was a young man of 24. years old ; ſcorning riches, and honours, which were offered to him, if he would turne Chriſtian. They who ſay he was a traytor, do lye egregiouſly; for he did defend that place where he was Governour, moſt valiantly; as ours do deport themſelves in thoſe fortified places which are committed to their charge. The ſame Martyrdom was undergone at *Lima*, by *Eli Nazarenus*, in *Ann.* 1639. *Janu.* 23. who after he had lived 14 whole years in priſon, all which time hee eat no fleſh, leſt he ſhould defile his mouth ; he called himſelfe by that name, after he had circumciſed himſelfe. Such a Martyr alſo, this year, was *Thomas Terbinon* in the City of *Mexico*.

SECT. 31.

IF the Lord fulfilled his word in calamities, he will fulfill it alſo in felicities. Therefore *Rabbi Aquibah* laughed, when hee ſaw a Fox run out of the Temple being deſtroyed, though his companions wept; he ſaying, Now is fulfilled that prophecy of *Jeremiah*, *Lament.* 5. 18. *And the foxes ſhall run therein*; and he added, and thoſe bleſſings alſo ſhall follow, which the Lord hath promiſed. We ſee all the curſes of God come to paſſe, which are mentioned in *Leviticus* and *Deuteronomy* ; as well as thoſe, which concerne our being ſcattered to the ends of the earth (which is *Portugall*) and thoſe concerning the calamities of the Inquiſition; and thoſe of our baniſhments, as I have opened in my booke, *De termino vitæ*; from whence it appears, that all the happy propheſies ſhall be fulfilled. And as we have periſhed, ſo alſo ſhall *Bozra* (that is, *Rome*) periſh. See *Iſa.* 34. 6.

SECT. 32.

SEcondly; The argument which we bring from our Conſtancy under ſo many evills, cannot be eluded, that therefore God doth reſerve us for better things. *Moſes* in *Levit.* 26. 44. ſaith, *Though they be in the land of their enemies, yet I will not caſt them away, neither will I abhor them to deſtroy them utterly, and to breake my covenant with them, for I am the Lord their God.* And truly theſe things are now fulfilled, for that in this captivity, and among the many reproaches which we Jewes ſuffer, yet many of ours are
ho-

honourably entertained by Princes, with a fingular affection. So *D. Ifhac Abarbanel*, who comes of *Davids* line, is Counfellor to the King of *Spaine*, and *Portugall*. By this alfo he hath got a great name, for that he compofed the differences, which arofe beene the King of *Portugall*, and the Republique of *Venice*. And from that Family of *Abarbanel* (which I note by the by) doe proceed my Children, by my wives fide. And in the houfe of his fonne, *D. Samuel Abarbanel*, and of his wife *Benuenida*, the Lady *Leonora de Toledo*, was brought up at *Naples*, who is the Daughter of *D. Peter de Toledo*, the Vice-roy of *Naples*; who afterwards was married to the moft eminent Duke *Cofmus de Medicis*, and having obtained the Dukedome of *Tofcani*, fhe honoured *Benuenida* with as much honour, as if fhe were her mother.

That peace, which the *Venetians* made with the Emperour *Sultan Selim*, 75. yeares agone, was made, and ratified by a certaine Jew *Don Selomo Rophe*, who was fent Ambaffadour to *Venice*, and received with great pomp, by the *Venetians*. At *Conftantinople* D. *Ben Jaefe, Anaucas*, and *Sonfinos* are of great authority with the *Turk*. In *Ægypt* the *Jewes* were alwayes *Saraph baxas*, and alfo at this day is *D. Abraham Alholn*. Who knowes not that *D. Jofephus Naffi*, otherwife called *Joannes Michefius*, about the 66. yeare of the former age, was Duke of *Naccia*, Lord of *Milum*, and of the feven Iflands, of whom fee *Famian. Strada* in *Hiftor. Belgic. part.* 1. *lib.* 5. He was raifed to thefe honours by *Sultan Selim*. As alfo by *Sultan Amurat, Jacob Aben Jaes*, otherwife called *Alvoro Mendez*, was made Governour of *Tyberias*; witneffe *Boterus* in *Relation. part.* 3. *lib.* 2. in *Barbary*, the Lords *Rutes* were always Governours of *Sekes, Phes*, and *Taradanta*. In *Ann.* 1609. *D. Samuel Palaxe* was fent Ambaffadour to the States, by *Mulai Zidan* the King of *Maracco*. But he dyed at the *Haghe* in *Anno*. 1616. And the moft eminent Prince *Maurice*, and the Nobles, were at his Funerall. In *Perfia* who knowes not of what account they are? There, thirty years fince, *Elhazar* was fecond to the King, and as it were Governour. Now *David Jan* fucceeds him, to whom others alfo being joyned, they live in the Court. And that muft not be forgot, that when the moft eminent Duke of *Holftein* fent *Otto Burchmannus* Ambaffadour to *Perfia*, in *Ann.* 1635. he defired commendatory letters from our *Jewes* at *Hamburgh*, to them, who (as we have already told you) doe live there in the Court, that they would

G   make

make way there, for him that was a ſtranger: that he might diſpatch his affaires: Which was alſo performed. By which means ours, who are in *Perſia*, diſmiſſed *Burchmannus*, with rich gifts, and with Letters to the moſt eminent Duke of *Holſtein*, which the twelve Chuzæ, or Princes, had ſubſigned. A copy of which Letters the moſt excellent *D. Benjamin Muſſapha*, one familiar with the Prince helped me to. Alſo *Claudius Duretu en ſon threſor des langues, fol.* 302. faith, that there are almoſt an infinite number of *Jewes* in *Aſia*, eſpecially in *India*, and that King *Cochini* is their great favourer. Yea *Linſchotes* faith (where he treats of *Cochini*) that they have Synagogues there, and that ſome of them are of the Kings Counſell. At *Prague*, *Mordocheas Maiſel* had Armes given him by the Emperour *Matthias*, who alſo knighted him. Which honour *Iacob Bathſebah* alſo had, under the Reigne of *Ferdinand*; and many other Families are graced with other honours. And in this very captivity (who could thinke it) they are ſo wealthy, that (Gods providence favouring them) they may challenge to themſelves a place among the moſt Noble.

SECT. 33.

WHo can enumerate the number of ours, who are renowned by fame, and learning? The learned *R. Moſes bar Maimon* was Phiſician to *Saladin* the King of *Ægypt*. *Moſes Amon* to the Emperour *Sultan Bajaſeth*. *Elias Montalto* to the moſt eminent Queen of France, *Loyſia de Medicis*; and was alſo her Counſellor. At Padua *Elias Cretenſis* read Philoſophy; and *R. Abraham de Balmas*, the Hebrew Grammer. And how much honour had *Elias Grammaticus* at *Rome?* And almoſt all the Princes of *Italy* honoured him with all kinde of honour, *Abraham Kolorni*; as appeares by a Letter writ to him by *Thomas Garzoni nella ſua piazza univerſale del mundo*. *Picus Mirandula* (who uſeth to ſay, *That he had but ſmall underſtanding, who only looked after his owne things, and not after other mens*) and others, had Hebrew teachers. *David de Pomis* dedicated his Book to Pope *Sextus* the fifth, who lovingly, and courteouſly received both the Author, and work. So at this day we ſee many deſirous to learne the Hebrew tongue of our men. Hence may be ſeene that God hath not left us; for if one perſecute us, another receives us civilly, and courteouſly; and if this Prince treats us ill, another treats us well; if one baniſheth us out of his coun-

try,

try, another invites us by a thoufand priviledges; as divers Princes of *Italy* have done, the moft eminent King of *Denmarke*, and the mighty Duke of *Savoy* in *Niffa*. *And doe we not fee, that thofe Republiques doe flourifh, and much increafe in Trade, which admit the Ifraelites?*

S E C T. 34.

MOfes faith in his laft fong, that God would revenge the bloud of his people who are fcattered. And *Ieremiah* faith, in chap. 2. 3. *Ifrael is the Lords holy thing, the firft fruits of his increafe; all who devoure him fhall be found guilty; evill fhall come upon them, faith the Lord.* And that the Hiftories of divers times, even from *Nebuchadnezzar* to thefe very times, doe teftifie. Have not the Monarchies of great Princes been deftroyed? Confider with me the miferable ends of *Antiochus,* of *Pompey,* of *Sifibuthus,* of *Philip* the King of *France,* of A*lonfus* the fonne of *Iohn* the fecond. And we may remember, how King *Sebaftian* with his fourth Generation, and with all his Nobles, was flaine in a battell of A*frica,* in that fame place, in which he had caufed the *Iews* to be banifhed. *Ferdinand,* and *Ifabel* were the great Perfecutors of our Nation, but how did both he, and fhe dye? as for him his Son-in-law, and his owne Subjects did perfecute him; and his only fonne dyed (leaving no iffue) on his Wedding-day, being feventeen yeares old. His daughter being Heire of the Kingdome, and of her Fathers hatred, would not marry to *Emanuel* King of *Portugal,* unleffe he would compell us to be banifhed, and change our Religion. But fhe dyed in Child-birth of her Sonne *Saragoci,* and alfo her Son, before he was halfe a yeare old; and the fucceffion was devolved upon the Kingdome of *Spaine.* It is not long fince, that the *Spaniards* exercifed upon us at *Mantua,* what ever cruelties they could invent; what fhall we fay of that at *Madrid* in the yeare 1632, was done by the Inquifition, the King, and Princes of the Kingdome concurring; but in the very fame month dyed the Infant *Charles,* and their Kingdome declined. What wonder is it if God hath chaftifed divers Kingdomes by fundry wayes: but of this I treat farther in my Hiftory of the *Iewes.* Let us conclude therefore, that that good, which God hath promifed, will fhortly come, fince we fee that we have fuffered thofe evils, which he hath threatned us with, by the Prophets.

G 2   S E C T.

S E C T. 35.

3ly, **T**He fhortneffe of time (when we beleeve our redemption fhall appeare) is confirmed by this, that the Lord hath promifed that he will gather the two Tribes, *Iudah*, and *Benjamin*, out of the foure quarters of the World, calling them *Nephuffim*. From whence you may gather, that for the fulfilling of that, they muft be fcattered through all the corners of the World; as *Daniel* faith, *Dan.* 12. 7. *And when the fcattering of the holy people fhall have an end, all thofe things fhall be fulfilled.* And this appeares now to be done, when as our Synagogues are found in *America.*

S E C T. 36.

4ly, **T**O thefe, let us adde that, which the fame Prophet fpeakes, in ch. 12. ver. 4. *That knowledge fhall be encreafed;* for then the prophecies fhall better be underftood, the meaning of which we can fcarce attaine to, till they be fulfilled. So after the *Otteman* race began to flourifh, we underftood the prophefie of the two leggs of the Image of *Nebuchadnezzar,* which is to be overthrowne by the fifth Monarchy, which fhall be in the World. So *Jeremiah* after he had handled in Chap. 30. the redemption of *Ifrael,* and *Judah,* and of the war of *Gog,* and *Magog* (of which *Daniel* alfo fpeakes in ch. 12.) when he treats of the Scepter of the Meffiah the fon of *David,* of the ruine of the Nations, of the reftoration of *Judah,* of holy *Jerufalem,* and of the third Temple, he adds in ver. 24. *The fierce anger of the Lord fhall not returne, till he hath executed it, and till he hath performed the intents of his heart; in the latter dayes ye fhall underftand it.* From whence followes what we have faid, that the time of redemption is at hand. And becaufe *Jeremiah* in that Chapter makes an abridgement of all things that fhall be, therefore it is faid in ver. 2. *Write thee all the words which I have fpoken to thee in a book.* By this meane making the Prophecie clearer, by relating in a cleare ftyle, whatever the Prophets had fore-told; imitating *Mofes,* the laft words of whofe fong are, *Sing, O ye Nations, with his people,* in *Deut.* 32. 43. Alfo the laft words which he fpake, after that he had bleffed the Tribes, are thefe, *Happy art thou, O* Ifrael: *who is like to thee, O people? faved by the Lord, who is the fheild of thy help, and the fword of thy excellency; and*
thine

*thine enemies ſhall be found lyars to thee, and thou ſhalt tread up-
on their high places,* in *Deut.* 33. 29. From whence it appeares,
that God will revenge the bloud of *Iſrael,* which had been ſhed.
Joel confirmes the ſame in ch. 3. 19. *Ægypt ſhall be a deſolation,
and* Edom *ſhall be a filthy deſert, for the violence, and injury offered to the* Jewes, *and becauſe they have ſhed innocent bloud in their
Land.* And as they ſhall be puniſhed by the juſt judgement of God,
who wiſh us evill: ſo alſo God will give bleſſings upon them who favour us. And thoſe are the trees of the field which then ſhall rejoyce. So God ſaith to *Abraham,* in *Gen.* 12. 3. *I will bleſſe them
who bleſſe thee, and curſe them that curſe thee.*

S E C T. 37.

THeſe are the things which I could gather concerning this matter,
which hath not been heretofore handled ; from whence theſe
conſequences may be deduced.

1. That the *Weſt-Indies,* were anciently inhabited by a part of
the ten Tribes, which paſſed thither out of *Tartary,* by the Streight
of *Anian.*

2. That the Tribes are not in any one place, but in many; becauſe
the Prophets have fore-told their return ſhall be into their Country,
out of divers places; *Iſaiah* eſpecially ſaith it ſhall be out of eight.

3. That they did not returne to the ſecond Temple.

4. That at this day they keep the *Jewiſh* Religion.

5. That the prophecies concerning their returne to their Country,
are of neceſſity to be fulfilled.

6. That from all coaſts of the World they ſhall meet in thoſe two
places, ſc. *Aſſyria,* and *Ægypt* ; God preparing an eaſie, pleaſant
way, and abounding with all things, as *Iſaiah* ſaith, ch. 49. and from
thence they ſhall flie to *Jeruſalem,* as birds to their neſts.

7. That their Kingdome ſhall be no more divided; but the twelve
Tribes ſhall be joyned together under one Prince, that is under *Meſ-
ſiah* the Son of *David*; and that they ſhall never be driven out of their
Land.

S E C T. 38.

I Returne to the relation of our *Montezinus,* which I prefer before
the opinions of all others as moſt true For that *Peru* ſhould be derived from the name *Ophir,* as *Gulielmus Poſtellus, Goropius in Orte-*

lius, Bozius de signis Ecclef. lib. 2. *c.* 3. *Marinus in arca Noah, P. Sa. in* 3. *Reg. Pomarius* in his *Lexicon,* and *Poffevinus lib.* 2. *Biblith. c.* 8. do think, cannot be proved; as *Pineda* hath wel obferved, in *Job, c.* 28. *p.* 500. for we have faid out of *Garcilaffo de la Vega,* that that name was unknown to them of *Peru. Ophir* then is *Eaft-India,* if we beleeve *Jofephus, lib.* 8. *Antiquit. Judaic. c.* 6. & *Acofta* in *lib.* 1. *Hiftor. Ind.* from whence *Solomon* fetched gold, and precious ftones. But what *Gomara in part* 1. *hift. Ind. fol.* 120. and *Zarate in procem. hift. Peru,* would have, that ours did paffe over that famous, and much praifed Ifland (by *Plato* in *Critia,* and *Timæus*) of *Atlantis,* and fo went into the neighbour Iflands of *Barlovent,* and from thence to the firm land, and at laft to the Kingdom of *Peru,* and *New-Spain;* it is defervedly exploded as fabulous; and *Acofta* laughs at it, *in lib.* 1. *hift.* Ind. *c.* 22. But *Marcilius Ficinus in comment. in Timeum, c.* 4. & *Critia,* that he might defend *Plato,* thinkes (and his Difciples, *Porphiry, Origen,* and *Proclus* doe follow him) that all that which is in *Critia,* and in *Timæus,* is to be underftood allegorically. And who will beleeve *Lefcarbotus,* who faith that they are the *Canaanites,* who fled thither for feare of *Jofhua?* For I cannot be perfwaded that they fought out Countries fo far remote. They who will have them of *Peru* to have come out of *Norwey,* or *Spain,* may be confuted by their very form, manners and the unlikeneffe of their Languages. But that is more falfe, that they are *Ifraelites,* who have forgot circumcifion, and their rites. For they are of a comly body, and of a good wit, as faith Doct. *Johannes Huarte,* in his book which is called, *Examen ingenior. c.* 14. But contrarily all men know that the *Indians* are deformed, dul, and altogether rude. And we have abundantly fhown, with how great ftudy, and zeal, the *Ifraelites* have kept their Language, and Religion, out of their Country.

S E C T. 39.

MOntezinus then fpeaks moft likely; that as other people forced the *Ifraelites* to betake them to the mountains: fo *America* being firft of all inhabited by the perfecuting *Tartars,* they were driven to the mountains of *Cordillere,* where at laft they were hid, as God would have it. Truly, comparing the *Ifraelites* themfelves, or their Laws, with other people, I fee not anything that comes nearer truth. Perhaps alfo *America* was not of old contiguous to *Afia* on the North fide. It doth not feeme to me fuch an abfurdity, to fay, that the

Ifraelites

Ifraelites went out of *Tartary* into *America* by land; and afterward, that God, to preferve his, among other miracles, alfo wrought this, to make that a Sea, where now is the ftreight of *Anian*. Yea that might be don without a miracle, by accident, as we know that more than once, the Sea by a violent ftorm hath carryed away the Land, and made I- flands. *Xenophon in fuis æquivoc.* mentions the inundations of *Ægypt*, which happened in the days of *Prometheus*, and *Hercules*. Alfo *Berofus in lib. 5.* and *Diodorus li. 6.* mentions the inundation of *Attica*, in which *Athens* ftands. *Pliny in lib. 2. c. 85. & lib. 13. c. 11. Strabo in l. 1. & l. 12.* and *Plutarch in Alexandr.* relate the drowning of the Ifle *Pharaonica*; of which *Luther* fpeaks fo elegantly in *lib. ultimo.* Befides, who knows not how many, and how great Cities have at divers times been almoft wholly ruined by feveral earthquakes? *Sueton, in Tiberio, c. 48.* writes, that under *Tiberius*, twelve Cities in *Afia* have been by this means ruined. *Orofius lib. 7. c. 4.* and *Dion Caffius lib. 57.* do affirm the fame, though they differ about the time. *Tacitus in lib. 14*, and *Eufebius in Chron.* relate the deftruction of that famous and rich City of *Laodicea*. *Origen tom. 28. in Joan* and *Baronius tom. 2. Annal. Ecclefiaft, Ann. 340*: do fpeak of other earthquakes, which have deftroyed divers, and very many men, and Cities. And *P. Alonfus in fuo manual. tempor.* relates, that the fame hath happened in our dayes; faith he, In the year 1638. *A great Earthquake happened in the Iflands of the Terceræ, but efpecially in St. Michael, where the Governour dwells; for that unheard of fhaking of the earth, and houfes, ftruck fo great terror into the Inhabitants, that al fled out of their houfes & lived in the fields, a little after, two miles from thence, they faw the Sea vomit up abundance of fiery matter, which made a very thicke fmoake, which covered the very clouds; and it caft up many great ftones which feemed like rocks; part whereof falling downe againe, made an Ifland in the Sea which was halfe a mile over, and fixty fathom high, & an hundred & fifty fathom deep. That hot exhalation which that fiery mountain fent forth, pierced the very waters, and ftifled fo many fifhes, that two Indian fhips could not carry them.* The fame Ifland two years after, was fwallowed up again of the Sea.

S E C T. 40.

HEE that doth ferioufly weigh thofe things, may (I think) well gather, that the Sea of the Streight of *Anian* was an inundation. By affirming which, this doubt may be anfwered, *fc.* That after

ter the univerfall Flood, man-kinde encreafed againe, and all beafts, which had been preferved in the Arke. But how could fo many kinds of beafts, (which come by propagation, and are not bred out of the earth) be found in thofe Countries? Some did fwim thither, fome were brought thither by fome huntfmen, fome were bred out of the earth, as *Auftin* thinks it happened in the firft Creation. But what Land-beaft can fwim over fo great a Sea? And would Huntf-men carry Lyons thither, and other fuch kind of beafts, oftentimes to the great hazzard of their lives? And if God would have created thofe beafts out of the earth, he would not have commanded *Noah* to have kept them in the Ark. I am fully perfwaded, that the beafts which are found there paffed that way into *America*; unleffe any thinks that this new world is joyned to the old, on fome other fide, as *Herrera* be-leeves *Dec.* 3. *lib.* 11. *c.* 10.

S E C T. 41.

AS for the other things in the relation of our *Montezinus*, they fay nothing which favours of falfhood. For their faying that the *Semah*, truly it is the cuftom of our people, in what part foever of the world they live; and it is the abridgement of the confeffion and religion of the Jewes. That revelation of the Magicians whom they call *Mo-hanes*, it agrees with thofe things which in 2 *Efdras* you may fee, concerning the Miracles which God wrought for the Ifraelites, as they paffed over *Euphrates,* concerning thofe conditions of not revealing fecrets to any, but fuch an one who hath feen three hundred Moons, (which make twenty five years) it appeares to be true, by what the famous *De Laet* tells in many parts of *America*, that the *Indi-ans* do compute their years by Moones. That a fecret muft be told in the Field, doth not that argue a *Jewiſh* cuftome, which the ancients have obferved in *Jacob*? who being about to depart from *Laban*, he called his Wives into the field.

I now conclude this difcourfe, in which this only was in my inten-tion, that I might briefly, and compendioufly declare mine, and the Rabbies opinion, concerning thofe things which I have handled. I hope that this my indeavor will not be unacceptable, being defired by many men famous both for Birth, and for Learning; not unprofitable, having therein explained the relation of *Montezinus*, with what bre-vity I could. The Name of God be bleffed for ever. *Amen.*

CONSI-

CONSIDERATIONS
Upon the Point of the
CONVERSION
OF THE
JEWES:

GOD hath promifed to doe great things in thefe laft days, as namely, to fubdue all his Enemies, to releive his people, to deftroy all Tyranny and Oppreffion both civil and ecclefiafticall, and to ampliate the Bounds of Chrifts Kingdom, by a plentifull pouring forth of his fpirit, and by converting the multitudes both of Jews and Gentiles. Herein he doth what the Ruler of the Feaft faid to the Bridegroome in *John* 2. 10. *he keepes the beft wine till the laft*; he makes the laft Act, the beft part of the Comedy. Whereas the method of the Devill, and the World, is contrary; reprefented by *Nebuchadnezzars image*, whofe head, or beginning, was of gold; but the feet, or ending, was of iron, and clay. And of thefe great good things (we being now upon the borders of the long-looked-for-*Canaan*) God hath given us fome earneft (which is a fmall proportion, with the whole for kind) a bunch of grapes; *Og*, and the *Amorites* fubdued. For he hath in our days arrefted the *Turks* greatneffe; abated the formidableneffe of the *German-Auftrian Beaft*; revealed in good meafure the hypocrifie and lies of the falfe Prophet, who hath his feat at *Rome*; and hath brought to light the fubtilties of Satan, who had fhifted himfelfe into feverall dreffes of pretended Reformation. Hee is rifen up like a mighty Gyant, againft his enemies among

H   mong

(57)

mong us, and elfewhere, and hath pleaded his peoples caufe fo fignally, that all but thofe whofe judgement it is to be wilfully blind, will fay, *The Lord is on our fide.* He hath alfo fcattered *Light,* and *Truth* in an unwonted meafure, among all forts of people; he hath given forth his owne good Spirit more plentifully than formerly (except in thofe extraordinary primitive times of Chriftianifm;) and hath inftated us into liberty for our fpirits; which though too many abufe, and turne into licentioufneffe, or a liberty to finne, yet that is no difpraife, but a commendation to the thing; for it is a figne that liberty is exceeding good in itfelfe, feeing the corruption or abufe of it, is a thing fo bad, but fo hedged in by feverall Fences, as it hath pleafed God in much mercy to direct the wifdome of our State to, it is a choyfe mercy, and fuch as is fuitable to our Principles both Humane, and Chriftian; Thus we have a Day-ftar to tell us that day is at hand; fomething prodromous concerning almoft all the great things promifed, and looked for, as might be more largely fhowne, if that were my proper work. But yet nothing concerning *the returning of the Shulamite,* in *Cant.* 6. *ult.* which Mr. *Brightman* interprets to be the *Jewes* turning Chriftian, the clock of their converfion hath not yet given warning; it is as midnight with them ftill, as it was a thoufand yeares agone. Upon which, fome ground the hopelefneffe of their repentance, but I dare not owne that Logick, but rather conclude thus; That therefore their Converfion fhall be the work of God (of which more anon) with whom all difficulties are no hinderance; and though *Ifrael* be bond-men in *Ægypt,* and fealed up to it by the darkneffe of a midnight, yet let but God fpeake, and they are immediately at liberty, and fent away without waiting for the comming of the day.

Now we ought much to minde their Converfion, exercifing thereupon our faith, our prayers, and alfo our enquiries, and that for thefe following reafons:

Firft, becaufe they have the fame Humane nature with us; from this ground we fhould wifh well to all men, whether *Jew,* or *Gentile;* which is the precept of the Apoftle, in 2 *Pet.* 1. 7. *To adde love to brotherly kindneffe;* that is, not only to love Saints, but to love Men (though the Saints with a choyfe, and peculiar love.) Yea it is Gods owne practife, in *Mat.* 5. 45. There is a φιλανθρωπία in God (as *Paul* faith to *Titus*) a love to Man-kinde. *Plutarch* could obferve that God is not called φίλιππος, he beares another manner

ner

ner of love to men, than to horſes; ſo ought we to doe, and even upon this generall account, to love the *Iewiſh* Nation.

Secondly, becauſe of their extraction; Their root is holy, though now the Branches be degenerate and wilde; ſo in *Rom.* 11. verſ. 16, 17. Some good turnes are due to the bad children of good Parents for the Parents ſake; and this *Paul* expreſly urgeth, in *Rom.* 11. 28. *that they are beloved for the Fathers ſake;* yea the chief root, or head of their Nation, *Abraham* is myſtically our ſubſtituted Father, as in *Gal.* 4 laſt; *If ye be Chriſts, then are ye* Abrahams *ſeed, and heires according to the promiſe.* The *Iewes* are children, and heires of the fleſh of *Abraham,* but we of his faith; they by the Bond-woman, but we by the Free; but notwithſtanding, *Abraham* is our common Father, and therefore we ſhould love as brethren.

Thirdly, becauſe Gods covenant with the *Iewes* is not nulled, or broken, but only ſuſpended. It is with them as it was with *Nebuchadnezzars* tree, the leaves, fruit, and boughes were all ſcattered and broken, yet there was a chaine of braſſe upon the root, to reſerve that for future hopes; ſo though all true fruitfulneſſe, beauty, and ſymptoms of life are long ſince gone, yet there is a root, a ſeed, which ſhall bring forth in Gods time; and this ſeemes a maine ſcope of *Paul* in *Rom.* 11. To this purpoſe may that be alledged of *Mat.* 24. 22. *Except thoſe dayes ſhould be ſhortned, no fleſh ſhould be ſaved, but for the Elects ſake thoſe dayes ſhall be ſhortned;* that is, ſo great ſhall the ſlaughter of the *Iewes* be, at the deſtruction of *Ieruſalem,* that if thoſe deſtroying dayes ſhould laſt a little longer, their whole Nation would faile, and be cut off; which ſhall not be, becauſe God hath elect ones to be borne of that People in future times. Hence you ſee, that in their loweſt ebbe, that is, in the midſt of their greateſt guilt, and ſoreſt puniſhments, God hath ſtill an eye upon a number of elect ones of that Nation; and Gods Covenant was never ſo with them, or with any People, as to take the whole of them for his inheritance. In *Ier.* 31. 36, 37. Gods Covenant with *Iſrael* is ſurer than the Lawes of Nature (which we know, remaine unviolable to the Worlds end) and he ſaith, that muſt come to paſſe, before he will caſt off the Seed of *Iſrael,* for all that they have done; yea in *Iſa.* 54. 9, 10. God confirmes it to *Iſrael,* not only by the firmeneſſe of the Lawes of Nature, but alſo by an Oath; now what God ratifies with an Oath, is his abſolute and poſitive Wil, that which makes the concluſion immutable; as in *Heb.* 6. 18. And in this caſe God is ever too ftrong for all hardneffe of heart, difobedience, unbeleefe, and any impediments that can be. See alfo that full place of *Levit.* 26. 42. 44. and *ver.* 45. for I beleeve that place Propheticall, of times, and things not yet fulfilled.

Fourthly, We *Gentiles* were gainers by their cafting away, the whirlwind of Gods wrath that threw them downe, brought us much profit, even falvation itfelfe, *Rom.* 11. 12. *The fall of them becomes the riches of the World,* ver. 15. *The cafting away of them is the reconciling of the World;* implying, that we *Gentiles* were poore, and miferable, till made rich, and happy by the *Jewes* fpoyles, who by this meanes are as wretched as we formerly had been. Which confideration muft needs move an ingenuous fpirit, to pitty thofe fo undone. Our Lord faith to a *Gentile,* in *Mark,* 7. 27. *Let the Children firft be filled, for it is not meet to take the Childrens bread and to caft it to the Doggs:* They were Children, and we were Doggs, and we Doggs have got the Childrens meat before their bellies were full; which, as it fhould make us not to be high-minded; fo alfo to pitty them, whofe bread being taken away, and given to us, are brought to a ftarving condition.

Fifthly, We fhall be gainers by their receiving againe; it fhould be motive sufficient to us, that God fhall be gainer by it, and that not only by the acceffion of a whole Nation to him, and alfo of that Nation, which is as the loft Sheep, the finding of which is a matter of great joy, *Luke* 15. But alfo becaufe as it is faid in *Pfal.* 102. 16. *When the Lord fhall build up* Zion, *he fhall appeare in his glory.* Now glory is a manifeftation of excellency, and at that time Gods excellency fhall fhine forth, which is now much hid, and vailed; the excellency of his mercy, of his truth and faithfulneffe, to remember an ancient Covenant made about foure thoufand yeares fince, and his old friend *Abraham,* and the Patriarks; all which have feemed to be afleep for many Generations together. So alfo in *Ifa.* chap. 12. compared with chap. 11. But not only God (which might have been a diftinct reafon) but we alfo fhall receive great advantages thereby; for then there fhall be not only an enlargement of good to us *Gentiles,* as a concomitant and fynchronifm with the *Jewes* converfion (the miftake about which, hath, and doth caufe black thoughts in fome) as in *Apoc.* 7. 9. after the fealing of the hundred, and forty, and foure thoufand (which relates to the time of the forty two moneths) a great multitude, and innumerable, of all Nations,

Kindred,

Kindred, Tongues, and people ſtood before the Lambe, and were
cloathed with white Robes; now theſe numbers of all Gentile-Nati-
ons are to be converted at that time when the *Jewes* are to be brought
home; for it is to be at the founding of the ſeventh Trumpet. But
beſide, the *Jewes* converſion ſhall in ſome ſort be the cauſe of it,
elſe what meanes the Apoſtle in *Rom.* 11. 12. *How much more ſhall
their fulneſſe be the riches of the Gentiles?* and in verſ. 15. *What
ſhall the receiving of the* Jewes *be* (to the *Gentiles*) *but life from
the dead?* The Apoſtle heightens the expreſſion of the benefit by
their receiving, to an higher degree than what we got by their fall.
It is obſervable, that the Goſpel did in ſome ſenſe, firſt goe out of
Sion, for the Spirit who enabled the Diſciples to preach and propagate it was there given; and *Micah* ſpeaking of the times yet looked
for, ſaith in *Mic.* 4. 2. *The Law ſhall goe forth out of* Sion, *and the
Word of the Lord out of Jeruſalem*; that is, the fulneſſe of the
Spirit, and knowledge of Chriſt ſhall ſtreame through the *Jewes* to
the *Gentiles.* So that as it was in the firſt giving of the holy Spirit, he
was firſt given to the *Jewes,* then to the *Gentiles*; yea by the *Jewes*
to the *Gentiles*; ſo ſhall it be in the laſt dayes, fulfilling what *Paul*
ſaith in *Rom.* 2. to the *Jew* firſt, and alſo to the *Gentile,* When God
ſhall be reconciled to *Iſrael,* their condition wil be greatly changed; for
they who are now actually the moſt accurſed people, then as in *Mic.*
5. 7. *The remnant of* Jacob *ſhall be in the midſt of many people as
dew from the Lord*; *as the ſhowres upon the graſſe, that tarry not
for man, nor waite for the ſons of men.* Dew, and Showers in thoſe
hot Countries are Heavens bounty, a *cornucopia* of all good things;
ſuch ſhall the *Jewes* be to the places where they ſhall be, when they
ſhall owne the Lord Jeſus.

Sixthly, They were Gods firſt Wife (as I may ſay) for a conſiderable time they were a faithfull people; and many of them have
been Martyrs for God. And theſe things God will thinke on, though
we may ſleight them.

They were Gods firſt Wife. Did God ever aſſay to take any Nation before them, to be his owne people? Yea, did he take any beſide them, for two thouſand yeares together? In *Iſa.* 54. 6. *I have
called thee as a woman forſaken, and grieved in ſpirit, and a wife of
youth, when thou waſt refuſed, ſaith the Lord*; and what follows,
verſ. 7. *For a ſmall moment have I forſaken thee, but with great
mercies will I gather thee.* And in verſe 8. *With everlaſting kind-*

neffe will I have mercy upon thee. We fee God forgets not, though men may, and doe.

They were a faithfull people. As great was their unfaithfulneffe; fo there were times when great was their faithfulneffe. In *Jer.* 2. 2. *I remember thee, the kindneffe of thy youth, the love of thy efpou-* *fals, when thou wenteft after me in the Wilderneffe, in a Land that* *was not fowne.* It was fomething to follow God in fuch a Country forty years; and for fo long a time to expofe themfelves, wives, and children daily to almoft al forts of deaths; and you fee, God remembers it in after times; and if he did in *Jeremiahs* time, when thofe who in perfon had been fo faithfull, had been long dead; and that race of the *Jewes* then were very provoking, and corrupt; why not alfo now, in this prefent fucceeding generation of them:

They were Martyrs for God. To prove this, read the Hiftory of the *Maccabees,* and if we like not fo farre to owne what is Apocry-phall, turne to *Heb.* 11. which is a booke of the *Jewifh* Martyrs, a Catalogue of them that fuffered under *Antiochus,* and thofe *Syrian* Tyrants. And they were not few that fuffered, but many; nor light punifhments, but unfpeakeable torments. Now God takes it fo kind-ly that we give up our lives to torments, and to death for his Name, that commonly he owes that perfon a good turne in his pofterity. And if upon thefe accounts God hath an eye upon them, we alfo fhould be like minded, and love them too.

Seventhly, It is a duty which we owe to Gods expreffe command, for fo I take that in the literall fence, in *Ifa.* 62. 6, 7. *Ye that make* *mention of the Lord, keep not filence, and give him no reft, till he* *eftablifh, and till he make* Jerufalem *a praife in the earth.* This duty the Prophet himfelfe performed in verf. 1. *For Sions fake I will* *not hold my peace, and for* Jerufalems *fake I will not reft, till the* *righteoufneffe thereof goe forth as brightneffe, &c.* And alfo the Church in her affliction, *Pfal.* 137. 5, 6. And now that *Sion* is in the duft, if we that beleeve among the *Gentiles,* did pitty her, and com-paffionate her in her ruines, it were an argument that God is about to arife, and have mercy upon her; as may be urged from Pfalme 102. 13, 14.

Laftly, They minded our converfion to God. This appeares in the writings of almoft all their Prophets, efpecially in the Pfalmes, *Ifaiah, Jeremiah, Hofeah, Malachi.* Now then for us to love the notion, and in what we may, help forward their returne,

what

what is it but an honeſt and juſt retaliation?

Having diſpatched the Reaſons, two things yet remaine about their Converſion, which I muſt ſpeake ſomewhat to, and thoſe are the *Time,* and the *Manner*; as for the *time when,* the determining of that is hard, though not impoſsible. I beleeve that it is punctually ſet downe in Scripture, and God wil be as criticall in looking after times as things; but all the difficulty of knowing it is from the darkneſſe, and defects of our underſtanding, and not from a ſuppoſed uncertainty in the thing. So that I am equally adverſe as to the common practiſe of the *Iewes,* who becauſe they are unwilling to owne Gods accomplifhments, doe therefore diſ-allow his computations, and expreſly hold that man accurſed who buſieth himſelfe in that ſtudy. So to the too common opinion of thoſe who ſay, That oft in ſuch computations God puts a certaine number for an uncertaine. No, there is an infallibility in the ſet times of Scripture; only the Well is deep, and the cord to our Bucket is but ſhort! yet this difficulty ſhould not cauſe deſpondency, but quicken our induſtry. All that I ſhall now ſay to it is this, I judge the time not farre off; this preſent age will ſee thoſe things fulfilled which we have waited and prayed for. *R. Maimonides* ſaith of Jeſus Chriſt, That ſince *Moſes* his time none ſo like to the Meſsiah as the Chriſt of the Chriſtians; ſo I ſay, ſince Chriſt, no period of time ſo like to be that, in which the *Iewes* ſhall be called, as this in which we live. And perhaps it is nearer than we are aware of, being the more comfortably perſwaded of it, by that excellent Treatiſe called, *The Revelation revealed,* newly publiſhed by a Gentleman of an indefatigable Spirit for God and publick good, Mr. S. *Hartlib,* in which Apocalypticall computations are explained the moſt harmoniouſly, and clearly, that I have read in any diſcourſe of that nature. He ſaith poſitively, that at the ending of the laſt yeare of 1655. the ſeventh Trumpet ſhall ſound; whoſe effect will be as much good to Gods elected ones, whether *Iewes,* or *Gentiles,* as our hearts can wiſh for. I ſhall adde this, The age in which we live, hath been eyed by many Generations paſt, for the time wherein the *Iewes* ſhall be received to mercy; many of their owne Writers, and alſo of Chriſtian Authors have pitched upon it; And I beleeve that God will be as gracious to them in this their laſt, and greateſt reſtauration, as he was to them in that of their returne out of *Babylon*; now concerning that there were three computations and epochaes of the beginning (and conſequently of the ending) of the ſeventy yeares of

cap-

captivity; and obferve, that thofe feventy yeares ended, and the *Iewes* returned, not at the lateft computation, but with the firft, for there were but feventy yeares from *Jechoniahs* carrying to *Babylon,* (which was the firft Captivity) to the releafe by the Proclamation of *Cyrus.* And as God ended that Captivity with the fooneft, fo I hope that he will doe this; efpecially confidering, that fpeaking of thefe mercies to them, in *Ifa.* 60. in verfe laft, he faith, *I the Lord will haften it in its time;* which he fhould not doe, if he fhould ftay the longeft calculation, and utmoft period of time. O let us be Gods Remembrancers to put him in minde of this his promife.

For the *manner* how, and *meanes* whereby their converfion fhall be compaffed; this alfo is a depth equall to the former. And as it is in things Propheticall, the event will beft determine it; yet I fhall fay fomething to it, according to what I have attained. That of the ordinary way of Chriftianizing a perfon, or people, feemes to me not of ufe here; which hath been by Difcourfes, written or printed Books, Preachers, or the will and command of a Conquerour; for all thefe have had their efficacy in (at leaft a feeming and out-fide) converfion of many Nations. But after the application of thefe to the *Jewes,* for many ages together, yet we muft fay as *Gehazi* did to *Elifha,* when he had laid his ftaffe on the *Shunamite* her Son, thereby to bring him to life; *The childe is not awaked.* I then conclude, that their converfion fhall be in an extraordinary way, it fhall be the worke of our Lord Jefus, and of his good Spirit. As *Paul* was turned by the appearing of Chrift to him; fo fhall they. He will manifeft himfelfe to them eminently, powerfully, and gracioufly, to forme them to be a people to himfelfe. Whether this his prefence to them fhall be perfonall, or only in the Spirit, I will not now fay, but leave the Reader to make a judgement, as he fees moft caufe, out of the Scriptures which I bring. Confider that of *Mat.* 23. 38, 39. *Behold your houfe is left unto you defolate, for I fay unto you, ye fhall not fee me hence-forth, till ye fhall fay, Bleffed is he that comes in the name of the Lord.* Here you have their doome fore-told, *their houfe fhall be defolate,* the Temple and *Jerufalem fhall be deftroyed;* alfo their converfion, in thofe words, their faying, *Bleffed is he that comes, &c.* the *medium* to compaffe it, fc. *their feeing Iefus Chrift; ye fhall not fee me,* &c. In the order of caufes, Chrifts difcovering himfelfe to them fhall be firft, and fhall produce their relenting towards him. And for a further proofe, let thofe two places be joyned toge-

together, as bearing the fame fence; that of *Mat.* 24. 30. 31. and of *Apoc.* 1. 7. both which are taken out of *Zechar.* 12. 10. And all three not to be underftood of Chrifts appearing to Judgement; for here, faving repentance is the effect of his appearance; but repentance will be then too late when the Judge is come; that fhall be a night to all finners, in which no worke can be done. Againe, there are but three grand periods mentioned in *Mat.* 24. namely, the deftruction of *Jerufalem,* Chrifts comming (when, and whereby the *Jewes* fhall be converted, who though they have refifted him, when he came in the flefh, yet they fhall not, they cannot, when he comes in the Spirit) and the end of the World. Now the fignes of the firft of thefe are in verf. 14, 15. 21, 22. Of the fecond in verf. 29, 30, 31, &c. And of the laft, in verf. 36, &c. So that this of ver. 30, 31. muft concerne fome other thing than the end of the World. And that the three fore-named Scriptures are properly to be underftood of the *Jews,* the texts doe fhow; for that of *Zechariah,* (from whence the other two places are taken) exprefly faith, *I will poure upon the houfe of* David, *and the inhabitants of* Jerufalem, *&c.* and other paffages to the fame purpofe in verf. 11, 12, 13. of *Zechar.* 12. And in the two places of *Mat.* 24. and *Apoc.* 1. it is exprefly applyed to the *Jewes*; for in *Mat.* it is, *All the Tribes of the earth fhall mourn, and fee him*; that is, All the twelve Tribes fcattered upon the face of the whole earth, and thefe fhall be gathered by the Angels from the foure winds. And that of *Apoc.* 1.7. is clearly to be applyed alfo to them, for it is faid, *They that pierced him, fhall fee him*; that is, the *Jewes*; and *All the Tribes* (for fo the word φυλαὶ ought to be rendred) *of the earth fhall waile*; that is, the twelve Tribes fcattered throughout all places. Now the *meane* whereby thefe *Jewes* fhall be converted, is, *And they fhall fee him*; that is, Jefus Chrift, for thofe words are in all the three Scriptures. It fhall be fuch a fight, as the *Ifraelites* had of the Brazen Serpent in the Wildernefle, it was healing to them. Such a fight as *Paul* had of Chrift in Heaven, upon which he faith, that he had feene the Lord. For particularities about this fight. I fhall leave them, knowing that *fecret things doe belong to God.*

And becaufe after that I had publifhed in *Englifh,* about laft Autumne, the Booke of *Menaffeh Ben Ifrael,* called, *The Hope of Ifrael,* I received a Letter from an Honourable Perfon, concerning that Booke, to which I wrote an Anfwer, and both containe

I   fome

fome further difcourfe about the *Jewes,* and their Converfion; therefore I thought good to give you them, and they are thefe which follow.

To the Tranflator of *Menaffeh; Ben Ifraels fpes Ifraelis.*

SIR:

I Defire to be acquainted with you, becaufe we have both fallen upon one Booke, with the fame intentions to convert the Jewes, *though we take not one way; I defire therefore to conferre with you, to fee who taketh the righteft way. You by your Tranflation feeme to me to prize the learned* Jewes *writing too much, which will beget pride, and not humility in him, without which he will not turne, repent, and be faved. Therefore for his good, and alfo for the Chriftians, and for the credit of us who are Parliamentarians, I would not fee them too much yeelded unto. You juftly perftringe him in his thirtieth Section, wherein he talkes fo wildly of his goodly Martyrs, and truly if you marke him in his Difcourfe upon the Sabatticall River, which where it is he knownes not, you will finde him as faulty and dangerous, if we have any of the race of the* Thraskytes *left among us; but Sir, in that you thinke that the* Jewes *fhall now be called as a Nation, and not only by particulars, and would have them have an earthly Kingdome againe; you doe more for the ten Tribes then he would have himfelfe,* Sect. 25. p. 79. 80. *and for the other two, of* Judah, *and* Benjamin, *it is not fo likely they fhould have a fecond Call, feeing that Chrift and his Apoftles preached to them, and all that were of the Election were then converted, as you may fee by many texts, and after their rejection of the Gofpell, their Country-men,* Paul, *and* Peter *turned to the Gentiles. Therefore thofe two Tribes who Crucified our Lord, and perfecuted his Apoftles, are not fo likely to be called againe as the ten Tribes who did neither, except fome few who returned into the holy Land; neither did many of them fo much as heare of it, you might fee your owne fentence fulfilled then. Firft,*
the

*the Jew was called, and then the Gentile. But now looke not for it,
but for their ſingle converſions, though numbers may be called upon
one day, one Sermon as they were heretofore ; but they muſt not exalt themſelves as a Nation, for they muſt be ingrafted againe upon
that branch, or Vine, Chriſt Jeſus, and we muſt have one
Shepheard, and be one flock.* See Rom. 11. ver. 31. *which you cite.*
Through your mercy they may alſo obtain mercy; *I had writ it* (ſhall)
but it is only (may:) *ſee the place to which this relates,* Iſa. 59. v.
19, 20, 21. *where you ſhall finde that all their hope is in eternalls,
not in temporalls ; and looke upon* Rom. 11. 24. *concerning the en-
grafting, and clearly, (unleſſe you be a Millenarian) you will finde
no ſuch Nationall glory of the* Jewes ; *therefore I pray you take
heed you fall not into the ſame ſnare wherein the* Jewes *are, to looke
for a temporall reigne, which you ſeeme to intimate, and too many
were, and are of that opinion. Aſſure your ſelfe that Chriſt will
come to ſuch as a theife in the night, though his comming will be
very glorious, yet it will be ſuddaine; the learned* Jew *can finde no
text punctuall in all his Booke, but whatſoever he citeth, the ſame
Chapter makes againſt him, and ſpeakes not of temporallity, but of
eternity, and the new Jeruſalem. I reſt, deſirous of your friendſhip.*

Octob. 5. 1650. E. S.

Poſtſcript.

I Have it from a good hand, that *Maſter* Jo. Dury *is the
Tranſlator of that Booke, and I have ſome Arguments to beleeve
it to be ſo, becauſe he ſeemes to be of the ſame minde in his Epiſto-
licall Diſcourſe before Mr:* Thorowgoods *pious Booke, which I
have gained ſince I wrote this Letter. But truly if it be ſo, I muſt
move Mr.* Dury *both to amend his Tranſlation from groſſe faults,
and to make ſome retractions upon that Epiſtle, which upon conference I ſhall moſt plainely ſhew him, and in the meane time I deſire him, that he will read a Booke of a moſt reverend and pious
man, called,* The Revelation unrevealed ; *and thereby I beleeve he
will be convinced, and not looke for a fifth generall Monarchy upon earth ; for Chriſt reignes now, and hath ſo done ever ſince his
Aſcenſion, and ſo ſhall to the end of the World, untill he deliver
the Kingdome to the Father.*

Octob. 25. 1650.

I 2 SIR:

SIR: *The anfwer to the Letter.*

I Received a Letter directed, *To the Tranflator of Spes Ifraelis,* which worke thus corrected, as I here-with prefent to you, I confeffe mine. I left it with a friend to fee it printed, my felfe going into the Country; but his occafions called him from the City alfo, when it fhould have been reviewed; which is the reafon that though there be many *Errata's* in the Booke, that they are not gathered up at the end. At my owne reading of it, I found many, and mended thofe I found; and now I know that it hath farre fewer then it had, and may paffe tollerably; though neither I, nor what I doe, can be faid faultleffe. Concerning your defire of converting the *Jewes,* it is truly Chriftian, and a worke that fhall not loofe its reward. But you fay, We difagree about the way, that is very poffible, for apprehenfions are various, and men muft thinke, not as others doe, but as themfelves can, taking what is truth to them, to be their guide. But the *quære* is, Who lights on the beft way. For my part, I pretend not to any way to convert them, for I verily thinke that when it fhall be done, it will be Gods worke, and not mans; as much as Pauls converfion was wholly of God; which himfelfe makes the type, or patterne of the converfion of his Country-men; as Mr. *Mede* faith upon I *Tim.* I. 16. in his *Fragmenta facra,* which I know not whether they be in print, or no. You fay, I prize the learned *Iewes* writing too much, and that it will beget pride in them) Sir, pardon me, if I doe not recant till I fee my errour; but then I fhall freely doe it. I confeffe, I doe prize the Learned, whether *Iew,* or *Gentile,* for though I am not σοφὸς, yet I am φιλόσοφος and I doe beleeve the Author of *Spes Ifraelis* to be a very learned man; and I have it from thofe who are acquainted with him, that he is a very ingenuous and civill man; and others there are, and have been among them, not wanting a name for good learning. As for the fomenting their pride) truly that vice is fo evill, that I would not cherifh it, neither in my felf, nor in others. But Sir, whether is a more likely way to gaine upon men, to ufe them civilly, and with the fpirit of meekneffe, or to be fupercilious and tart towards them? What got *Auftine* the Monke by ufing the Brittaines of *Bangor* fo Lordly as he did? and (to come to latter dayes) did Mr. *Broughton* gaine upon a learned Rabbi, in a Conference at *Dort,* where Mr. *Forbes* was Moderator, by his high and peremptory language? This he reaped, to fet the *Iew* at a greater diftance from Chriftianifme, and an abating of his owne efteeme, in

the

the judgement of wiſe men. As for *Menaſſeh's* Sabbaticall river, I know many Authors have ſaid it, but whether true, or falſe, that is nothing to the Tranſlator; and I am as farre from beleeving that ſtory, as I am from the wilde opinions of Mr. *Thraſk*. But theſe are of leſſe concernment; you fall upon the maine of your judgement which relates to them, and pardon me if I deale as roundly in my anſwer; for I deſire to have reſpect to Truth, and not to man. I doe firmly beleeve, and feare not to profeſſe it; That the *Jewes* ſhall be called as a Nation, both *Judah* and *Iſrael*, and ſhall returne to their owne Land, and have an earthly Kingdome againe. For the proofe of which, I could ſay much, but ſhall now but little; and if poſſibly I cite any thing which *Menaſſeh Ben Iſrael* brings for himſelfe, beleeve me that I have it not from him, but from my owne obſervations out of Scripture, ſome yeares ſince. There is weight in that place of *Mic.* 4. 8. *The firſt dominion, the Kingdome ſhall come to the daughter of Jeruſalem*; and this is ſpoken of times after Chriſts incarnation, and not yet performed. See that of *Zech.* 10. 6, 7, 8, 9, 10. there is *Judah* and *Ephraim* fore-told to be brought to *Gilead*, and *Lebanon*, and they ſhall ſo encreaſe, that they ſhall want room. Say not this was done in the returne of thoſe few from the Captivity of *Babylon*; for thoſe of the ten Tribes that then returned, were but ſome gleanings of them; and of *Judah* it ſelfe, there returned but about one halfe: now God doth not promiſe Mountaines, and performe but Mole-hils; yea in verſ. 6. *God will ſave and ſtrengthen the houſe of* Judah, *and of* Joſeph, *and they ſhall be as though I had not caſt them off.* Which, if ſince that Propheſie, it hath been made good of *Judah*, yet be ſure not of *Joſeph*. And in v. 7. *They of* Ephraim *ſhall be like a mighty man*, but ſince the captivity of *Salmanaſſar* to this day, what might hath *Ephraim* ſhown? yea is he not poore, weak, ſcattered, and unknowne? And in ver. 8. *I will gather them, and they ſhall encreaſe as they have encreaſed*; hath this been fulfilled of *Ephraim?* Where is his fruitfulneſſe, which his name imports? much leſſe hath there been a time ſince their great captivity, in which they have encreaſed to their numbers and ſtrength, mentioned in the dayes of *Moſes, Joſhua, David, Solomon*, and under their owne Kings, after the defection from the houſe of *David*. See that noted place of *Ezek.* 37. 16, 17. 22. 24, 25. Sir, in good earneſt, hath this Scripture been fulfilled? hath *Judah* and *Ephraim* been *but one ſtick in Gods hand, but one Nation, ſo that they ſhall be no more two Na-*

tions, as in ver. 22. Surely to this day they have been from their laſt
difperſion not only two, but many Nations. Neither will it be an anfwer to fay, That now they are no Nation, therefore they are not two;
yes, Hiſtorians report them many Nations; though perhaps fcarce after the juſt rules of Nations. And that phrafe hath not a negative, but
a poſitive fence, not that they ſhould be nothing, but that they ſhould
be one Nation. More-over, in ver. 24. *Judah* and *Ephraim* were fo to
be one Nation, that *David* (that is Jefus Chriſt) was to be King over
them: And when did *Judah* and *Iſrael* ever to this day, as a Nation
acknowledge the Soveraignty of Jefus Chriſt? and he to be their
Prince for ever, as in ver. 25. But I muſt not too much enlarge. I
ſhall only adde this; That as many places of the Old, fo many in the
New Teſtament agree thereto, as *Rom.* 11. ver. 12. 15. 25, 26. 28.
Though this of the *Romans,* chiefly proves one point, *fc.* their generall or Nationall converſion. Give me leave briefly to anfwer your
objeĉtions. You fay, The call of *Judah* and *Benjamin* is not fo likely,
becaufe Chriſt and the Apoſtles preached to them already. I anfwer;
that by their preaching, all of thofe living, who were eleĉted, were converted; but after-ages have a new race, and God hath his number a-
mong them too; yea the words run high, then *All Iſrael ſhall be faved.* You fay, thofe two Tribes who crucified Chriſt, not fo likely to
be converted. I anfwer, by how much their fin is greater, by fo much
the greater will Gods mercy be; *Et Dei noviſſima erunt optima, &
maxima.* You fay, Their converſion ſhall be fingle, that is anfwered
already; but I adde, that *Iſaiah* is contrary to it, in *Ifa.* 66. 7, 8.
which Chapter I doubt not but it points to times after our Saviour. As
for their being engraffed upon the Vine Chriſt, or being brought to
one ſheep-fold, what doth that hinder but that they may be a Nation
of Converts brought to their owne Land? You objeĉt that of *Rom.*
11. 31. *That through your mercy they may obtaine mercy.* I anfwer, that I beleeve the maine of their converſion will be from Heaven,
and extraordinary; though the *Gentiles* by provoking them to emu-
lation, and alfo by their gifts and graces, may fome way be auxiliary
to them. After this you are pleafed to put the term *Millenarian* upon me; which, though for what I have writ, I need not owne, yet I
will not difclaime; they are not Names that affright me, but reall fal-
fities. The term *Chiliaſt,* as it congregates the many odde, and falfe
opinions of them of old, I explode; though to beleeve thofe thoufand
yeares in *Apoc.* 20. to be yet unfulfilled, that, I willingly owne. To

put

put that ſenſe upon them, as that they imply the thouſand yeares of eternity,I can thinke little leſſe of it then to be a contradiction.Againe, if the thouſand yeares be the eternity in Heaven,what meanes that in ver. 3. *Till the thouſand yeares be fulfilled, and after that he muſt be looſed for a little ſeaſon;* I pray, what little ſeaſon is that that is after eternity? neither doth Chriſts *comming ſuddenly in the night as a theife,* hinder, but that when he doth come, he may ſtay a thou-ſand yeares. But whether that time be *ante,in,* or *poſt diem judicii,* is not my taske to determine,or maintaine. As for what you adde in the Poſt-ſcript,not to looke for a fifth Monarchy, becauſe Chriſt reignes now. I anſwer,that though he reignes *de jure,* yet not *de facto;* for expreſly in Scripture the Devill is called κοσμοκράτωρ he is the grand Tyrant,and great Uſurper,and the whole world κεῖται ἐν πῷ πονηρῷ yet I am farre from denying to Chriſt a Kingdome now in being,*ſc.* Spirituall,and Inviſible, but I looke for a viſible one to come. In the cloſe (as alſo at the beginning) you are pleaſed to deſire my acquain-tance; but Sir, I look not upon my ſelf as a Star of ſo conſiderable a magnitude, as to preſent my ſelfe to your eyes; but if I might be ſo happy as to be capable to ſerve you really,none ſhould be more deſi-rous of it (both as you are a Gentleman of Learning, by which you have obliged the publick; and alſo a Member of that Houſe which I ſo much honour) than Sir,

Novemb. 5. 1650.   *Your moſt humble Servant*
                                                            M. W.

SIR:

I Doe now very highly *eſteeme of my intereſt in your converſation, and thanke you very much for your kinde viſitations, which I ſhal endeavour to repay, and deſire by theſe you will tell me where, if you be in town; I ſhall continue in town till monday noone be paſſed, and will meet you at the Stationers, or any where elſe you ſhall ap-point; very neceſſary, and too urgent occaſions hindred my comming to — untill laſt night. I have ſomewhat thought with my ſelf of the faire propoſition of re-printing what concernes* Ben Iſrael, *the con-verſion and generall call of the Jewiſh Nation, to which I now more perceive our ſerious endeavours and hopes doe encline. But I muſt needs ſay, that* Ben Iſraels *Booke gives very ſmall hopes of his con-verſion; Of which notwithſtanding neither you nor my ſelfe ought*
                                                                to

to defpaire, for Saul *the learned* Jew *from a fevere Perfecutor be-*
came a Paul, *a holy and remarkable Saint* ; *I fhall not at prefent*
enlarge my felfe unto you, leaft I fhould prove troublefome, or im-
pertinent till things be ripened between us by a conference, but if it
be neceffary you fhould print againe before I fee you, I only defire this
Letter of mine fhould be printed. For I embrace your candor and
ingenuity as much as you doe mine, and I hope love and knowledge
will ftill encreafe between us, and I fhall fay with the Pfalmift,
Let the righteous fmite me friendly, and reprove me, but let not their
precious balme breake my head ; *I have no defire to gaine applaufe*
of thofe who are without, or hazard their cenfure in that which
more learned men, but not fo loving, may fay, that I write flight
things, but I had rather firft fhew them that I can write ferious
things as well as flight, by tranflation of fome part of Peter Galatine & Reuchlin, *which is now my travaile, as I in part fhewed*
you; *I remaine*,

Febr. 21.   Your friend in the trueft intereft of
1650.   Chriftian love.

F I N I S.

Errata maximi momenti.

IN the fecond Epift. p. 2. l. 8. dele happy, in the 3 Epift. p. 1. l. 28. r. invironed, p.
2. l. 3. r. Carthagena, p. 3. l. 12. dele fo, p. 6, l. 2 1. r. thy, p. 18. l. 19. r. hating, p. 19. l.
16. r. away Hofhea, p. 22. l. 23. r. Hunni, p. 23. l. 10. r. there, p. 26. l. 3. r. were, p. 40.
l. 27. r. honoured *Abraham Kolorni*, with p. 44. l. 2 4. r. for thefe, p. 46. l. 16. dele the,
p. 49. l. 34. & he faith, thofe muft be nulled before.

TO

HIS HIGHNESSE

THE

LORD PROTECTOR

OF THE

COMMON-WEALTH OF
England, Scotland, *and* Ireland.

THE

HUMBLE ADDRESSES

OF

MENASSEH Ben Ifrael, *a Divine, and
Doctor of PHYSICK, in behalfe
of the Jewifh Nation.*

TO
His Highneſſe the Lord Protector
OF THE
Common-wealth of England,
Scotland, and Ireland.

The Humble Addreſſes of Menaſſeh Ben Iſrael, *a Divine and Doɛ̃or of Phyſick, in behalf of the Iewiſh Nation.*

Ive me leave, at ſuch a junɛ̃ure of time, to ſpeak to your Highneſſe, in a ſtyle and manner fitting to us *Jewes* and our condition. It is a thing moſt certaine, that the great God of *Iſrael*, Creator of Heaven and Earth, doth give and take away Dominions and Empires, according to his owne pleaſure; exalting ſome, and overthrowing others : who, ſeeing he hath the hearts of Kings in his hand, he eaſily moves them whitherſoever himſelfe pleaſeth, to put in execution his Divine Commands. This, my Lord, appeares moſt evidently out of thoſe words of *Daniel*, where he, rendring thanks unto God, for revealing unto him that prodigious Dreame of *Nebuchadnezar*, doth ſay : *Thou that removeſt Kings, and ſets up Kings.* And elſe-where, *To the end the living might know, that the Higheſt hath dominion in Mans Kingdome, and giveth the ſame to whom he pleaſe.* Of the very ſame-minde are the *Thalmudiſts* likewiſe, affirming that a good Government, or Governor, is a Heavenly Gift, and that there is no Governor, but is firſt called by God unto that dignity : and this they prove from that paſſage of *Exodus : Behold I have called Bazale'l by name,* &c. all things being governed by Divine Providence, God diſpenſing rewards unto Vertues, and puniſhment unto Vices, according to his owne

A 2   good

(75)

good Will. This the Examples of great Monarchs make good; efpecially of fuch, who have afflicted the people of *Ifrael:* For none hath ever afflicted them, who hath not been by fome ominous *Exit*, moft heavily punifh-ed of God Almighty; as is manifeft from the Hiftories of thofe Kings, *Pharaoh, Nebuchadnezar, Antiochus, Epiphanius,Pompey,*and others. And on the contrary, none ever was a Benefactor to that people, and cherifhed them in their Countries, who thereupon hath not prefently be-gun very much to flourifh. In fo much that the Oracle to *Abraham (I will bleffe them that bleffe thee, and curfe them that curfe thee)* feemeth yet daily to have its accom-plifhment. Hence I, one of the leaft among the *Hebrews,* fince by experience I have found, that through Gods great bounty toward us, many confiderable and eminent per-fons both for Piety and Power, are moved with fincere and inward pitty and compaffion towards us, and do com-fort us concerning the approaching deliverance of *Ifrael,* could not but for my felf, and in the behalf of my Coun-trey men, make this my humble addreffe to your Highnefs, and befeech you for Gods fake, that ye would, according to that Piety and Power wherein you are eminent beyond others, vouchfafe to grant, that the Great and Glorious Name of the Lord our God may be extolled, and folemn-ly worfhiped and praifed by us through all the bounds of this Common-wealth; and to grant us place in your Coun-trey, that we may have our Synagogues, and free exercife of our Religion. I nothing doubting, but that your Clemen-cy will eafily grant this moft equitable Petition of ours. Pa-gans have of old, out of reverence to the God of *Ifrael;* & the efteem they had to his people, granted moft willingly free liberty, even to apoftated *Jewes;* as *Onias* the High Prieft, to build another Temple in their Countrey, like unto that at *Jerufalem:* how much more then may we, that are not Apoftate or runagate *Iewes*, hope it from your

Highneffe

Highneſſe and your Chriſtian Councill, ſince you have ſo great knowledge of, and adore the ſame one onely God of *Iſrael*, together with us. Beſides, it increaſes our confidence of your bounty towards us, in that ſo ſoon as ever the rumour of that moſt wiſhed-for liberty, that ye were a thinking to grant us, was made known unto our Countrey-men; I, in the name of my Nation, the *Iewes*, that live in *Holland*, did congratulate and entertaine their Excellencies, the Ambaſſadors of *England*; who were received in our Synagogue with as great pomp and applauſe, Hymns and cheerfulneſſe of minde, as ever any Soveraigne Prince was. For our people did in their owne mindes preſage, that the Kingly Government being now changed into that of a Common-wealth, the antient hatred towards them, would alſo be changed into good-will: that thoſe rigorous Laws (if any there be yet extant, made under the Kings) againſt ſo innocent a people, would happily be repealed. So that we hope now for better from your gentleneſs, & goodneſs, ſince, from the beginning of your Government of this Common-wealth, your Highneſſe hath profeſſed much reſpeƈt, and favour towards us. Wherefore I humbly entreat your Highneſſe, that you would with a gracious eye have regard unto us, and our Petition, and grant unto us, as you have done unto others, free exerciſe of our Religion, that we may have our Synagogues, and keep our own publick worſhip, as our brethren doe in *Italy*, *Germany*, *Poland*, and many other places, and we ſhall pray for the happineſſe and Peace of this your much renowned and puiſſant Common-wealth.

A 3　　　　　　　A

A DECLARATION

TO THE
Common-wealth of England,

BY

Rabbi Menaſſeh Ben ISRAEL, ſhewing
the Motives of his coming into England.

 *Aving ſome yeares ſince often perceived that
in this Nation, God hath a People, that is
very tender-hearted, and well-wiſhing to our
ſore-afflicted Nation ; Yea, I my ſelfe having ſome Experience thereof, in divers
Eminent perſons, excelling both in Piety and
Learning: I thought with my-ſelf, I ſhould do no ſmall ſervice
to my owne Nation, as alſo to the People and Inhabitants of
this Common-wealth, if by humble addreſſes to the late Honourable Parliament, I might obtaine a ſafe-Conduct once to
tranſport my ſelfe thither. Which I having done, and according to my deſire, received a moſt kinde and ſatisfactory Anſwer, I now am come. And to the end all Men may know the
true Motives and Intent of this my coming, I ſhall briefly
comprehend and deliver them in theſe particulars.*

First and formoſt, *my Intention is to try, if by Gods
good hand over me, I may obtaine here for my Nation the Liberty of a free and publick Synagogue, wherein we may daily
call upon the Lord our God, that once he may be pleaſed to remember his Mercies and Promiſes done to our Fore fathers,*

forgiving

(78)

forgiving our trespasses, and restoring us once againe into our fathers Inheritance; and besides to sue also for a blessing upon this Nation, and People of England, *for receiving us into their bosomes, and comforting* Sion *in her distresse.*

My second *Motive is, because the opinion of many Christians and mine doe concurre herein, that we both believe that the restoring time of our Nation into their Native Countrey, is very neer at hand; I believing more particularly, that this restauration cannot be, before these words of* Daniel, Chap. 12. ver. 7. *be first accomplished, when he saith,* And when the difperfion of the Holy people fhall be compleated in all places, then fhall all thefe things be compleated: *fignifying therewith, that before allbe fulfilled, the People of God muft be first difperfed into all places & Countreyes of the World. Now we know, how our Nation at the prefent is fpread all about, and hath its feat and dwelling in the moft flourifhing parts of all the Kingdomes, and Countreys of the World, as well in* America, *as in the other three parts thereof; except onely in this confiderable and mighty Ifland. And therefore this remains onely in my judgement, before the* MESSIA *come and reftore our Nation, that firft we muft have our feat here likewife.*

My third *Motive is grounded on the profit that I conceive this Common wealth is to reap, if it fhall vouchfafe to receive us; for thence, I hope, there will follow a great bleffing from God upon them, and a very abundant trading into, and from all parts of the World, not onely without prejudice to the Englifh Nation, but for their profit, both in Importation, and Exportation of goods. Yet if any fhall doubt hereof, I truft their Charity towards the people of God, will fatisfie them, efpecially when they fhall reade the enfuing Treatife.*

The fourth *Motive of my coming hither, is, my fincere affection to this Common wealth, by reafon of fo many Worthy, Learned, and Pious men in this Nation, whofe loving kindneffe and Piety I have experience of: hoping to finde the like*
                                                              affection

affection in all the People generally; the more, because I al-
wayes have, both by writing and deeds, professed much incli-
nation to this Common-wealth; and that I perswade my selfe
they will be mindfull of that Command of the Lord our God,
who so highly recommends unto all men the love of ſtrangers;
much more to thoſe that profeſſe their good affection to them.
For this I deſire all may be confident of, that I am not come to
make any diſturbance, or to move any diſputes about matters
of Religion ; but onely to live with my Nation in the feare
of the Lord, under the ſhadow of your protection, whiles we
expect with you the hope of Iſrael *to be revealed.*

How Profitable

The Nation of the Iewes are.

 *Hree* things, if it pleafe your Highneffe, there are that make a ftrange *Nation* wel-beloved a-mongft the Natives of a land where they dwell: (as the defect of thofe *three* things make them hatefull.) viz. *Profit*, they may receive from them; *Fidelity* they hold towards their Princes; and the *Noblenes* and purity of their blood. Now when I fhall have made good, that all *thefe three* things are found in the *Iewifh Nation*, I fhall certainly perfuade your High-neffe, that with a favorable eye, (Monarchy being changed into a Republicq) you fhall be pleafed to receive again the Nation of the Iews, who in time paft lived in that Ifland : but, I know not by what falfe Informations, were cruelly handled and banifhed.

Profit is a moft powerfull motive, and which all the World pre-ferres before all other things : and therefore we fhall handle that point firft.

It is a thing confirmed, that merchandizing is, as it were, the pro-per profeffion of the Nation of the Iews. I attribute this in the firft place, to the particular Providence and mercy of God towards his people: for having banifhed them from their own Country, yet not from his Protection, he hath given them, as it were, a naturall in-ftinct, by which they might not onely gain what was neceffary for their need, but that they fhould alfo thrive in Riches and poffef-fions; whereby they fhould not onely become gracious to their Princes and Lords, but that they fhould be invited by others to come and dwell in their Lands.

Moreover, it cannot be denyed, but that neceffity ftirrs up a mans ability and induftry; and that it gives him great incitement, by all means to trie the favour of Providence.

A   Befides,

Befides, feeing it is no wifedome for them to endeavour the gaining of Lands and other immovable goods, and fo to imprifon their poffeffions here, where their perfons are fubject to fo many cafualities, banifhments and peregrinations; they are forced to ufe marchandizing untill that time, when they fhall returne to their own Country, that then as God hath promifed by the Prophet Zachary, *Their fhall be found no more any marchant amongft them in the Houfe of the Lord.*

From that very thing we have faid, there rifeth an infallible Profit, commodity and gain to all thofe Princes in whofe Lands they dwell above all other ftrange Nations whatfoever, as experience by divers *Reafons* doth confirme.

I. The Iews, have no oportunity to live in their own Country, to till the Lands or other like employments, give themfelves wholy unto merchandizing, and for contriving new Inventions, no Nation almoft going beyond them. And fo 't is obferved, that wherefoever they go to dwell, there prefently the Traficq begins to florifh. Which may be feen in divers places, efpecially in Ligorne, which having been but a very ignoble and inconfiderable City, is at this time, by the great concourfe of people, one of the moft famous places of Trafique of whole Italy.

Furthermore, the Inventor of the famous *Scala de Spalatro* (the moft firme and folid Traficq of Venice) was a Iew, who by this his Invention tranfported the Negotiation from a great part of the Levant into that City.

Even that very fame is feene likewife at this day in Nizza and in other innumerable places more, both in Europe and Afia.

II. The Nation of the Iews is difperfed throughout the whole World, it being a chaftifement that God hath layd upon them for their Idolatries, Deut. 28,69. Ezech. 20,23. Nehem. 1,8. Pf. 107,27. and by other their finnes their families fuffer the fame fhipwrack.

Now in this difperfion our Fore-fathers flying from the Spanifh Inquifition, fome of them came in Holland, others got into Italy, and others betooke themfelves into Afia; and fo eafily they credit

dit one another ; and by that meanes they draw the Negotiation where-ever they are, where with all of them marchandifing and having perfeᶜt knowledge of all the kinds of Moneys, Diamants, Cochinil, Indigo, Wines, Oyle, and other Commodities, that ferve from place to place; efpecially holding correfpondence with their friends and kinds-folk, whofe language they underftand; they do abundantly enrich the Lands and Countrys of ftrangers, where they live, not onely with what is requifite and neceffary for the life of man ; but alfo what may ferve for ornament to his civill condition.   Of which *Traficq*, there arifeth ordinarily *Five* important benefits.

1. The augmentation of the Publiq Tolls and Cuftomes, at their coming and going out of the place.

2. The tranfporting and bringing in of marchandifes from remote Countries.

3. The affording of Materials in great plenty for all Mechaniqs; as Wooll, Leather, Wines; Jewels, as Diamants, Pearles, and fuch like Merchandize.

4. The venting and exportation of fo many kinds of Manifaᶜtures.

5. The Commerce and reciprocall Negotiation at Sea, which is the ground of Peace between neighbour Nations, and of great profit to their own Fellow-cittizens.

III. This reafon is the more ftrengthened, when we fee, that not onely the Iewifh Nation dwelling in Holland and Italy, trafficqs with their own ftock, but alfo with the riches of many others of their own Nation, friends, kinds-men and acquaintance, which notwithftanding live in Spaine, and fend unto them their moneys and goods, which they hold in their hands, and content themfelves with a very fmall portion of their eftate, to the end they may be fecure and free from danger that might happen unto them, in cafe they fhould fall under the yoke of the Inquifition ; whence not onely their goods, but oftentimes alfo their lives are endangered.

IV. The love that men ordinarily beare to their own Country

A 2　　　　　and

4

and the defire they have to end their lives, where they had their be-
gining, is the caufe, that moft ftrangers having gotten riches where
they are in a forain land, are commonly taken in a defire to returne
to their native foil, and there peaceably to enjoy their eftate; fo that
as they were a help to the places where they lived, and negotiated
while they remained there; fo when they depart from thence, they
carry all away, and fpoile them of their wealth : tranfporting all into
their own native Country : But with the Iews the cafe is farre different ; for where the Iews are once kindly receaved, they make a
firm refolution never to depart from thence, feeing they have no
proper place of their own : and fo they are alwayes with their goods
in the Cities where they live, a perpetuall benefit to all payments.
Which reafons do clearly proove, that it being the property of Cit-
tizens in populous and rich countries, to feeke their reft and eafe
with buying lands and faire poffeffion of which they live; many of
them hating commerce, afpire to Titles and Dignities : therefore
of all ftrangers, in whofe hands ordinarily Trafique is found, there
are none fo profitable and beneficiall to the place where they trade
and live, as is the Nation of the Iews. And feeing amongft the people of Europ, the chiefeft riches they poffeffe, fom from Spain, thofe
neighbour Nations, where the Iews fhall finde liberty to live according to their own Iudaicall Laws, they fhall moft eafily draw that
benefit to themfelves by means of the induftry of our Nation, and
their mutuall correfpondance.

From hence (if it pleafe your Highnes) it refults, that the Iewifh
Nation, though fcattered through the whole World, are not therefore a defpifable people, but as a Plant worthy to be planted in the
whole world, and received into Populous Cities : who ought to
plant them in thofe places, which are moft fecure from danger ;
being trees of moft favory fruit and profit, to be alwayes moft favoured with Laws and Priviledges, or Prerogatives, fecured and
defended by Armes. An Example of this we have in our times. His
Majefty, the Illuftrious King of Denmark, invited them with fpeciall Priviledges into Geluckftadt : the Duke of Savoy into Nifa of
Pro-

(84)(84)

Provence; and the Duke of Modina in Retio, allowing them fuch conditions and benefices, as like never were prefented unto them by any other Prince, as appeareth by the copy of thofe Priviledges, which I have in my hands. But fuppofing it would be a matter of too large extention, if I fhould make a relation of all the places under whofe Princes the Iews live, I will onely fpeake briefly of the two Tribes Iudah and Benjamin. Thefe in India in Cochin have 4 Synagogues, one part of thefe Iews being there of a white colour, and three of a tawny; thefe being moft favoured by the King. In the year 1640. dyed Samuel Caftoel, Governour of the City, and Agent for the King, and David Caftoel his fonne fucceeded in his place. In Perfia there is a great number of Iews, and they live indifferent freely : there are alfo amongft them that are in favour and great refpect by the King, and who live there very bravely. Some years paft, there was Elhazar Huza, the Viceroy, and now there is David Ian; if yet he be living. In the year 1636. the Saltan Amarat took in Bagdad, and puting all to the fword, he commanded that they fhould not touch the Iews, nor their houfes, and befides that, he freed them from one half of the tribuit they were wont to pay to the Perfian.

But the chiefeft place where the Iews life, is the Turkifh Empire, where fome of them live in great eftate, even in the Court of the Grand Turke at Conftantinople, by reafon there is no Viceroy, or Governour, or Baffa, which hath not a Iew to manage his affaires, and to take care for his eftate : Hence it cometh that in fhort time they grow up to be Lords of great revenues, and they moft frequently bend the minds of Great ones to moft weighty affaires in government.

The greateft Viceroy of whole Europe is the Baffa of Egypt; this Baffa always takes to him, by order of the Kingdome, a Iew with the title of Zaraf-Baffa (*Threfurer*) viz. of all the Revenues of that government, who receaves purfes full of money, feals them, and then fends them to the King. This man in a fhort time grows very rich, for that by his hands as being next to the Baffa, the 24 Go-
vern-

vernments of that Empire are fould and given, and all other bu-
fineſſes managed.   At preſent he that poſſeſſeth this place, is called S^r. Abraham Alhula.   The number of the Iews living in this
Kingdome of the Great Turke, is very great, and amounts to many Millions.   In Conſtantinople alone there are 48 Synagogues,
and in Salaminque 36, and more then fourefcore thoufand foules
in theſe two Cities alone.

The firſt King gave them great priviledges which they enjoy
untill this day : for befides the liberty, they have every-where, of
trading with open ſhops, of bearing any Office and poſſeſſing of
any goods, both mooveable and immooveable, he yet graunted
them power to judge all Civill caufes according to their own Laws
amongſt themſelves.   Moreover they are exempted from going to
Warres, and that fouldiers ſhould be quartered in their houfes, and
that Juſtice ſhould take no place upon the death of any one that left
no heir to his Eſtate.

In all which they are preferred before the naturall Turks themſelves.   For which caufe they pay in fome Cittys to the King three
Patacons, and in others two and a half by the pole.

In this eſtate fome of the Iews have grown to great fortunes; as
Joſeph Naſino, unto whom Amatus Luſitanus dedicated his fifth
and ſixth Centuriæ, was by Sultan Solime made Duke of Maccia,
Earle of Andro, Seignor of Millo, and the feaven Iſlands: And Jacob Ben-Iaes by Sultan Amurat, was made Governour of the Tiberiades: fo likewife others were exalted to very great and Eminent
Dignities: as was that Selomo Rofe, that was fent for Ambaſſador
at Venice, where he confirmed the laſt Peace with Amurat. In Germany, there lives alfo a great multitude of Jews, efpecially at Prague,
Vienna and Franckfurt, very much favoured by the moſt mild and
moſt gracious Emperours, but defpifed of the people, being a Nation not very finely garniſhed by reafon of their vile cloathing: yet
notwithſtanding there is not wanting amongſt them perfons of
great quality. The Emperour Matthias made Noble both Mardochai Mairel, and Ferdinando Jacob Bar Seba.

But

But yet a greater number of Iews are found in the Kingdome of Poland, Pruffia and Lethuania, under which Monarchy they have the Jurifdiction to judge amongft themfelves all caufes, both Criminal and Civil; and alfo great and famous Academies of their own. The chief Cities where the Nation liveth, are Lublin and Cracow, where there is a Iew, called Ifaac Iecells, who built a Synagogue, which ftood him in one hundred thoufand Francs, and is worth many tons of gold. There is in this place fuch infinite number of Iews; that although the Cofaques in the late warres have killed of them above one hundred and fourefcore thoufand; yet it is fuftained that they are yet at this day as innumerable as thofe were that came out of Egypt. In that Kingdome the whole Negotiation is in the hand of the Iews, the reft of the Chriftians are either all Noble-men, or Ruftiques and kept as flaves.

In Italy they are generally protected by all the Princes: their principall refidence is in the moft famous City of Venice; fo that in that fame City alone they poffeffe about 1400 Houfes; and are ufed there with much courtefy and clemency. Many alfo live in Padoa and Verona; others in Mantua, and alfo many in Rome it felf. Finally they are fcattered here and there in the chief places of Italy, and do live there with many fpeciall priviledges.

In the Government of the great Duke of Tufcany, they are by that Prince moft gracioufly & bountifully dealt with, having power from him graunted, to have their Judicatory by themfelves, and to judge in all matters, both Civill and Criminall; befides many other Priviledges, whereof I my felf have the Copies in hand. The rich and illuftrious families that flourifhed in thefe Countries are many, viz. The Thoraces, who being three Brethren, fhared betwixt them above 700 thoufand Crowns. In Ferrara were the Viles, whofe ftock was above 200 thoufand Crowns. The Lord Jofeph de Fano, Marquis de Villependi, was a man much refpected of all the Princes in Italy, and was called by them, The Peace-maker and appeafer of all troubles; becaufe he, by his authority and entremife, was ufed to appeafe all troubles and ftrife rifing amongft them.

Don

Don Daniel Rodrigues, becaufe of his prudency and other good qualities, was fent in the year 1589 from the moft Excellent Senat of Venice into Dalmatia, to appeafe thofe tumults and fcandals given by the Vfquoquibs in Cliffa: which he moft manly effected, and caufed all the women and children, that were kept cloofe prifoners, to be fet at liberty, brought alfo to an happy iffue many other things of great moment, for which he was fent. Alphonfo II. the Duke of Ferrara, fent alfo for his Ambaffador to the Imperiall Majefty, one Abraham de Bondi, to pay and difcharge Invefti-ture of the States of Modena and Reggio. The Prince of Safol and the Marquis of Scandia likewife, had to their Factors men of our Nation.

In the Kingdome of Barbary, their lives alfo a great number of Iews, who-ever cruelly and bafely ufed by that Barbarous Nation, except at Marrocco, the Court and Kings houfe, where they have their Naguid or Prince that governs them, and is their Iudge, and is called at this day, Seignor Mofeh Palache: and before him was in the fame Court, that Noble family Ruthes, that had power and Iurifdiction of all kinde of punifhment, onely life and death excepted.

In the Low-Countries alfo, the Iews are received with great Charity and Benevolency, and efpecially in this moft renowned City of Amfterdam, where there are no leffe then 400 Families; and how great a trading and Negotiation they draw to that City, experience doth fufficiently witnefs. They have there no leffe then three hundred houfes of their own, enjoy a good part of the Weft and Eaft-Indian Compagnies; and befides have yet to fet forth their Trafiq fuch a ftock. that for fetting a fide, onely one duit of every pound Flemifh for all kind of commodities that enter, and again as much for all what goes out of this town, and what befides we pay yearly of the rents we get from the Eaft-Indian Compagnie to the reliefe and fuftenance of the poore of our Synagogue, that very money amounts ordinarily every year, unto the fumme very neare of 12000 Franks; whereby you may eafely conceive what a migh-

ty

ty ſtock it is they trade with, and what a profit they needs muſt bring into this City.

In Hambourg likewiſe, a moſt famous City of Holſace in Germany, there lives alſo a hundred families, protected by the Magiſtrat, though moleſted by the people. There reſides Sir Duarte Nunes d'Acoſta, Reſident for his Majeſty the King of Portugal: Gabriel Gomes, Agent for his Majeſty the King of Danemarck: David de Lima, a Ieweller, for the ſame his Majeſty; and Emanuel Boccaro Roſales, created by the Emperour a Noble-man and a Count Palatin.

In all theſe places the Iews live (in a manner) all of them Merchants, and that without any prejudice at all to the Natives: For the Natives, and thoſe eſpecially that are moſt rich, they build themſelves houſes and Palaces, buy Lands and firme goods, aime at Titles and Dignities, and ſo ſeek their reſt and contentment that way: But as for the Iews, they aſpire at nothing, but to preferre themſelves in their way of Marchandize; and ſo employing their *Capitals*, they ſend forth the benefit of their labour amongſt many and ſundry of the Natives, which they, by the trafick of their Negotiation, do enrich. From whence it's eaſy to judge of the profit that Princes and Common-wealths do reap, by giving liberty of Religion to the Iews, and gathering them by ſome ſpeciall priviledges into their Countries: as Trees that bring forth ſuch excellent fruits.

So that if one Prince, ill adviſed, driveth them out of his Land, yet another invites them to his; & ſhews them favour: Wherein we may ſee the prophecy of Iacob fulfilled in the letter: *The ſtaffe (to ſupport him) ſhall not depart from Iacob, untill Meſſias ſhall come.* And this ſhall ſuffice concerning the Profit of the Iewiſh Nation.

B   How

How Faithfull

The Nation of the Iewes are.

He Fidelity of Vaffals and Subjects, is a thing that Princes moft efteem off: for there-on, both in Peace and Warre, depends the prefervation of their eftates. And as for this point, in my opinion, they owe much to the Nation of the Iews, by reafon of the faithfulneffe and loyalty they fhow to all Potentates that receive and protect them in their Countries. For fetting afide the Hiftories of the Ptolomies, Kings of Egypt, who did not truft the Guard of their perfons, nor the keeping of their Forts, nor the moft important affairs of their Kingdome to any other Nation with greater fatisfaction then to the Iews; the Wounds of Antipater fhewed to Iulius Cæfar in token of his loyalty, and the brafen Tables of our Anceftours amongft the Romans, are evident witneffes enough of their fidelity fhewed unto them.

In Spaine the Iews of Burgos; as the Chronicles do declare, moft generoufly fhewed the very fame fidelity in the times of Don Henrique; who having killed his Brother, the King, Don Pedro de Cruel, made himfelf Lord of all his Kingdomes, and brought under his obedience all the Grandees and people of Spaine: Only the Iews of Burgos denyed to obey him, and fortified themfelves within the City, faying, *That God would never have it, that they fhould deny obedience to their Naturall Lord Don Pedro, or to his rightfull fucceffours.* A conftancy that the prudent King, Don Henriques, very much efteemed of, faying, that fuch Vaffals as thofe were, by Kings and great men, worthy of much account, feeing they held greater refpect to the fidelity *they ought to their King, although conquered and dead, than to the prefent fortune of the Conquerour:* And a while after, receiving very *honourable conditions, they gave themfelves over.*

In Spain alfo (as you may fee in Mariana) many Iewes for the fame fidelity were appointed Governours of the Kingdome, and Tutors

(90)

tors of Noble-mens children, jointly to others of the Nobility upon the death of their Parents.

The Chronicles of the Xarifes, dedicated to King Philip the second, King of Spaine, alleagues for an example of great fidelity and vertue, how the rifing of the Xarifes againſt the Morines, their killing and ſpoyling them of the Kingdome, was ſuch a great grief unto Samuel Alvalenſi, one of thoſe baniſhed out of Spaine, and much favoured by the King of Fez, deſcended from the houſe of the Morines; that joyning himſelf with other Magiſtrates, and ſubjects of the Morines, arming ſome ſhips and going himſelf Captain over all, he came ſuddenly with 400. men, and fell by night upon the Army of the Xarifes, that were more then 3000. men, beſieging Copta, and without loſing one man, killed of them above 500. and cauſed them to raiſe the ſiege.

Many the like Examples may be brought of times paſt; but for our preſent; and modern times there is no Exemple ſo evident, as in the beſieging of Mantua for the Emperour in the year 1630, where the Iews fought moſt valiantly, and reſcued it from the Natives. As likewiſe in the Seignory of Braſil, where the ſame thing was done: for one of the ſame Nation, a Dutchman, having delivered the Cape unto the Portugals, there was found in our Nation there not only loyalty, but alſo ſuch diſcretion, that had they taken their adviſe, the buſineſs had not ſo proceeded.

This may be ſeen more clearly yet in their being baniſhed out of Caſtile, in the dayes of Ferdinand & Iſabella. Their number at that time was ſuppoſed to have been half a Milion of men, amongſt whom were many of great valour, & courage (as Don Iſaac Abarbanel, a Counſellor of State, doth relate) & yet amongſt ſo great a number, there was not found any one man, that undertook to raiſe a party to free themſelves from that moſt miſerable baniſhment. An evident ſign of the proper and naturall reſolution of this Nation, and their conſtant obedience to their Princes.

The ſame affection is confirmed by the inviolable cuſtome of all the Iews whereſoever they live : for on every Sabbath or feſti-

B 2   vall

12

vall Day, they every where are ufed to pray for the fafety of all
Kings, Princes and Common-wealths, under whofe jurifdiction
they live, of what profeffion-foever : unto which duty they are
bound by the Prophets and the Talmudifts ; from the Law, as by
Ieremie chap. 29. verf. 7. *Seek the peace of the City unto which I have
made you to wander : and pray for her unto the Lord, for in her Peace
you fhall enjoy peace.* He fpeaks of Babylon, where the Iews at that
time were captives. From the Talmud ord. 4. tract. 4. Abodazara
pereq. 1. *Pray for the peace of the Kingdome, for unleffe there were
feare of the Kingdome, men would fwallow one the other alive,* &c.

From the continuall and never broken Cuftome of the Iews
wherefoever they are, on the Sabbath-Day, or other folemn Feafts;
at which time all the Iews from all places come together to the Synagogue, after the benediction of the Holy Law, before the Minifter of the Synagogue bleffeth the people of the Iews; with a loud
voice he bleffeth the Prince of the Country under whom they live,
that all the Iews may hear it, and fay, Amen. The words he ufeth
are thefe, as in the printed book of the Iews may be feen : *He that
giveth falvation unto Kings, and dominion unto Lords, he that delivered his fervant David from the fword of the Enemy, he that made a way
in the Sea, and a path in the ftrange waters, bleffe and keep, preferve and
refcue, exalt and magnify, and lift up higher and higher, our Lord.*
[And then he names, the Pope, the Emperour, King, Duke, or any
other Prince under whom the Iews live, and add's :] *The King of
kings defend him in his mercy, making him joyfull, & free him from all
dangers and diftreffe. The King of kings, for his goodnefs fake, raife up
and exalt his planetary ftar, & multiply his dayes over his Kingdome.
The King of kings for his mercies fake, put into his heart, and into the
heart of his Counfellers, & thofe that attend and adminifter to him, that
he may fhew mercy unto us, & unto all the people of Ifrael. In his dayes
and in our dayes, let Iudah be fafe, and Ifrael dwell fecurely, and let the
Redeemer come to Ifrael, and fo may it pleafe God. Amen.* Thefe are the
very formalities fet down word for word, which the Iewes, by the
command of God, received from the Talmud, do ufe in their prayers

(92)

yers for Princes, under whofe government they refide. And therefore wife Princes are wont to banifh from their Courts falfe reports. And moft wife *R. Simon Ben-Iochai*, in his excellent book called *Zoar* in Sarafa Pecudi, relates, that *it is a Tradition received from Heaven, that the Kings of the Nations of the world, Princes, Governours, that protect the Iews in this world, or do them any good, that the fame fhall enjoy certain degrees of glory, or eternall reward; as on the other fide, they that do to the Nation of the Iews any harm, that they fhall be punifhed with fome particular eternal punifhment.* As appeareth alfo out of Efa. the laft chapter.

Thus you fee the Fidelity of the Iews to wards their Governours clearly proved. Now, that no man may think that their banifhment out of Spaign & Portugal, proceeded from any fufpition or faults of theirs, I fhall clearly rehearfe the reafon of fo fudden a determination, and what the thoughts of many Chriftian Princes have been there-upon. The bufinefs was thus: Ferdinand and Ifabella, Governours of Caftile, having gained the Kingdome of Granada, of which they took poffeffion on the fifth of Ianuary, they refolved to thruft out all the Iews that lived in their Kingdomes, and fo on the laft of March, they made an Edict in the fame City, in which they expreffed: *That feeing the Iews in their Countries drew many Chriftians to turn Iews, and efpecially fome Noble-men of their Kingdome of Andaluzia, that for this caufe they banifhed them under moft heavy penalties, &c.* So that the caufe of their banifhment was not any difloyalty at all.

Now what amongft many others in all Chriftendom, one famous Lawyer in Rome, and Oforius an excellent and moft eloquent Hiftorian have thought, I fhall here relate. In the year 1492 (faith the Lawyer) Ferdinand, called the Catholick, being King of Spain, drove out of his Country all the Iews that were living there from the time of the Babylonian and Roman Captivity, and were very rich in houfes and goods: and that upon pain, if they went not away within the term of fix moneths, that all their houfes and goods fhould be confifcated unto the Exchequer, which as

we have faid, were very great. Whereupon they leaving the Kingdome of Caftile, they went over many of them into Portugal, as being the neareft place. In the year 1497, there being an Alliance con-
tracted between the Kings of Caftile and Portugal; the Jews at the
requeft of the faid King Ferdinand, were banifhed out of Portugal;
but it being againft the will of Emanuel, King of Portugal, to have
them banifhed out of his Country, he refolved to oblidge them to
become Chriftians, promifing never to moleft them, neither in
Criminall matters, nor in the loffe of their goods; and exempted
them from many burdens, and Tributs of the Kingdome. This E-
manuel being dead, John III, fucceeded in his place in the Kingdome of Portugal, who being excited by others, faid, That what his
Father Emanuel had done, concerning the not-troubling them, was
of no valew, becaufe they lived not as was convenient, & that without the authority of the Pope of Rome, his father could not graunt
any fuch thing: for which caufe he would that for thofe that lived
amiffe, they fhould be proceeded againft, as againft the Mores in
Caftile: And fending to Rome to difanull the faid promifes, it was
not onely not graunted to him, but moreover they reprooved his
appearance there, and praifed and approoved the promifes made
by his Father Emanuel to the Jewes, publifhing a generall pardon to
all that were taken, which were about 1500, and they all were fet
free. Which Bull was graunted by Clement VII. by the intervention of all the Confiftory of Cardinals. Afterwards the faid king
John fent once again to defire the former Licence with fo many re-
plications and triplications, that at length the Pope granted it: But
a few daies after it was revoked again with a generall Pardon to all
that were taken, which were 12000, with fuch a determination,
that the fame Licence fhould never be graunted, as being againft all
right and reafon. This troubled Don John the King very much,
and withall the Cardinal his brother, who came in thefe laft dayes
to be King of Portugal himfelf. Great Paul III. of the houfe of
Farnefia, fucceeding to Clement the VII. there was a requeft rendred to the Pope for power to bring in the Inquifition into this
King-

Kingdome. The Pope would not graunt it, faying: He could not, and that it was a thing againft reafon and Iuftice, but on the contrary confirmed the promifes made by the King Don Emanuel, his Father; and pardoned all the delinquents fince the time of violence unto that day. Don Iohn feeing this, fent an Embaffadour meerly for that bufineffe to the Pope, but could obtain nothing at all: for which caufe King Iohn refolved to entreat the Emperour Charles the V. then paffing for Rome, as Conquerour over the Turks, having wonn Tunis and Goleta, that in this his Triumph he would take occafion to defire this favour from the Pope, that the King of Portugal might fet up the Inquifition in his Kingdome, it being an old cuftome that thofe that triumphed, fhould aske fomething of the Pope that they moft defired. The Emperour than having defired this, the Pope anfwered him, that he could not do it by reafon of the agreement made, and the promifes of the King Don Emanuel; which he had found by an Apoftolicall Nuntio in Portugal in the year 1497, at which time the Iewes were forced and compelled to become Chriftians. The Emperour replyed, Let that finne fall on him, and the Prince his fonne, the Apoftolicall feat fhall be free from it. So the Pope graunted it; becaufe the Emperour Charles the V. was brother in law to King Don Iohn of Portugal; and befides they treated at that time to enter further in affinity, and to marry their children, which fince was effected. After Paul the III. graunted this, there was a new Pardon given in generall to all that were taken unto that time, amounting the Number unto 1800. But the King refufing to obey the Pardon, and to free the Prifonners, the Pope tooke it very ill, and fent for this onely bufineffe for his Nuntio, one Monfegnor Monte Paliciano, who fince was Cardinal of the Church of Rome. And the King for all this not obeying, the Pope made the Nuntio to fix the Pardon upon the doores of the Cathedrall Churches, and the Nuntio caufed the Prifons to be opened, and there were fet free about 1800 prifoners. He that follicited this bufineffe at Rome was one Seignor Duarte de Paz, a Cavallier of the Order

of

of St. Iohn: whom to fearch out there were appointed at Rome ten men difguifed ; thefe having found him, gave him fifteen wounds, and left him for dead : thus wounded, he was carried to the houfe of Seignor Philip Eftrozi : This being reported to the Pope, Paul the III. he caufed him to be carried to the Caftle of S. Ange-lo, where he gave order to have him nobly cured.   That fame Sei-gnor was by the Pope, by all the Cardinals and the whole Court in great refpeƈt. At the fame time that this man was hurt, the Empe-rour Charles the V. was at Rome with his Army.   On the time when he began to treat of this bufineffe with Clement the VII. fee-ing the Kings importunity, he made a Bull and gave licence to all the Portugals of that Nation of the Iews; that they might go and live in the Church-Dominions, & whofoever will come in the faid Dominions, that he fhall have freedom to live, as at the firft, in his Iewifh profeffion, and that at no time they fhould be enquired into, but after the fame manner as they were wont to live in Portugal, fo they fhould live there.   The faid Bull paffed all the Confiftory; and being confirmed and received by the faid Portugals, they began fome of them to depart to live in Ancona, being a fea-port more commodious then others: which being known by the King and Cardinal of Portugal, they caufed to be proclaimed in all the King-dome, that upon paine of death, and loffe of all their goods, no man fhould dare depart the Kingdome. Clement being dead, in his place fucceeded (as we have faid) Pope Paul the III. who confir-med the fame Priviledges: Afterwards in the year 1550. Paul the III. died, and Julius the III. fucceeded, who ratified the fore-men-tioned Priviledges given by his Predeceffours, and the whole Apo-ftolike Seat inviolably. In thofe times there were many Doƈtors that wrote on this matter, amongft whom the chiefeft were Alciat, and the Cardinal Parifius in 2 & 3 *parte Confiliorum pro Chriftianis no-viter converfis;* fhewing by reafon and law, that confidering they were forced and not converted willingly, that they had not fallen nor do fall under any Cenfure.   Thefe reafons being confidered of by the Princes of Italy, they graunted likewife the fame Priviledges:

viz.

viz. Cofmo the Great, Duke of Florence, and Hercules, Duke of
Ferrare, and within few years Emanuel Felibert, Duke of Savoye;
and were by all his fucceffours confirmed. In the year 1492, when
they were banifhed from Caftile, we read in the Chronicles of that
Kingdome, that the Lords of that place did complain that their Cities and Towns were deftroyed and dis-inhabitated; and had they
believed any fuch thing, that they would have oppofed the Kings
decree, and would never have given their confent to it. That
was the caufe, that Don Emanuel of Portugal, feeing on the one
fide apparent dammage, fhould he let them depart his Kingdome; and on the otherfide, not being able to break his promife made to the King of Caftile, he caufed them to be compelled to the Faith, upon paine of Death, that they fhould not
depart out of his Dominions. The Catholiq King was blamed
of all Chriftian Princes, and efpecially by the Senate of Venice, (as Marcus Antonius Sabellicus doth write) for having banifhed a Nation fo profitable to the Publicq and Particular good,
without any kind of pretence. And fo the Parliament of Paris likewife did extreamly wonder at fuch a determination. And truely
good reafon there was to wonder; for we fee fince, what the Senat
of Venice hath done, who never deliberats or puts into execution
any thing, without great judgement: having the advantage of all
Republicqs in their Government and leaving behind them
the Romans, Carthagenians, Athenians, and moft learned La-
cedemonians, and that Parliament of Paris, which in the Government of affaires was alwayes moft prudent. Moft of thofe
that were banifhed paffed to the Levant, who were embraced by
the Ottoman-family, all the fucceeding Kings wondring at it, that
the Spanjards, who make profeffion to be a politiq Nation, fhould
drive out of their kingdomes fuch a people. Moreover Sultan
Bajazet, and Sultan Soliman, received them exceeding well, the
coming of the Iews to them being very acceptable: and fo did likewife all their fucceffours, confidering of how great a profit and benefit their refiding in their Dominions was. And in the year 1555.

C Paul

Paul the IV. being chosen Pope of Rome, who before was called Cardinal de Chiesi, an intimate to the Cardinal of Portugal, caused the Iewes to be held in Ancona, & other places of the Church, according to the Priviledges graunted to them by the Popes, his Predecessours in the name of the Apostolical Roman seat. Licurgus, Solon and Draco, and all Founders of Commonwealths, gave counsell that strangers ought to be loved and much made of, as in the Discourses of *Se. in 7 de Legibus de Rep.* is amply to be seen. And by the Divine Law (as Moses commanded us) we ought not to trouble a stranger, but he sayes, *Remember you were strangers in the Land of Egypt.*

In summe, to the same purpose might be brought many other and more powerfull reasons, but because they are out of our consideration, we passe them over. And here to declare some particulars, worthy to be known for advise and example, that befell our Nation in those bitter banishments; part whereof Hieronymus Oforius recites more at large, in the first of his elegant two Books de Rebus Emanuelis. The first title he giveth to those miserable successes, is this, which he puts for a Postil in the margent of his booke, *Iudæorum Liberi per vim ad Christianismum pertracti:* and than rehearses, how that in the year 1496 the King decreed, that all the Iewes and Mores, that dwelt in his Kingdome, and would not become Christians, should depart his Dominions in a short time; which being past, all that should be found in his Kingdome, should loose their liberty, and become slaves to the King. The time being now at hand (as Oforius proceeds) in which the Iewes, that would not turne Christians, were to depart the Kingdome, and all of them as many as they were, had with all their power provided, and taken a firme resolution to be gone: which the King seeing, and not able to endure it, thought upon a businesse (as he saith) *facto quidem iniquam & injustam,* which to do was really wicked and unjust, and that was to command that all the children of the Israelites, that were not above 14 years old, should be taken out of the power of their own Parents; & when they had them, they should force them

to

to become Chriftians; a new thing that could not be done without
a wonderfull alteration of their minds: for it was (as Oforius fpeaks)
a horrid and miferable fpectacle, to fee the tender Infants wreftled
out of the arms and brefts of their lamenting mothers, to dragge a-
long their poore fathers that held them faft, and to give them
many wounds and blows to draw them out of their handes; to hear
their cryes that afcend to heaven, their groanes, lamentations, and
complaints every-where, fo that this cruelty was the caufe, that
many of thofe diftreffed Fathers threw their children into wells,
and others killed themfelves with their own hands, that they might
not fee fo bitter a thing with their eyes. The cruelty of Emanuel ended not here, but going on with compulfion and revilings, gave
caufe to his owne Chronographer to make the fecond title or poftil, with thefe words; *Vis & Dolus Iudæis illata*: That is, The force
and deceit ufed towards the Iewes. And fo he goes on, declaring
how he had promifed in the condition they had made, that he
would affigne them three Ports in his Kingdome to embarque at,
viz. Lisbon, Setuval, and Puerto: and neverthelеffe he forbad them
afterwards to embarque themfelves in any place but Lisbon: for
which caufe all the Iewes of the Kingdome came to that City, from
whence befides a thoufand moleftations and extortions, he drove
them (as Vafquo faith) as fheep in the ftalls, and there forced
their afflicted bodies to counterfeit, that which their foules and
thoughts never meant nor approoved of. Works, of which his
own Chronologer faith, *Fuit hoc quidem neque ex Lege, neque ex
religione factum*. That is, This was done neither according to Law,
nor Religion. Let men of clear mind, and free from paffion confider for Gods fake, if fuch violences can work any good impref-
fion or character in men: or what Law, either Humain or Divine,
National or Modern, can bear, that the fouls of men (which the
Moft High hath created free) be forced to believe what they believe not, and to love what they hate? This cruelty was reproved
and cenfure of many Princes of the world and learned men. And
his own Chronologer reprehends it with a new poftil, and fpeaks

C 2

freely;

freely; *Regis in* Iudæos *facinorum reprehenſio*. That is, A cenſure of the Kings wickedneſſe againſt the Iews. Truely with juſt reaſon doth Oſorius call the works, which the King did unto us, I*niquities and injuſtices, deceitfull violences, and wicked attempts :* and ſo goes on, reproving them with moſt elegant Reaſons.

Further what happened to the Iews under other Princes in other Kingdomes and Countries, is notorious and enough known to all the world, and therefore not neceſſary here to relate. So farre concerning their Banniſhment.

Now, I will not conceale to ſay, but that alwayes there have bene found ſome calumniators, that endeavouring to make the Nation infamous, laid upon them *three moſt falſe reports*, as if *they were dangerous to the Goods, the Lives*, and withall to *the very Souls of the Natives*. They urge againſt them their *uſuries*, the *ſlaying of infants* to celebrate their Paſſe-over, and the *inducing Chriſtians to become* Iews. To all which I ſhall anſwer briefly.

1. As for *uſury*, ſuch dealing is not the eſſential property of the Iews, for though in Germany there be ſome indeed that practiſe uſury; yet the moſt part of them that live in Turky, Italy, Holland and Hamburg, being come out of Spaigne, they hold it infamous to uſe it; and ſo with a very ſmall profit of 4. or 5. per Cent, as Chriſtians themſelves do, they put their money ordinarily in Banco : for to lay out their money without any profit, was commanded only toward their brethren of the ſame Nation of the Iews; but not to any other Nation. And however by this Charity is not hurt: for it ſtands in good reaſon, that every on ſhould gain and get ſome advantage with his money, to ſuſtaine his own life: and when any one to ſupply his own wants, doth take ſome courſe of Marchandiſe, by which he hopes to gaine by other mens moneys taken up on truſt, 'tis no inhumanity to reckon and take from him uſe : For as no man is bound to give his goods to an other; ſo is he not bound to let it out, but for his own occaſions and profit, and not to leave himſelf deſtitute of the profit he could make

of

of the monyes. Onely this muft be done with moderation, that the ufury be not biting and exorbitant, which the Chriftians themfelves ufe, amongft themfelves; as even in the Mounts of Piety at Padua, Vicenza and Verona is to be feen, where they take 6 par Cent, and elfewhere yet much more. This in no manner can be called Robbery, but is with confent and will of the Contracter; and the fame Sacred Scripture, which allows ufury with him that is not of the fame Religion, forbids abfolutely the robbing of all men, whatfoever Religion they be of. In our Law it is a greater finne to rob or defraud a ftranger, than if I did it to one of my own profeffion: becaufe a Jew is bound to fhew his charity to all men: for he hath a precept, not to abhorre an Idumean, nor an Egyptian; and that he fhall love and protecta ftranger that comes to live in his land. If notwithftanding there be fome that do contrary to this, they do it not as Iewes fimply, but as wicked Iewes, as amongft all nations there are found generally fome Ufurers.

2. As for *killing of the young children of Chriftians;* it is an infallible truth what is reported of the Negros of Guinea and Brazil, that if they fee any miferable man that hath efcaped from the danger of the fea, or hath fallen or fuffered any kind of ill-fortune, or Shipwrake, they perfecute and vex him fo much the more, faying, *God curfe thee.* And wee that live not amongft the Blacke-moors and wild-men, but amongft the white and civilized people of the world, yet wee find this an ordinary courfe, that men are very prone to hate and defpife him that hath ill fortune; and on the other fide, to make much of thofe whom fortune doth favour. Hereof the Chriftians themfelves have good experience; for during the times of their fuppreffion and perfecution under the Roman Empire, they were falfely flandred of divers Emperours and tyrannicall Princes. Nero accufed them, that they had fet Rome on fire; Others, that they were Witches and Conjurers; and others againe that they flew their children to celebrate their Ceremonies, as wee find in divers Authors. Even fo likewife it is with the Jewifh Nation, that now is difperfed and afflicted, though they have

C 3   mo-

22

moneys: There is no flander nor calumny that is not caft upon
them, even the very fame ancient fcandall that was caft of old upon
the innocent Chriftians, is now laid upon the Jews. Whereas the
whole world may eafely perceive, it is but a meer flander, feeing
it is known that at this day, out of Jerufalem, no facrifice nor blood
is in any ufe by them, even that blood which is found in an Egg is
forbidden them, how much more mans blood? Moreover I could
produce divers memorable examples which out in our own times
in Araguza to a Jew: how he was accufed of this fame wickednefs,
and not confeffing it, how they imprifoned him betwixt to walls,
and being in that diftreffe, how he cited before God all the Judges
to anfwer there for what they did; and how within a year after,
many of the Iudges died, and thofe that lived, fearing the like might
befall them, and loofe their lives, fet him free: But I muft not be too
prolix; it may fuffice to fay, that by the Pope himfelf it was defined
in full Counfell the accufation to be falfe; and fo likewife judged
all the Princes of Italy; as alfo Alphonfo the Wife, King of Spain,
and that it was onely a meer invention to drink the blood, and to
fwallow up the goods of the harmleffe Iews.

3. As for the *third* Point, I fay, that although Ferdinand & Ifa-
bell, giving colour to fo indifcreet a determination, faid, that they
induced the Nobles to become Iews, yet truely this cannot be faid,
but by fome falfe informations. For if fo be, amongft thofe difficulties and impoffibilities, it may happen, that fome of the Sect of
the Papifts, of a better mind, embrace the Iewifh Religion; it cannot therefore be prefumed, that they were induced thereunto by
the Iews; feeing the Iews do not entice any man to profeffe their
Law: But if any man of his own free-will come to them, they by
their rites & Ceremonies are obliged to make proof of them, whether they come for any temporall intereft, and to perfuade them to
look well to themfelves what they do: that the Law unto which
they are to fubmit themfelves, is of many precepts; and doth oblige the tranfgreffor to many fore punifhments. And fo we follow
the example of Nahomi, cited in the Sacred Scripture, who did
not

23

not perfuade Ruth to go along with her; but faid firſt to her: *Orpa thy ſiſter returned to her Nation and her Gods; go thou and follow her.* But Ruth continuing conſtant, then at length ſhe received her.

Befides this, the Iews indeed have reaſon to take care for their own preſervation; and therefore will not go about by ſuch wayes to make themſelves odious to Princes and Common-wealths, under whoſe Dominions they live.

Now, becauſe I beleive, that with a good conſcience I have diſcharged our Nation of the Iews of thoſe three ſlanders or calumnies, as elſewhere I have more at large written about it; I conceive I may from thoſe two qualities, of Profitableneſſe and Fidelity conclude, that ſuch a Nation ought to be well entertained, and alſo beloved and protected generally of all. The more, confidering they are called in the Sacred Scriptures, the Sons of God; and 'tis faid by all the Prophets, that they who ſhall wrong them, ſhall be moſt ſeverely puniſhed; and that he that toucheth them, toucheth the apple of Gods eye. And at leaſt, it was alwayes the opinion of Auguſtine, as he made it appear in his works *Libr. de Doctrina Chriſtiana cap.* 28. where he faith, *Quod omnes homines æque diligendi ſunt.* That all men are equally to be beloved.

Now, having proved the two former Points. I could adde a third, viz. of the Nobility of the Iews: but becauſe that Point is enough known amongſt all Chriſtians, as lately yet it hath been moſt worthily and excellently ſhewed and deſcribed in a certain Book, called, *The Glory of Iehudah and Iſrael,* dedicated to our Nation by that worthy Chriſtian Miniſter Mr. *Henry Ieſſey, (*1653. in Duch) where this matter is ſet out at large: And by Mr. *Edw. Nicholas* Genleman, in his Book, called, *An Apologie for the Honorable Nation of the* Iews, *and all the Sons of Iſrael*(1648. in Engliſh.) Therefore I will here forbeare, and reſt on their ſaying of our King Salomon, the wifeſt on earth, *Let another mans mouth praiſe thee, and not thine own.* Which is the cloſe of *Rabbi Meneſſe Ben-Iſrael,* a Divine, and Doctor in Phyfick, in the *Strand* over againſt the *New-Exchange* in *London.*

F I N I S.

(103)

Menasseh ben Israel.

from a portrait by Rembrandt
now in the Hermitage Collection. S.t Petersburg.

VINDICIÆ

JUDÆORUM,

OR A

LETTER

In Anſwer to certain Queſtions propounded by
a Noble and Learned Gentleman, touching
the reproaches caſt on the Nation of the
JEVVES; wherein all objections are
candidly, and yet fully cleared.

By Rabbi Menaſſeh Ben Iſrael *a Divine
and a Phyſicyan.*

Printed by *R. D.* in the year 1656.

Moſt Noble, and Learned Sir,

 Have received a letter from your worſhip, which was welcome to me; and I read it, becauſe yours, with great delight; if you will pleaſe to allow for the unpleaſantneſſe of the ſubject. For I do aſſure your worſhip, I never met with any thing in my life which I did more deeply reſent, for that it reflecteth upon the credit of a nation, which amongſt ſo many calumnies, ſo manifeſt, (and therefore ſhamefull) I dare to pronounce innocent. Yet I am afraid, that whilſt I anſwer to them, I ſhall offend ſome, whoſe zeal will not permit them to conſider, that ſelf vindication, as defenſive armes, is naturall to all; but to be wholly ſilent, were to acknowledge what is ſo falſly objected. Wherefore that I may juſtifie my ſelf to my own conſcience, I have obeyed your worſhips commands: for your requeſt muſt not be accounted leſſe, at leaſt by me. I preſume your worſhip cannot expect either prolix, or polite diſcourſes upon ſo ſad a ſubject; for who can be ambitious in his own calamity? I have therefore diſpatcht onely ſome conciſe, and brief relations, barely exceeding the bounds of a letter; yet ſuch as may ſuffice you, to inform the Rulers of the *English* nation, of a truth moſt reall, and ſincere; which I hope they will accept in good part, according to their noble, and ſingular prudence and piety. For innocencie being alwayes moſt free from ſuſpecting evil, I cannot be perſwaded, that any one hath either ſpoken, or written againſt us, out of any particular hatred that they bare us, but that they rather ſuppoſed our coming might prove prejudiciall to their eſtates, and intereſts; charity alwayes beginning at home. Yet notwithſtanding I propounded this matter under an argument of profit (for this hath made us welcome in other countries) and

A 2

therefore I hope I may prove what I undertake. However, I have but fmall encouragement to expect the happy attainment of any other defign, but onely that truth may be juftified of her children. I fhall anfwer in order to what your worfhip hath propofed.

THE FIRST SECTION.

ANd in the firft place, I cannot but weep bitterly, and with much anguifh of foul lament that ftrange and horrid accufation of fome Chriftians againft the difperfed, and affli-&ted *Iewes* that dwell among them, when they fay (what I tremble to write) that the *Iewes* are wont to celebrate the feaft of unleavened bread, fermenting it with the bloud of fome Chriftians, whom they have for this purpofe killed : when the calumniators themfelves have moft barbaroufly and cruelly butchered fome of them. Or to fpeak more mildly, have found one dead, and caft the corps, as if it had been murdered by the *Iewes*, into their houfes or yards, as lamentable experience hath proved in fundry places : and then with unbridled rage and tumult, they accufe the innocent *Iews*, as the committers of this moft execrable fact. Which deteftable wickedneffe hath been fometimes perpetrated, that they might thereby take advantage to exercife their cruelty upon them ; and fometimes to juftifie, and patronize their maffacres already executed. But how farre this accufation is from any femblable appearance of truth, your worfhip may judge by thefe following arguments.

1. It is utterly forbid the *Iewes* to eat any manner of bloud whatfoever, *Levit.* Chapter 7. 26. and *Deuter.* 12. where it is exprefly faid וכל דם, *And ye shall eat no manner of bloud,* and in obedience to this command the *Iewes* eat not the bloud of any animal. And more then this, if they find one drop of bloud in an egge, they caft it away as prohibited. And if in eating a piece of bread, it happens to touch any bloud drawn from the teeth, or gummes, it muft be pared, and cleanfed from the faid bloud, as it evidenely appeares in *Sulhan Haruch* and our rituall book. Since then it is thus, how can it enter into any mans heart to believe

lieve

lieve that they fhould eat humane bloud, which is yet more deteftable, there being fcarce any nation now remaining upon
earth fo barbarous, as to commit fuch wickedneffe ?

2. The precept in the Decalogue *Thou shalt not kill* is of generall extent; it is a morall command. So that the *Iewes* are bound
not onely, not to kill one of thofe nations where they live, but
they are alfo oblig'd by the law of gratitude, to love them. They
are the very words of R. *Mofes* of *Egypt* in *Iad a Razaka*, in his
treatife of Kings, the tenth Chapter, in the end, *Concerning the na-*
tions,the ancients have commanded us to vifit their fick and to bury their
dead,as the dead of Ifrael,and to relieve,and maintain their poor,as we
do the poor of Ifrael, becaufe of the wayes of peace, as it is written,
God is good to all, and his tender mercies are over all his works. Pfal.
145. 9. And in conformity hereto, I witneffe before God bleffed for ever, that I have continually feen in *Amfterdam* where I refide, abundance of good correfpondency, many interchanges of
brotherly affeﬅion, and fundry things of reciprocall love. I
have thrice feen when fome *Flemine* Chriftians have fallen into
the river in our ward, called *Flemburgh,* our nation caft themfelves into the river to them, to help them out, and to deliver
their lives from death. And certainly he that will thus hazard
himfelf to fave another, cannot harbour fo much cruell malice,
as to kill the innocent, whom he ought out of the duty of huma-
nity to defend and proteﬅ.

3. It is forbidden *Exodus* 21. 20. to kill a ftranger; *If a man*
fmite his fervant, or his maid with a rod, and he die under his hand, he
shall furely be punished,notwithftanding,if he continue a day or two, he
shall not be punished, for he is his money. The text fpeaks of a fervant
that is one of the Gentile nations, becaufe that he onely is faid to
be the *money* of the *Iew,* who is his mafter, as *Aben Ezra* well notes
upon the place. And the Lord commands, that if he die under
the hand of his mafter, his mafter fhall be put to death, for that as
it feems, he ftruck him with a murderous intent. But it is otherwife
if the fervant dies afterwards, for then it appeares, that he did not
ftrike him with a purpofe to kill him ; for if fo, he would have killed
him out of hand, wherefore he fhall be free, and it may fuffice for
punifhment that he hath loft his money. If therefore a *Iew* cannot
A 3

kill

kill his fervant, or flave that is one of the nations, according to the law, how much leffe fhall he be impowred to murder him that is not his *enemy*, and with whom he leads a quiet and a peaceable life? and therefore how can any good man believe that againft his holy law, a *Iew* (in a ftrange countrey efpecially) fhould make himfelf guilty of fo execrable a fact?

4. Admit that it were lawfull (which God forbid) why fhould they eat the bloud? And fuppofing they fhould eat the bloud, why fhould they eat it on the Paffeover? Here at this feaft, every confection ought to be fo pure, as not to admit of any leaven, or any thing that may fermentate, which certainly bloud doth.

5. If the *Iewes* did repute, and hold this action (which is never to be named without an epethite of horrour) neceffary, they would not expofe themfelves to fo eminent a danger, to fo cruell and more deferved punifhment, unleffe they were moved to it by fome divine precept; or at leaft, fome conftitution of their wife men. Now we challenge all thofe men who entertain this dreadfull opinion of us, as obliged in point of juftice, to cite the place of Scripture, or of the Rabbins, where any fuch precept, or doctrine is delivered. And untill they do fo, we will affume fo much liberty, as to conclude it to be no better then a malicious flander.

6. If a man, to fave his life, may break the Sabbath, and tranfgreffe many of the other commands of the law, as hath been determined in the Talmud; as alfo confirmed by R. *Mofes* of E*gypt*, in the fifth Chapter of his treatife of the fundamentalls of the law; yet three are excepted, which are, *idolatry, murther,* and *adultery* ; life not being to be purchafed at fo dear a rate, as the committing of thefe heinous fins : an innocent death being infinitely to be preferred before it. Wherefore if the killing of a Chriftian, as they object, were a divine precept, and inftitution, (which far be it from me to conceive) it were certainly to be null'd and rendred void, fince a man cannot perform it, without indangering his own life; and not onely fo, but the life of the whole congregation of an entire people; and yet more, fince it is directly a violation of one of thefe three precepts, *Thou shalt do no murder :* which is intended univerfally of all men, as we have faid before.

7. The

7. The Lord, bleſſed for ever, by his prophet *Ieremiah* Chap. 29. 7. gives it in command to the captive Iſraelites that were diſperſed among the heathens, that they ſhould continually pray for, and endeavour the peace, welfare and proſperity of the city wherein they dwelt, and the inhabitants thereof. This the *Iewes* have alwayes done, and continue to this day in all their Synagogues, with a particular bleſſing of the Prince or Magiſtrate, under whoſe protection they live. And this the Right Honourable my Lord *St. Iohn* can teſtifie; who when he was Embaſſadour to the Lords the States of the united Provinces, was pleaſed to honour our Synagogue at *Amſterdam* with his preſence, where our nation entertained him with muſick, and all expreſſions of joy and gladneſſe, and alſo pronounced a bleſſing, not onely upon his honour, then preſent, but upon the whole Common-wealth of *England*, for that they were a people in league and amity ; and becauſe we conceived ſome hopes that they would manifeſt towards us, what we ever bare towards them, *viz.* all love and affection. But to return again to our argument, if we are bound to ſtudy, endeavour, and ſollicite, the good and flouriſhing eſtate of the city where we live, and the inhabitants thereof, how ſhall we then murder their children, who are the greateſt good, and the moſt flouriſhing bleſſing that this life doth indulge to them.

8. The children of Iſrael are naturally mercifull, and full of compaſſion. This was acknowledged by their enemies, *Kings* 1. 20, 31. when *Benhadad* King of *Aſſyria* was diſcomfited in the battel, and fled away, he became a petitioner for his life to King *Ahab*, who had conquered him ; for he underſtood that *the Kings of the houſe of Iſrael were mercifull Kings ;* and his own experience confirmed it, when for a little affection that he pretended in a complement, he obtained again his life and fortunes, from which the event of the warre had diſentitled him. And when the *Gibeonites* made that cruell requeſt to *David*, that ſeven of *Sauls* ſons who were innocent, ſhould be delivered unto them, the prophet ſaies, *now the Gibeonites were not of the children of Iſrael*, Sam. 2. 21, 2. as if he had ſaid, in this cruelty, the piety of the Iſraelites is not ſo much ſet forth, as the tyranny, and implacable rage of the Gentiles, the *Gibeonites*. Which being ſo, and experience
withall

withall declares it, *viz.* the fidelity which our nation hath inviolably preferved towards their fuperiours, then moft certainly it is wholly incompatible, and inconfiftent with the murdering of their children.

9. There are fome Chriftians, that ufe to infult againft the *Iewes*, as Chriftian homicides, that will venter to give a reafon of thefe pretended murtherous practifes. As if the accufation were then moft infallibly true, if they can find any femblance of a reafon why it might be fo. As they fay, that this is practifed by them in hatred and deteftation of Jefus of Nazareth. And that therefore they fteal Chriftian Children, buffeting them in the fame manner that he was buffetted; thereby to rub up, and revive the memory of the aforefaid death. And likewife they imagine that the *Iewes* fecretly fteal away croffes, crucifixes, and fuch like graven images, which Papifts privately and carefully retein in their houfes, and every day the *Iewes* mainly ftrike, and buffet, fhamefully fpitting on them, with fuch like ceremonies of defpight, and all this in hatred of Jefus. But I admire what they really think, when they object fuch things as thefe, laying them to our charge. For furely we cannot believe, that a people, otherwife of fufficient prudence, and judgement, can perfwade themfelves into an opinion that the *Iewes* fhould commit fuch practifes, unleffe they could conceive they did them in honour and obedience to the God whom they worfhip. And what kind of obedience is this they perform to God bleffed for ever, when they directly fin againft that fpeciall command *Thou shalt not kill?* Befides, this cannot be committed without the imminent, and manifeft perill of their lives aud fortunes, and the neceffary expofing themfelves to a juft revenge. Moreover, it is an *Anathema* to a *Iew* to have any graven images in his houfe, or any thing of an idol, which any of the nations figuratively worfhip, *Deut.* 7. 26.

10. *Matthew Paris* p. 532. writes, how that in the year 1240. the *Iewes* circumcifed a Chriftian child at *Norwich,* and gave him the name *Iurnin,* and referved him to be crucified, for which caufe many of them were moft cruelly put to death. The truth of this ftory will evidently appear upon the confideration of its circumftances. He was first circumcifed, and this perfectly conftitutes

him

him a *Iew*. Now for a *Iew* to embrace a Chriftian in his armes, and fofter him in his bofome, is a teftimony of great love and affection. But if it was intended that fhortly after this child fhould be crucified, to what end was he firft circumcifed? If it fhall be faid it was out of hatred to the Chriftians, it appears rather to the contrary, that it proceeded from deteftation of the *Iewes*, or of them who had newly become profelytes, to embrace the *Iewes* religion. Surely this fuppofed pranck (ftoried to be done in popifh times) looks more like a piece of the reall fcene of the Popifh *Spaniards* piety, who firft baptiz'd the poor *Indians*, and afterwards out of cruel pity to their fouls, inhumanely butchered them; then of ftrict-law-obferving *Iewes*, who dare not make a fport of one of the feales of their covenant.

11. Our captivity under the Mahumetans is farre more burdenfome, and grievous then under the Chriftians, and fo our ancients have faid, *it is better to inhabit under Edom then Ifmael,* for they are a people more civill, and rationall, and of a better policie, as our nation have found experimentally. For, excepting the nobler, and better fort of *Iewes*, fuch as live in the Court of *Conftantinople*, the vulgar people of the *Iewes* that are difperfed in other countries of the Mahumetan Empire, in *Afia* and *Africa*, are treated with abundance of contempt and fcorn. It would therefore follow, that if this facrificing of children be the product and refult of hatred, that they fhould execute and difgorge it much more upon the Mahumetans, who have reduced them to fo great calamity and mifery. So that if it be neceffary to the celebration of the Paffeover, why do they not as well kill a *Mahumetan?* But although the *Iewes* are fcattered, and difperfed throughout all thofe vaft territories, notwithftanding all their defpite againft us, they never yet to this day forged fuch a calumnious accufation. Wherefore it appeares plainly, that it is nothing elfe but a flander, and fuch a one, that confidering how the fcene is laid, I cannot eafily determine whether it fpeak more of malice, or of folly: certainly Sultan *Selim* made himfelf very merry with it, when the ftory was related him by *Mofes Amon* his chief Phyficyan.

12. If all that which hath been faid is not of fufficient force to wipe off this accufation, becaufe the matter on our part is

B purely

purely negative, and fo cannot be cleared by evidence of witneffes, I am conftrained to ufe another way of argument, which
the Lord, bleffed for ever, hath prefcribed *Exod.* 22. which is an
oath ; wherefore I fwear, without any deceit or fraud, by the moft
high God, the creatour of heaven and earth, who promulged his
law to the people of Ifrael, upon mount *Sinai*, that I never yet to
this day faw any fuch cuftome among the people of Ifrael, and
that they doe not hold any fuch thing by divine precept of the
law, or any ordinance or inftitution of their wife men, and that
they never committed or endeavoured fuch wickedneffe, (that I
know, or have credibly heard, or read in any Jewifh Authours)
and if I lie in this matter, then let all the curfes mentioned in *Leviticus* and *Deuteronomy* come upon me, let me never fee the bleffings and confolations of Zion, nor attain to the refurrection of
the dead.   By this I hope I may have proved what I did intend, and
certainly this may fuffice all the friends of truth, and all faithfull
Chriftians to give credit to what I have here averred.   And indeed our adverfaries who have been a little more learned, and
confequently a little more civill then the vulgar, have made a halt
at this imputation.   *Iohn Hoornbeek* in that book which he lately
writ againft our nation, wherein he hath objected againft us, right
or wrong, all that he could any wayes fcrape together, was notwithftanding afhamed to lay this at our door, in his *Prolegomena*
pag. 26. where he fayes, *An autem verum fit quod vulgò in hiftoriis lega-
tur, &c. i.e.* whether that be true which is commonly read in hiftories, to aggravate the I*ewes* hatred againft the Chriftians, or rather the Chriftians againft the I*ewes,* that they fhould annually
upon the preparation of the Paffeover, after a cruell manner facrifice a Chriftian child, privily ftollen, in difgrace, and contempt
of Chrift, whofe paffion, and crucifixion the Chriftians celebrate,
I will not affert for truth ; as well knowing, how eafy it was for
thofe times wherein thefe things are mentioned, to have happen'd, (efpecially after the Inquifition was fet up in the Pope-
dome) to forge, and fain ; and how the hiftories of thofe ages, according to the affection of the writers, were too too much addi-
cted, and given unto fables and figments.   Indeed I have never
yet feen any of all thofe relations that hath by any certain experiment

periment proved this fact, for they are all founded; either upon the uncertain report of the vulgar, or elfe upon the fecret accufa-tion of the Monks belonging to the inquifition, not to mention the avarice of the informers, wickedly hanquering after the *Iewes* wealth, and fo with eafe forging any wickedneffe. For in the firft book of the *Sicilian* conftitutions tit. 7. we fee the Emperour *Frederick* faying, *Sivero Iudæus, vel Saracenus fit, in quibus prout certò perpendimus Chriftianorum perfecutio minus abundat ad præfens*, but if he be a *Iew* or a *Saracen,* againft whom, as we have weighed, the perfecution of the Chriftians do much abound, *&c.* thus taxing the violence of certain Chriftians againft the *Iewes.* Or if perhaps it hath fometimes happened, that a Chriftian was kill'd by a *Iew*, we muft not therefore fay that in all places where they inhabit, they annually kill a Chriftian Child. And for that which *Thomas Cantipratenfis* lib. 2. cap. 23. affirms, *viz.* that it is certainly known, that the *Iewes* every year, in every province, caft lots what city or town fhall afford Chriftian bloud to the other cities. I can give it no more credit then his other fictions and lies where-with he hath ftuffed his book. Thus farre *Iohn Hoornbeek.*

13. Notwithftanding all this, there are not wanting fome hi-ftories, that relate thefe and the like calumnies againft an afflicted people, For which caufe the Lord faith, *He that toucheth you touch-eth the apple of my eye*, Zach. 2. 6. I fhall curfolarily mention fome paffages that have occurred in my time, whereof, I fay not that I was an eye witneffe, but onely that they were of generall report and credence, without the leaft contradiction. I have faithfully noted both the names of the perfons, the places where, and the time when they happened, in my continuation of *Flavius* Jofephus, I fhall be the leffe curious therefore in reciting them here. In *Vi-enna* the Metropolis of *Auftria, Frederick* being Emperour, there was a pond frozen, according to the cold of thofe parts, wherein three boyes (as it too frequently happens) were drowned. when they were miffed, the imputation is caft upon the Jewes, and they are incontinently indicted, for murthering of them, to cele-brate their Paffeover. And being imprifoned, after infinite pray-ers and fupplications made to no effect, three hundred of them were burnt, when the pond thawd, thefe three boyes were found,

B 2   and

and then their innocency was clearly evinc'd although too late, after the execution of this cruelty.

In *Araguza* about thirty yeares ago, there was a Chriftian woman, into whofe houfe there came a little girle (of eleven yeares of age, daughter to a neighbouring gentleman) richly adorned with jewels : this wretched woman, not thinking of a fafer way to rob her, then by killing her, cut her throat, and hid her under her bed, the girle was prefently mift, and by information they underftood that fhe was feen to go into that houfe, they call a Magiftrate to fearch the houfe, and find the girle dead, fhe confeft the fact, and as if fhe fhould have expiated her own guilt by deftroying a I*ew*, though never fo innocent, fhe faid, fhe did it at the inftigation and perfwafion of one *Ifaac Jeshurun,* for that the J*ewes* wanted bloud to celebrate their feaft: fhe was hang'd, and the J*ew* was apprehended, who being fix times cruelly tortur'd, they employing their wits in inventing unheard of, and infufferable torments, fuch as might gain *Perillous* the eftimation of mercifull and compaffionate, ftill cryes out of the falfhood of the accufation, faying, that that wickedneffe which he never committed, no not fo much as in his dreams, was malicioufly imputed to him, yet notwithftanding he was condemned to remain clofe prifoner for twenty yeares, (though he continued there onely three,) and to be fed there through a trough, upon the bread and water of affliction, being clofe manacled, and naked, within a four fquare wall, built for that purpofe, that he might there perifh in his own dung. This mans brother *Jofeph Jefhurun* is now living at this time in *Hamborough.* This miferable man calling upon God, befeeching him to fhew fome fignall teftimony of his innocencie, and citing before his divine tribunall the Senatours who had with no more mercy, then juftice, thus grievoufly and inhumanely afflicted him ; the bleffed God was a juft Judge, for the Prince died fuddenly at a banquet, the Sunday next enfuing the giving of the fentence, and during the time of his imprifonment, the aforefaid Senatours by little and little dropt away, and died, which was prudently obferved by thofe few that yet remain'd, wherefore they refolved to deliver themfelves by reftoring him to his liberty, accounting it as a particular divine

vine providence: this man came out well, paffed throughout all *Italy*, where he was feen, to the admiration of all that had cognizance of his fufferings, and died a few yeares fince at *Jerufalem*.

14. The act of the faith (which is ordinarily done at *Toledo*) was done at *Madrid*, *Anno* 1632, in the prefence of the King of *Spain*, where the Inquifitors did then take an oath of the King and queen, that they fhould maintain and conferve the Catholick faith in their dominions. In this act it is found printed, how that a family of our nation was burnt, for confeffing upon the wrack the truth of a certain accufation of a maid fervant, who, (provoked out of fome difguft) faid, that they had fcourged, and whip't an image, which by the frequent lafhes, iffued forth a great deal of bloud, and crying with an out ftretched voice, faid unto them, why do you thus cruelly fcourge me? the whole nobility well underftood that it was all falfe, but things of the inquifition all muft hufh.

15. A very true ftory happened at *Lisbon*, *Anno* 1631. A certain Church miffed one night a filver pixe or box, wherein was the popifh hofts. And forafmuch as they had feen a young youth of our nation, whofe name was *Simao pires folis*, fufficiently noble, to paffe by the fame night, not farre from thence, who went to vifit a Lady, he was apprehended, imprifoned, and terribly tortured. They cut off his hands, and after they had dragged him along the ftreets, burnt him. one year paffed over, and a thief at the foot of the gallowes confeffed how he himfelf had rifled and plundered the fhrine of the hoft, and not that poor innocent whom they had burnt. This young mans brother was a Frier, a great Theologift, and a preacher, he lives now a Jew in *Amfterdam*, and calls himfelf *Eliazar de folis*.

16. Some perhaps will fay, that men are not blame worthy for imputing to the Jewes, that which they themfelves with their own mouthes have confeft. But furely he hath little underftanding of wracks, and tortures that fpeaks thus. An Earle of *Portugal*, when his Phyficvan was imprifoned for being a Jew, requefted one of the inquifitors, by letter, that he would caufe him to be fet at liberty, for that he knew for certain that he was a very good Chriftian, but

he not being able to undergo the tortures inflicted on him, confeffed himfelf a *Iew*, and became a penitentiary. At which the Earl being much incenft, feins himfelf fick, and defires the inquifitor by one of his fervants, that he would be pleafed to come and vifit him. when he came, he commanded him that he fhould conleffe that himfelf was a *Iew*, and further, that he fhould put it down in writing with his own hand, which when he refufed to do, he charges fome of his fervants to put a helmet that was red hot in the fire, (provided for this purpofe) upon his head; at which, he not being able to endure this threatned torment, takes him afide to confeffe, and alfo he writ with his own hand that he was a *Iew*: whereupon the Earl takes occafion to reprove his injuftice, cruelty, and inhumanity, faying, in like manner as you have confeft, did my Phyficyan confeffe. Befides that, you have prefently, onely out of fear, not fence of torment, confeft more. For this caufe in the Ifraelitifh Senate, no torture was ever inflicted, but onely every perfon was convicted at the teftimony of two witneffes. That fuch like inftruments of cruelty may enforce children that have been tenderly educated, and fathers that have lived delicioufly to confeffe that they have whipt an image, and been guilty of fuch like criminall offences, daily experience may demonftrate.

17. Others will perchance alledge, thefe are hiftories indeed, but they are not facred, nor canonicall. I answer, Love and hatred fayes *Plutarch,* corrupt the truth of every thing, as experience fufficiently declares it; when we fee that which comes to paffe, that one and the fame thing, in one and the fame city, at one and the fame time, is related in different manners. I my felf in my own Negotiation here have found it. For it hath been rumoured abroad, that our nation had purchafed S. *Pauls* Church for to make it their Synagogue, notwithftanding that it was formerly a temple confecrated to the worfhip of *Diana.* And many other things have been reported of us that never entred into the thoughts of our nation; as I have feen a fabulous Narrative of the proceedings of a great Council of the *Iewes,* affembled in the plain of *Ageda* in *Hungaria,* to determine whether the Meffiah were come or no.

18. And

18. And now, fince that it is evident that it is forbidden the *Iewes* to eat any manner of bloud, and that to kill a man is directly prohibited by our law, and the reafons before given are confentaneous and agreeable to every ones underftanding, I know it will be inquired by many, but efpecially by thofe who are more pious, and the friends of truth, how this calumnie did arife, and from whence it derived its firft originall. I may anfwer, that this wickedneffe is laid to their charge for divers reafons.

Firft, *Ruffinus* the familiar friend of S. *Hierome* in his verfion of *Iofephus* his fecond book that he writ againft *Apion* the Grammarian (for the Greek text is there wanting) tells us how *Apion* invented this flander to gratifie *Antiochus,* to excufe his facriledge, and juftifie his perfidious dealing with the *Iewes,* making their eftates fupply his wants. *Propheta vero aliorum est Apion* &c. *Apion* is become a Prophet, and faid that *Antiochus* found in the temple, a bed, with a man lying upon it, and a table fet before him, furnifhed with all dainties both of fea and land, and fowles, and that this man was aftonifhed at them, and prefently adores the entrance of the King, as coming to fuccour and relieve him, and proftrating himfelf at his knees, & ftretching out his right hand, he implores liberty; whereat the King commanding him to fit down and declare who he was, why he dwelt there, and what was the caufe of this his plentifull provifion? the man with fighs and tears, lamentably weeps out his neceffity: and tells him that he is a *Grecian,* and whilft he travelled about the province to get food, he was fuddenly apprehended, and caught up by fome ftrange men, and brought to the temple, and there fhut up, that he might be feen by no man, but be there fatted with all manner of dainties, and that thefe unexpected benefits wrought in him at the firft joy, then fufpicion, after that aftonifhment, and laft of all, advifing with the Minifter that came unto him, he underftood that the *Iewes* every year, at a certain time appointed according to their fecret and *ineffable* law, take up fome Greek ftranger, and after he hath been fed delicately for the fpace of a whole year, they bring him into a certain wood, and kill him. Then according to their folem rites and ceremonies, they facrifice his body, and every one tafting of his intrails, in the offering

ing up of this Greek, they enter into a folemn oath, that they will bear an immortall feude and hatred to the Greeks. And then they caft the reliques of this perifhing man into a certain pit. After this *Apion* makes him to fay, that onely fome few dayes remained to him, before his execution, & to defire the King that he, fearing and worfhipping the Grecian gods, would revenge the bloud of his fubjects upon the *Iewes*, and deliver him from his approaching death. This fable (faith *Iofephus*) as it is moft full of all tragedy, fo it abounds with cruell impudence, I had rather you fhould read the confutation of this flander there, then I to write it in this place, you will find it in the *Geneva* edition of *Iofephus*, pag. 1066.

Secondly, The very fame accufation and horrid wickedneffe of killing children, and eating their bloud, was of old by the ancient heathens, charg'd upon the Chriftians, that thereby they might make them odious, and incenfe the common people againft them, as appeares by *Tertullian* in his *Apologia contra gentes*, *Iuftin Martyr in apologia* 2. *ad Anton. Eufebius Cæfareenfis* l. 5. cap. 1. & 4. *Pineda* in his *Monarchia Ecclefiaftica* l. 11. c. 52. and many others, as is known fufficiently. So that the imputation of this cruelty, which as to them continues onely in memory, is to the very fame purpofe, at this day charged upon the *Iewes*. And as they deny this fact, as being falfly charged upon them, fo in like manner do we deny it, and I may fay perhaps with a little more reafon, forafmuch as we eat not any manner of bloud, wherein they do not think themfelves obliged.

Now the reafon of this flander was alwayes the *covetous ambition* of fome, who defiring to gain their wealth, and poffeffe themfelves of their eftates, have forg'd and introduc'd this enormous accufation, to colour their wickedneffe, under a fpecious pretence of revenging their own bloud. And to this purpofe, I remember that when I reproved a Rabbi (who came out of *Poland* to *Amfterdam*) for the exceffe of ufurie in *Germany*, and *Poland*, which they exacted of the Chriftians, and told him how moderate they in *Holland* and in *Italy* were, he replyed, we are of neceffity conftrained to do fo, becaufe they fo often raife up falfe witneffes againft us, and levie more from us at once, then we are able to

get

get again by them in many yeares. And fo, as experience fhews, it ufually fucceeds with our poor people under this pretext and colour.

19. And fo it hath been divers times; men mifchieving the *Iewes* to excufe their own wickedneffe; as to inftance one precedent in the time of a certain King of *Portugal*. The Lord, bleffed for ever, took away his fleep one night, (as he did from King *Ahashuerus*) and he went up into a belcony in the palace, from whence he could difcover the whole city, and from thence (the moon fhining clear) he efpyed two men carrying a dead corps, which they caft into a *Iew's* yard. He prefently difpatches a couple of fervants, and commands them, yet with a feeming carelefneffe, they fhould trace and follow thofe men, and take notice of their houfe; which they accordingly did. The next day there is a hurly burly and a tumult in the city, accufing the *Iewes* of murder. Thereupon the King apprehends thefe rogues, and they confeffe the truth; and confidering that this bufineffe was guided by a particular divine providence, calls fome of the wife men of the *Iewes*, and asks them how they tranflate the 4. verfe of the 121 Pfalm, and they anfwered, *Behold, he that keepeth Ifrael will neither flumber nor fleep.* The King replied, if he will not flumber then much leffe will he fleep, you do not fay well, for the true tranflation is, *Behold, the Lord doth not flumber, neither will he fuffer him that keepeth Ifrael to fleep.* God who hath yet a care over you, hath taken away my fleep, that I might be an eye witneffe of that wickedneffe which is this day laid to your charge. This with many fuch like relations we may read in the book called *Scebet Iehuda*, how fundry times, when our nation was at the very brink of deftruction, for fuch forged flanders, the truth hath difcovered it felf for their deliverance.

20. This matter of bloud hath been heretofore difcuffed and difputed before one of the Popes, at a full councell; where it was determined to be nothing elfe but a mere calumnie: and hereupon gave liberty to the *Iewes* to dwell in his countryes, and gave the princes of *Italy* to underftand the fame, as alfo *Alfonfo* the wife King of *Spain*. And fuppofe any one man had done fuch a thing, as I believe never any *Iew* did fo, yet this

C   were

were great cruelty to punifh a whole nation for one mans
wickedneffe.

21. But why fhould I ufe more words about this matter, feeing all that is come upon us, was foretold by all the prophets?
Mofes, Deut. 28. 61. *Moreover, every ficknefle and every plague which
is not written in the book of this law, them will the Lord bring upon
thee, &c. becaufe thou haft not hearkned to the voice of the Lord thy
God.* David in the 44. Pfalm make a dolefull complaint of thofe
evils, and ignominious reproaches, wherewith we are invironed
round about in this captivity, as if we were the proper center of
mifery, faying, *For thy fake are we killed all the day long, we are
counted as fheep for the flaughter.* The fame he fpeaks Pfalm 74. and
in other Pfalms.

Ezekiel more particularly mentions this calumnie; God, bleffed
for ever, promifing Chap. 36. 13. that in time to come the de-
vouring of men, or the eating of mans bloud fhall be no more
imputed to them, according to the true and proper expofition of
the learned *Don Ifaac Abarbanel.* The bleffed God, according to
the multitude of his mercies, will have compaffion upon his people, and will take away the reproach of Ifrael from off the earth,
that it may be no more heard, as is prophefied by *Ifaiah,* and let
this fuffice to have fpoken as to this point.

THE SECOND SECTION.

YOur worfhip defired joyntly, to know what ceremony, or
humiliation the *Iewes* ufe in their Synagogues, toward
the book of the Law; for which they are by fome igno-
rantly reputed to be idolaters. I fhall anfwer it in Order.

Firft, the *Iewes* hold themfelves bound to ftand up when the
book of the Law written upon parchment, is taken out of the
desk, untill it is opened on the pulpit, to fhew it to the people,
and afterwards to be read. We fee that obferved in *Nehemias,*
cap. 8. 6. where it is faid, *And when he had opened it, all the people
ftood up.* and this they do in reverence to the word of God, and
that facred Book.

For

For the fame caufe, when it paffeth from the desk toward the pulpit, all that it paffeth by, bow down their heads a little, with reverence; which can be no idolatry for thefe following reafons.

Firft, it is one thing *adorare, viz.* to *adore,* and another *venerari, viz.* to *worfhip.* For *Adoration* is forbidden to any creature, whether Angelicall, or Earthly; but *Worfhip* may be given to either of them, as to men of a higher rank, commonly ftiled *worfhip-full.* And fo *Abraham,* who in his time rooted out vain idolatry, humbled himfelf, and alfo proftrated himfelf before thofe three guefts, which then he entertained for *Men.* As alfo *Iofuah* the holy Captain of the people, did proftrate himfelf to another Angel, which with a fword in his hand, made him afraid, at the gates of *Iericho.* Wherefore if thofe were juft men, and if we are obliged to follow their example, and they were not reprehended for it, it is clear, that to worfhip the Law in this manner as we do, can be no idolatry.

Secondly, The *Iewes* are very fcrupulous in fuch things, and fear in the leaft, to *appear* to give any honour or reverence to images. And fo it is to be feen in the *Talmud,* and in R. *Mofes* of *Egypt* in his Treatife of idolatry: That if by chance any Ifraelite fhould paffe by a Church, that had images on the outfide, and at that time a thorn fhould run into his foot, he may not ftoop to pull it out, becaufe he that fhould fee him, might fufpeɕt he bowed to fuch an image. Therefore according to this ftriɕtneffe, if that were any appearance of idolatry to bow to the Law, the *Iewes* would utterly abhorre it; and fince they do it, it is an evident fign that it is none.

Thirdly, to *kiffe images* is the principall worfhip of idolatry, as God faith, in the 1 of *Kings* 19. 19. *Yet I have left me feven thoufand in Ifrael, all the knees that have not bowed unto Baal, and every mouth that hath not kiffed him.* But if that were fo, it would follow, that all men, who kiffe the Teftament after they are fworn, fhould be idolaters. But becaufe that is not fo, fince that aɕt is but a fimple worfhip, by the fame reafon it will follow, that to bow the head, cannot be reputed for idolatry.

Fourthly, Experience fheweth, that in all Nations the ceremonies

C 2   monies

monies that men ufe mutually one towards another, is to bow the head; And alfo there are degrees thereof, according to the quality of the perfon with whom they fpeak ; which fhew that in the opinion of all nations, it is no idolatry, and therefore much leffe, to reverence the Law with bowing of the body.

Fifthly, In *Afia* (and it is the fame almoft in all the world) the people receiving a decree, or order of the king, they take it, and kiffe it, and fet it upon the head. We owe much more to Gods word, and to his divine Commandments.

Sixthly, *Ptolomeus Philadelphus*, receiving the 72 *Interpreters* with the book of the Law, into his prefence, he rofe from his feat, and proftrating himfelf feven times, worfhipped it, (as *Ariftæus* affures us.) If a Gentile did this to a law which he thought did not oblige him, much more do we owe reverence to that Law which was particularly given unto us.

Seventhly, The I*fraelites* hold for the Articles of their Faith, that there is a God ; who is one in moft fimple unity; eternall, incorporeall; who gave the written Law unto his people Ifrael, by the hand of *Mofes*, the Prince, and chief of all the Prophets ; whofe Providence takes care for the world which he created ; who takes notice of all mens works, and rewardeth or punifheth them. Laftly, that one day *Mefsias* fhall come to gather together the fcattered Ifraelites, and fhortly after fhall be the refurrection of the dead.

Thefe are their Doctrines, which I believe contain not any idolatry; nor yet in the opinion of thofe that are of other judgements ; For, as a moft learned Chriftian of our time hath written, in a French book, which he calleth the *Rappel* of the I*ewes* (in which he makes the King of *France* to be their leader, when they fhall return to their country,) the I*ewes*, faith he, fhall be faved, for yet we expect a *fecond* coming of the fame *Mefsias* ; and the I*ewes* believe that that coming is the *firft*, and not the fecond, and by that faith they fhall be faved ; for the difference confifts onely in the circumftance of the time.

THE

THE THIRD SECTION.

Sir, I hope I have given fatisfaction to your worfhip, touching thofe points. I fhall yet further inform you with the fame fincerity, concerning the reft. *Sixtus Senenfis* in his *Bibliothæca*, lib. 2. *Titulo contra Talmud*, and others, as *Biatenfis, Ordine* 1. *Tract.* 1. *Titulo* Perachot. averre out of the *Talmud.* cap. 4. " that every *Iew*, thrice a day, curfeth all Chriftians, and prayeth " to God to confound, and root them out, with their Kings and " Princes. And this is efpecially done in the *Synagogue*, by the " *Iewes* Priefts, thrice a day. I pray let fuch as love the truth, fee the *Talmud*, in the quoted place; and they fhall find nothing of that which is objected : onely there is recited in the faid fourth Chapter, the daily prayer, which fpeaks of *Minim*, that is, *Hereticks, ordained* in *Talne*, (that is a town not farre from *Ierufalem*, between *Gath* and *Gazim*, &c.) the Talmud hath no more. Hence *Sixtus Senenfis* by diftillation, draws forth the forefaid calumnie, whenas, what the *Talmud* rehearfeth briefly, to be made onely by the wife men in the faid Town, he faith, was a conftitution in the *Talmud* long after.

Now let us fee what was done by thofe wife men in the faid Town; and let us examine, whether that may juftly offend the Chriftians.

There is in the daily prayers a certain Chapter where it is thus written, *la-Mumarim*, &c. that is, *For Apostates, let there be no hope, let all Hereticks be deftroyed, and all thine enemies, and all that hate thee, let them perish. And thou shalt root out the kingdome of pride forthwith, weaken, and put it out, and in our dayes.* This whole Chapter fpeaketh nothing of Chriftians originally, but of the *Iewes*, who fell in thofe times, to the *Zaduces*, and *Epicureans*, and to the Gentiles, as *Mofes* of *Egypt* faith, Tract. *Tephila.* cap. 2. For by Apoftates and Hereticks are not to be underftood all men, that are of a diverfe religion, or heathens, or Gentiles, but thofe renegado *Iewes*, who did abrogate the whole

Law of *Mofes*, or any Articles received thence; and fuch are properly by us called *Hereticks*.   For according to the Law of Chriftians, he is not properly an Apoftate, or Heritick, who is originally bred a fcholler and a candid follower from his youth of a
diverfe law, and fo continueth: otherwife native I*ewes* and *Hagarens*, and other Nations that are no Chriftians, nor ever were,
fhould be properly called Apoftates, and Hereticks in refpeſt
of Chriftians, which is abfurd, as it is abfurd for the *Iewes* to
call the Chriftians Apoftates, or Hereticks.   Wherefore it fpeaketh nothing of Chriftians, but of the fugitive *Iewes*, that is, fuch
as have deferted the ftandard, or the facred Law.

2. Laftly, neither the kingdomes, nor kings that are Chriftians, or *Hagarens*, or followers of other Seſts are curfed here, but
namely the kingdome of Pride.   Certain it is that in that time
(wherein, our wife men added to the daily Prayers the forefaid
Chapter) there was no kingdome of Chriftians. what therefore
that kingdome of pride was, fhould any man ask, who can plainly
ly fhew it ?   So much as we can conjeſture by it, it is the kingdome of the *Romans* which then flourifhed, which did rule over
all Nations tyrannically and proudly, efpecially over the *Iewes*.
For, after that, *Vefpafian*, with his fon *Titus*, had diffipated all *Iu-
dea*.   And though fom *Roman* Emperours after that became Chriftians, or had a good opinion of Chriftianity, yet the kingdome
of the *Romans* was heathenifh, and without diftinſtion, was proud,
and tyrannicall.   And however the *Iewes* repeated the fame words
of the prayer when the Prince was very good, and they lived under a juft government, that they did, onely of an ancient cuftome, without any malice to the prefent government.   And now
truly in all their books printed again, the forefaid words are wanting, left they fhould now be unjuftly objeſted againft the *Iewes*;
and fo for *Apoftates* and *Hereticks*, they fay, *fecret accufers, or betray-
ers* of the *Iewes*.   And for the *kingdome of pride*, they fubftitute
all Zedim, that is, *proud men*.

3. After this manner, to avoid fcandall, did the 72 Interpreters, who coming in *Leviticus*, to unclean beafts; in the place
of *Arnebeth* which fignifies the *Hare*, they put δασύποδα, that is,
rough foot : leaving the Name, and keeping the fenfe.   They would
not

not retein the Hebrew word *Arnebeth,* as they have done in fome
other appellatives, left the wife of *Ptolomy* whofe name was *Arne-*
bet, fhould think that the *Iewes* had mocked her, if they fhould
have placed her name amongft the unclean beafts. Neither would
they render it λαγωὸν *lagoon,* or λαγὸν *lagon,* which in the Greek language fignifies a *Hare,* left *Ptolomy* himfelf who was the fon, and
nephew of the *Lagi,* fhould be offended, to fee the name of his
family regiftred among the creatures that were unclean. Befides,
Plutarch records, how that it was deeply refented, as a very
high affront, and contempt, when one asked *Ptolomy,* who was
Lagus his father, as if it fcoffingly reflected upon his obfcure extraction and defcent.

4. The very like calumnie fell out concerning the very fame
Chapter of our Prayer, when *Mulet Zidan* reigned in *Morocco.*
A certain fugive *Iew,* to fhew himfelf conftant in the Mahumetan Religion, and an enemy to his own Nation, accufed the *Iewes*
before this king, faying, that they prayed to God for his deftruction, when they mention in their prayers all *Zedim,* as though
they would have all the Family of *Zidan* deftroyed. They excu-
fed themfelves with the truth, and affirmed, in praying againft
Zedim, that they prayed onely againft *proud men,* (as that word in
their Hebrew language properly fignifieth) and not againft his
Majefty. The King admitted of their excufe; but faid unto
them, that becaufe of the equivocation of the word, they fhould
change it for another.

5. For certain, the *Iewes* give no occafion, that any Prince,
or Magiftrate fhould be offended with them; but contrariwife,
as it feems to me, they are bound to love them, to defend, and
protect them. For, by their *Law,* and *Talmud,* and the inviolable
cuftome of the difperfed *Iewes,* every where, upon every Sabbath
day, and in all yearly folemnities, they have prayers for Kings
and Princes, under whofe Government the *Iewes* live, be they
Chriftians, or of other Religions, I fay by their *Law,* as *Iere-*
miah ch. 29. commandeth, *viz. Seek ye the peace of the city, whi-*
ther I have caufed you to be carried away captives, and pray for them,
unto the Lord, &c. By the *Talmud* ord. 4. Tract. 4. *Abodazara.*
cap. 1. *there is a prayer for the peace of the Kingdome,* from *cuftome,*
never

never intermitted of the Iewes. Wherefoever they are on the Sabbath day, and their annuall folemnities, the Minifter of the Synagogue before he bleffeth the people of the Iewes, doth with a loud voice, bleffe the Prince of the country under whom they live, that all the Iewes may hear it; and they fay Amen. You have feen the Form of the prayer in the book entitled The humble Addreffes.

6. In like manner the ancients obferve, that whereas God commands in *Numbers* 29. 13. that feventy bullocks fhould be facrificed upon the feven dayes of the feaft of tabernacles, that this was in refpect of the feventy nations (who fhall one day come up to Ierufalem, year after year, to keep this feaft of tabernacles, *Zechar.* 14. 16.) for whofe confervation they alfo facrificed. For they fay, that *all the nations of the earth shall be blessed in Abraham, and in his feed, not onely fpiritually, and in the knowledge of the one firft caufe, but alfo that at this time they fhall enjoy temporall, and earthly blefsings, by vertue of that promife.* And fo in the time of the fecond temple, they offered up facrifice for their confederate nations, as may appear by thefe enfuing inftances.

In *Megilat Tahanit.* cap. 9. it is reported, that when *Alexander* the great, at the inftigation of the *Samaritans*, that inhabited mount *Gerizim*, went with a refolution to deftroy the temple, *Simeon* the juft met him in the way, and amongft divers reafons that he urged to divert him from his purpofe, told him, *this is the place, where we pray unto God for the welfare of your felf, and of your kingdome, that it may not be deftroyed, and fhall thefe men perfwade you to deftroy this place?*

The like we find in the firft book of the *Maccabees*, cap. 7. 33. and in Iofephus his Antiq. *lib.* 12. *cap.* 17. when *Demetrius* had fent *Nicanor* the Generall of his army againft Jerufalem, the Priefts, with the Elders of the people went forth to falute him, and to fhew him the facrifice which they offered up to God for the welfare of the King.

In the fame hiftory *lib.* 2. 3. and in *Jofephus Gorionides* lib. 3. cap. 16. we may read, that *Heliodorus* Generall to *Selencus*, came to Jerufalem with the fame intent, *Onias* the High-prieft, befought him, not to deftroy that place, where they prayed to God for

the

the profperity of the King, and his iffue, and for the confervation of his kingdome.

In the firft Chapter of *Baruch,* the difciple of *Jeremiah,* we
find that the I*ewes,* who were firft carried captive into *Babylon*
with I*echonias,* made a collection of money, according to every
ones power, and fent it to J*erufalem,* faying, *Behold, we have fent
you money, wherewith ye shall buy offerings, and pray for the life of
Nebuchadnezzar, and for the life of Baltafar his fonne, that their dayes
may be upon earth as the dayes of heaven, and that God would give us
ftrength, and lighten our eyes, that we may live under their shadow,
that we may long do them fervice, and find favour in their fight.*

The I*ewes* in *Afia* did the fame, as is reported by J*ofephus Gorionides,* lib. 3. cap. 4. they fent letters, with a prefent to *Hircanus*
the High-prieft, defiring that prayers might be made for the life
of *Auguftus Cæfar,* and his companion *Marcus Antonius.*

Philo Judæus, in the book of his Embaffage to *Caius,* making
mention of a letter which *Caius* fent, requiring his ftatue to be fet
up in the facred temple, and *Agrippa's* anfwer thereupon, unto
the faid Emperour, reports, that there were thefe words in it, *viz.
The Iewes facrifice for the profperity of your Empire, and that not
onely upon their folemn feafts, but alfo every day.*

The like is recorded by J*ofephus,* (lib. 2. cap. 9. *De bello Judaico*)
the I*ewes* faid to *Petronius* Generall to the Emperour *Caius, we
daily offer up burnt offerings unto God, for the peace of the Emperour,
and the whole people of Rome.* And in his fecond book againft *Apion,* he fayes, *we Hebrews have allwayes accuftomed to honour Emperours with particular facrifices.*

Neither was this fervice ever entertained unthankfully, as appears by the decree of *Cyrus, Ezra* 6. 3. where alfo *Darius* commands, that *of the Kings goods, even of the tribute, expences should be
forth-with given unto the Elders of the Iewes &c. and that which they
had need of, both young bullocks, and rammes, and lambs for the burnt-
offerings of the Lord of heaven, and wheat, falt, wine, and oyl,* &c. *that
they might offer facrifices of a fweet favour, unto the God of heaven,
and pray for the life of the King, and of his fonnes.*

The fame alfo was commanded afterwards by *Artaxerxes,* who
alfo conferred liberally many large gifts, as well towards the

D   build-

building of the temple, as the maintaining of the facrifices. As for *Alexander* the great, he lighted down out of his chariot, and bowed himfelf at the feet of the High-prieft, defiring him to offer up facrifice to God on his behalf. And who can be ignorant of *Ptolomy Philadelphus,* how richly he endowed the temple, as is recorded by *Arifteas?* Nor did *Antiochus* king of the *Greeks* unlike this, when by a publick edict, he forbid *that any ftranger should enter the temple, to prophane that place, which the Hebrews had confecrated to religion, and divine worfhip.* (Jofephus *lib.* 12. *cap.* 3.) *Demetrius* did the like, (*Jofephus* lib. 13. cap. 5. 6.) To which may be added, that when they of *Ierufalem* contended with them of *Samaria,* about the honour and dignity of the temple, before *Alexander* the great, the *Ierufalem* Prieft in his plea, urged, *that this temple was ever had in great reverence by all the Kings of* Afia, *and by them enricht with fundry fplendid and magnificent gifts.* In the fecond book of *Iofephus* againft *Apion,* we read, that *Ptolomy Euergetes,* when he had conquered *Syria,* offered up *Euchariftically facrifices,* not to idols, and falfe Gods, but to the true God, at *Ierufalem,* according to the manner of the *Iewes. Pompey* the great, as is mentioned by *Iofephus de bello Iudaico* (lib. 1. cap. 5.) durft not fpoyl, no nor fo much as touch the treafures of the temple, not becaufe (as *Tully* in his Oration for *Plancius* fuppofeth, to whom *Auguftine* in his book *de civitate Dei affentos*) he feared left he might be thought too avaritious; for this feems in comparifon, very ridiculous, and childifh; for military law would foon have acquitted him for this; but becaufe of the reverence to the place with which his mind was fo affected. *Philo Iudæus,* (p. 102. 6.) relates a letter of *Agrippa's,* where he writes, that *Auguftus Cæfar* had the temple in fo great reverence, that he commanded a facrifice of one bullock, and two lambs, to be offered up every day out of his own revenues. And his wife *Iulia Augufta,* adorn'd it with golden cups, and bafons, and many other coftly gifts. Neither did *Cleopatra* Queen of *Egypt,* fall fhort of her liberallity. *Tiberius* throughout the 22 years of his Empire, commanded facrifices to be offered up unto God, out of his own tribute. The like did *Nero,* till the unadvifed rafhneffe of *Eleazar* in refufing his facrifice, alienated the mind of the Emperour, that he became the caufe of a bloudy perfecution. And

And by all this, we may the better interpret that 11 verfe of the
1. chap. of *Malachy*) who flourifht in the fecond temple,) The
words are, *From the rifing of the fun, even unto the going down of the
fame, my name fhall be great among the Gentiles, and in every place incenfe fhall be offered unto my name, and a pure offering; for my name
fhall be great among the heathen, faith the Lord of hofts.* For befides
that the heathens termed the temple *the houfe of the great God,*
(*Ezra* 5. 8.) they and their Monarchs, and Emperours, both of
Perfia, Grece, and *Rome,* defired, as we have heard, to have facrifices, and incenfe, offered for them in Gods name.

9. And let the reader be pleafed further to obferve, that the
Iewes were accuftomed, not onely to offer up facrifices, and prayers to God, for the Emperours, their friends, confederates, and
allyes, but alfo generally for the whole world.   It is the cuftome
(faith *Agrippa* to *Caius* according to *Philo* p. 1035.) for the High-
prieft, at the day of attonement, to make a prayer unto God, for
all mankind ; befeeching him to adde unto them another year,
with bleffing and peace.   The fame *Philo Iudæus* in his fecond book
of *Monarchy* faith, *The priefts of other nations pray unto God onely for
the welfare of their own particular nations, but our High-prieft prayes
for the happineffe and profperity of the whole world.*   And in his book
of facrifices, p. 836. he faith, *Some facrifices are offered up for our
nation, and fome for all mankind. For the daily facrifices, twice a day,
viz. at morning, and evening, are for the obtaining of thofe good things,
which God the chief good, grants unto them, at thofe two times of the
day.*

And in like manner, *Iofephus* in his fecond book againft *Apion*
faith, *We facrifice, and pray unto the Lord, in the firft place, for the
whole world, for their profperity, and peace, and afterwards more particularly for our felves, forafmuch (as we conceive) that prayer which
is firft extended univerfally, and is afterwards put up more particularly,
is very much acceptable unto God.*   Which words are alfo related by
Eufebius Cæfareenfis, in his *Præparatio Evangelica,* lib. 8. cap. 2.

10. 'Tis true, that no outward materiall glories are perpetuall ; and fo the *temple* had its period, and with the *pafchall lamb,* all
other facrifices ceafed : But in their ftead, we have at this day
prayer, and as *Hofeah* fpeaks Cap. 14. 2. For bullocks, we render

the calves of our lips. And three times every day, this is our humble fupplication, and requeft to God, *Fill the whole world, O Lord, with thy bleſſings; for all creatures are the works of thy hands; as it is written, the Lord is good to all, and his tender mercies are over all his works* Pſal. 145. 9.

11. Yea further, we pray for the converſion of the nations, and ſo we ſay in theſe moſt excellent prayers, upon *Roſ a ſana* and the day of attonement, *Our God, and the God of our Fathers, reign thou over the whole world in thy glory; and be thou exalted over all the earth, in thine excellency; cauſe thy influence to deſcend upon all the inhabitants of the world, in the glorious majeſty of thy ſtrength; and let every creature know that thou haſt created him; and let every thing that is formed, underſtand that thou haſt formed it; and let all that have breath in their noſtrills ſay, the Lord God of Iſrael reigneth, and his kingdome is over all dominions.* And again, *Let all the inhabitants of the earth know, and ſee, that unto thee every knee shall bow, and every tongue ſwear; before thee, O Lord our God, let them bow, and proſtrate themſelves; let them give honour to the honour of thy name, and let them all take upon them the yoak of thy kingdome,* &c. And again, *Put thy fear, O Lord, our God, upon all thy works, and thy dread upon all that thou haſt created; let all thy works fear thee, and let all creatures bow down before thee and let them all make themſelves one handfull,* (that is, with joynt conſent) *to do thy will with a perfect heart,* &c. A moſt worthy imitation of the wiſe King *Solomon,* who after he had finiſhed the building of the Temple, in that long prayer *King.* 1. 8. was not unmindfull of the Gentiles, but v. 41. he ſaith, *Moreover, concerning a ſtranger, that is not of thy people of Iſrael, but cometh out of a farre country, for thy names ſake, for they ſhall hear of thy great name, and of thy ſtrong hand, and of thy ſtretched-out arm, when he ſhall come, and pray towards this houſe, hear thou in heaven thy dwelling place, and do according to all that the ſtranger calleth to thee for, that all people of the earth may know thy name, to fear thee, as do the people of Iſrael, and that they may know that thy name is called upon this houſe which I have builded.* Where it may be obſerved, that when the Iſraelite comes to pray, he ſaith, 29. *and give every man according to his wayes;* but upon the prayer of a ſtranger, he ſaith, *and do according to all that the ſtran-*

ger

stranger calleth to thee for. And this distinction is made to this end, that by the evident, and apparent return, and answer of their prayers, all Gentiles might effectually be brought in to the truth, and knowledge, and fear of God, as well as the Israelites.

12. Moreover, since the holy prophets made prayers, and supplications for all men, as well for the *nations,* as the *Israelites,* how should not we do the same, for the nations, among whom we inhabit, as ingaged by a more especiall obligation, for that we live under their favour and protection? In *Deuteronomy* 23. 7. God commands *Thou shalt not abhorre an Egyptian,* notwithstanding the heavy burthens they afflicted us with, onely *becaufe thou waft a ftranger in his land,* becaufe that at the firft, they entertained, and received us into their country.

As on the other fide, *Ezek.* 23. 11. he faith, *As I live, faith the Lord God, I have no pleafure in the death of the wicked, but that the wicked turn from his way and live.* We ought therefore to imitate his actions, and not to hate any man, upon the mere account of religion, but onely to pray to the Lord for his converfion; and this alfo, without giving offence, or any kind of moleftation. To deteft, or abhorre thofe, to whom we owe that profperity which we enjoy, or who endeavour their own falvation, is a thing very unworthy, and ill becoming; but to abhorre their vices, and fins, is not fo. It was a very excellent obfervation, of a moft wife, and vertuous Lady, *Beruria,* who (as it is recorded in the *Talmud, Berachot* cap. 1. when her husband *R. Meir* was about to pray to God, to deftroy fome of his perverfe, and froward neighbours, that had no leffe grievoufly, then malicioufly vexed, and molefted him, gave him this feafonable admonition, that fuch a thing *ought not to be done in Ifrael; but that he should rather make his prayer, that they might return, and break off their finnes by repentance,* alledging that text, Pfal. 104. 35. *Let fin be confumed out of the earth;* it is not faid *finners,* but *finnes;* and then *the wicked shall be no more.*

13. We have now in this Section shewn, that it is a mere calumnie to imagine, that we *Iewes* should pray to God, fo as to give an offence to the Christians, or caufe fcandall, by any thing in

D 3

our

our prayers, unleſſe it be that we are not Chriſtians. we have declared to the contrary, how we daily pray for them. As alſo that
during the temple, we offered up ſacrifices, for nations confederate with us, and how all Emperours deſired this. Yea, and we
offered ſacrifices, not onely for particular princes, but for all
mankind in generall. How, ſince ſacrifices ceaſed, with the temple, we at this day, do the ſame in our prayers, and how we be-
ſeech God for their ſalvation, without giving any ſcandall, or
offence in reſpect of religion ; and how we think our ſelves obliged to perform all this, by the ſacred Scripture. By all which
layed together, I hope I have ſufficiently evidenced the truth,
of that I have aſſerted.

THE FOURTH SECTION.

BY conſequence, the accuſation of *Buxtorphius*, in his *Bibliotheca Rabbinorum*, can have no appearance of truth, concerning that which he puts upon us, *viz.* that we are *blaſphe-
mers*. I will ſet down the Prayer it ſelf.

"We are bound to praiſe the Lord of all things ; to magnifie
"him, who made the world, for that he hath not made us, as the
"Nations of the earth ; nor hath he placed us as the families of
"the earth ; nor hath he made our condition like unto theirs, nor
"our lot, according to all their multitude. For they humble
"themſelves to things of no worth, and vanity, and make their
"prayers to gods that cannot ſave them ; but we worſhip before
"the King of kings, that is holy, and bleſſed ; that ſtretch-
"ed forth the Heavens, and framed the Earth ; the ſeat of his glo-
"ry is in heaven above, and his divine ſtrength in the higheſt of
"the Heavens ; He is our God, and there is no other ; He is tru-
"ly, our King, and beſides him, there is no other ; as it is writ-
"ten in the Law. And know this day, and return into thine own
"heart, becauſe the Lord is God, in Heaven above, and upon the
"Earth beneath, there is no other.

Truly, in my opinion, it is a very ſhort, and moſt excellent
prayer,

prayer, and worthy of commendation. The *Sultan Selim*,
that famous conquerour, and Emperour of the *Mahumetans*,
made fo much account of it, that he commanded his Doctor *Mofes Amon*, (who tranflated the *Pentateuch* into the *Arabian* and *Perfian* languages) that he fhould tranflate our prayers. And when
he had delivered them to him in the *Turkish* Tongue, he faid to
him, what need is there of fo long prayers? truly this one might
fuffice, he did fo highly efteem and value it. This is like an other
prayer which was made at that time, *viz.*

    " Bleffed be our God, who created us for his honour, and fe-
" parated us from thofe that are in errours, and gave unto us a
" Law of truth, and planted amongft us eternall life. Let him
" open our hearts in his law, and put his love in our hearts, and
" his fear, to do his will, and to ferve him with a perfect heart,
" that we may not labour in vain, nor beget children of perdi-
" tion. Let it be thy will, O Lord our God, and God of our Fa-
" thers, that we may keep thy ftatutes, and thy laws in this world,
" and may deferve, and live, and inherit well, and that we may at-
" tain the bleffing of the world to come, that fo we may fing
" to thy honour, without ceafing. O Lord my God, I will praife
" thee for ever.

    But neither the one, nor the other is a *blafphemy*, or maledi-
ction againft any other Gods, for thefe reafons following.

    1. It is not the manner of the *Iewes* by their law to curfe other
gods by name, though they be of the *Gentiles.* So in *Exod.*
cap. 22. 27. *Thou shalt not revile the Gods.* Heb. אלהים, that is
Gods, or God, as *Philo Iudæus in libro de Monarchiâ,* doth interpret,
and not Judges, as *Onkelus* and *Ionathan* tranflate in their *Chald.
Paraphr.* Where *Philo* adds this reafon, which is, left they hearing
their own Gods blafphemed, fhould in a revengefull way of retaliation, blafpheme the true God of Ifrael. And we have examples
enough, how the idolatrous heathen ufed to revile, and defame
each others Gods, both in *Cicero*, and *Iuvenal.*

    And in that fenfe *Flavius Jofephus* in his book written againft
Apion, faith thefe words: " As it is our practife to obferve our
" own, and not to accufe, or revile others; fo neither may we de-
" ride, or blafpeeme thofe, which others account to be Gods.
                                         " Our

"Our Law-giver plainly forbad us that, by reafon of that com-
"pellation, Gods. According to this, by our own religion,
we dare not do that which *Buxtorfius* chargeth us with. And upon
this account the Talmudifts tell us, that we ought to honour, and
reverence, not onely the Kings of Ifrael, but all kings, princes,
and governours, in generall, forafmuch as the holy Scripture gives
them the ftile of gods, in refpect of the dignity of their
office.

2. The time wherein thefe, as alfo the other prayers were compofed, and ordered, was in the dayes of *Ezras*, who, with 120
men, amongft whom were three Prophets, *Haggai, Zechary, Malachy*, compofed them, as we have it in the *Talmud*. Wherefore he
cannot fay, that there is any thing intended againft honour, or
reverence of Chrift, who was not born till many yeares after.

Moreover, the *Iewes*, fince that calumny was firft raifed, (thouh
that was fpoken of the Gentiles, and their vain gods, *humbling
themfelves to things of no worth, and vanity*) becaufe they defire to
decline, and avoid the leaft occafion of fcandall, and offence, have
left off to print that line, and do not in fome books print any
part thereof. As *John Hoornbeek* alfo witneffes, in his fore-men-
tioned *Prolegomena*, and *William Dorftius*, in his obfervations upon
R. David Gawz, p. 269. and *Buxtorf* in his book of *Abbreviatures*.
And perhaps it will be worthy our obfervation, that all thefe three
witneffes fay, that it was firft made known to them, by one *Antonius Margarita*, who was a *Iew*, converted to the Chriftian faith.
That this part of the prayer was intended *Contra idola Papatus*,
againft the *Popish idols*, which they therefore, as by a neceffary
confequence, interpret, as againft *Chrift;* but how juftly, let the
unprejudiced and unbiafed reader judge.

3. If this be fo, how can it be thought, that in their *Synagogues*,
they name him with fcornfull fpitting, (farre be it from us.)
The Nation of the *Iewes* is *wife, and ingenius.* So faid the Lord,
Deut. cap. 4. 6. *The Nations fhall fay, furely this is a wife, and an underftanding people.* Therefore, how can it be fuppofed, that they
fhould be fo bruitifh in a ftrange land, when their Religion de-
pendeth not upon it? Certainly, it is much contrary to the precept we fpake of, to fhew any refemblance of fcorn. There was

never

never any fuch thing done, (as it is well known) in *Italy*, and *Holland*, where ordinarily the *Synagogues* are full of *Chriſtians*; which with great attention, ſtand conſidering, and weighing all their actions, and motions. And truly they ſhould have found great occaſion to find fault withall, if that were ſo. But never was any man heard thus to calumniate us, where ever we dwell and inhabite, which is a reaſon ſufficiently valid, to clear us. Wherefore, I ſuppoſe, that I have ſufficiently informed you, concerning our prayers, in which we purpoſe nothing, but to praiſe God, and to ask ſpirituall, and temporall bleſſings, and by our ſervice, and worſhip, implore the divine benevolence, protection, and defence.

THE FIFTH SECTION.

BUt foraſmuch as it is reported, that we draw, and ſeduce others to our religion, &c.

1. Never unto this day, in any part hath this been ſuſpected, where the *Iewes* are diſperſed; nor can it find place here. Truly, I have held friendſhip with many great men, and the wiſeſt, and moſt eminent of all *Europe*; and alſo they came to ſee me, from many places, at my houſe, and I had many friendly diſcourſes with them, yet did not this give occaſion to make us ſuſpected of any ſuch things. Yea, *Gaſpar Barleus*, the *Virgill* of our time, and many others, have written many verſes in my commendations, which I mention not, for vain glory (farre be it) but for vindication of my innocent repute.

2. By our rituall books we are clear of this ſeducing. For if any man offer to become a *Iew*, of what Nation ſoever he be, before we receive him, and admit him as a member of our Synagogue, we are bound to conſider, whether he be moved by neceſſity to do it, or if it be not for that he is in love with ſome of our nation, or for any other worldly reſpect. And when we find no reaſon to ſuſpect him, we have yet another obligation upon us, which is, to let him know the penalties he ſubjects himſelf unto, if he breaketh the

E   Sab-

Sabbath, or eateth bloud, or fat, which is forbidden *Levit.* 3. 17. or difannulleth any precept of the Law, as may be feen in the *Targum* upon *Ruth.* And if he fhew himfelf conftant, and zealous, then is he admitted and protected. Wherefore we do not feduce any one, but contrarily, avoid difputing with men, concerning religion, not for want of charity, but that we may as farre as it is poffible, avoid fcandall, and hate; and for this caufe we refufe to circumcife them that come to us, becaufe we will give no offence. Yea, I have known fome, that for this caufe have circumcifed themfelves. And if *Ferdinand* and I*fabella,* King and Queen of *Caſtile* did make an order to expell the I*ewes,* becaufe they feduced many Chriftians, and fome of the Nobility to become I*ewes,* this was but a pretence, and colour for their tyranny, and onely, as it is well known, having no other thing to object againft us. Truly, I do much commend that opinion, not onely of *Oforius, de rebus Immanuelis,* but of our *Flavius Iofephus,* the moft famous of all Hiftorians, which he relates in his hiftory of his own Life.

"At that time (faith he) there came unto me, two Noble men,
"of the *Trachomites,* fubjects of the king; bringing with them
"horfemen, with arms, and money. Thefe, when the I*ewes* would
"compell to be circumcifed, if they would live amongft them;
"I would not fuffer them to trouble them; maintaining that eve-
"ry man ought to ferve God, of his own free will, and not be for-
"ced thereto by others. For, fhould we do this thing (faith he)
"it might make them repent, that ever they fled unto us. And fo
"perfwading the multitude, I did abundantly afford unto thefe
"men, their food, according to their diet.

Truly, this was an action worthy of a noble, and wife man, and worthy of imitation, for defending common liberty, leaving the judgement, and determination to God alone. The *Spanish Inquiſitions,* with all their torments, and cruelties, cannot make any *Iew,* that falls into their power, become a *Chriſtian.* For unreafonable beafts are taught by blowes, but men are taught by reafon. Nor are men perfwaded to other opinions, by torments, but rather, on the contrary, they become more firm, and conftant in their Tenet.

THE

THE SIXTH SECTION.

HAving thus difcuffed the main exceptions, I will now proceed to fmaller matters, though leffe pertaining to my fa-
culty, that is to bufineffe of *Merchandife*. Some fay, that
if the *Iewes* come to dwell here, they will draw unto themfelves
the whole Negotiation, to the great damage of the naturall Inhabitants. I anfwer, that it hath been my opinion alwayes, (with
fubmiffion to better judgements) that it can be no prejudice at
all to the Englifh Nation: becaufe, principally in tranfporting
their goods, they would gain much, by reafon of the publick payments of cuftomes, excife, &c.

Moreover, they would alwayes bring profit to the people of the
land, as well in buying of commodities, which they would tranf-
port to other places, as in thofe they would trade in here.
And if by accident, any particular perfon fhould lofe by it, by
bringing down the price of fuch a commodity, being difperfed
into many hands; yet by that means the Commonwealth would
gain in buying cheaper, and procuring it at a leffer rate.

Yea, great emolument would grow to the naturall Inhabitants,
as well in the fale of all provifion, as in all things elfe that concern the ornaments of the body. Yea, and the native Mecha-
nicks alfo would gain by it, (there being rarely found among us,
any man that ufeth any fuch art.)

2. Adde to this, that as our nation hath failed into almoft all
parts of the world, fo they are alwayes herein profitable to a nation, in a readineffe to give their opinions, in favour of the people amongft whom they live. Befide that, all ftrangers do bring
in new merchandifes, together with the knowledge of thofe for-
reign Countries wherein they were born.

And this is fo farre from damnifying the natives, that it con-
duces much to their advantage; becaufe they bring from their
countryes new commodities, with new knowledge. For the great
Work-Mafter, and *Creatour* of all things, to the end, to make

E 2 com-

commerce in the earth, gave not to every place all things, but hath parted his benefits amongſt them; by which way, he hath made them all wanting the help of others. This may be ſeen in *England,* which being one of the moſt plentifull countries that are in the world, yet wanteth divers things for *shipping;* as alſo, wine, oyl, figs, almonds, raiſins, and all the drougs of I*ndia,* things ſo neceſſary for the *life of man.* And beſides, they want many o- ther commodities, which are abundant in other countries, with more knowledge of them; though it be true, that in my opinion, there is not in the world, a more underſtanding people, for moſt Navigations, and more capable of all Negotiation, then the *En- glish* Nation are.

3. Farther, there may be companies made of the natives, and ſtrangers, (where they are more acquainted) or elſe Factors. All which, if I be not deceived, will amount to the profit of the na- tives. For which, many reaſons may be brought, though I can- not comprehend them, having alwayes lived a ſedentary life, ap- plying my ſelf to my ſtudies, which are farre remote from things of that nature.

4. Nor can it be juſtly objected againſt our Nation, that they are deceivers; becauſe the generality cannot in any rationall way, be condemned for ſome particulars. I cannot excuſe them all, nor do I think, but there may be ſome deceivers amongſt them, as well as amongſt all other nations and people, becauſe poverty bringeth baſeneſſe along with it.

5. But if we look to that which we ought by our Religi- on, the morall precept of the Decalogue, *Thou shalt not steal,* it belongs in common to all I*ewes,* towards all *Gentiles.* As may be ſeen in Rab. *Moſes* of *Egypt,* Tract, *Geneba,* cap. 1. and *Gazela.* cap. 1. *It is a ſinne,* (ſaith he) *to rob any man, though he be a Gentile.* Nor can that be alledged out of the ſacred Hiſtory, concerning the jewells and houſhold ſtuff, of which the I*sraelites* ſpoiled the *Egyptians,* as I have heard it ſometimes alledged by ſome, to ſome men; becauſe that was a particular diſpenſation, and a divine pre- cept for that time. So it is recorded in the *Talmud,* in the *Tract of the Sanhedrim,* cap. 11. that in the time of *Alexander* the great, thoſe of *Alexandria* accuſed the I*ewes* for being thieves, and they de-

demanded reftitution of their goods. But *Guebia Ben Pefria* anfwered them, our Fathers went down into *Egypt* but feventy fouls,
there they grew a numerous nation, above 60000. and ferved
them in bafe offices, for the fpace of 210 yeares, according to
this, pay us for our labour, and make the accounts even, and you
fhall fee you are yet much in our debt. The reafon fatisfied *Alexander*, and he acquitted them.

6. By confequence, the *Iewes* are bound not to defraud, nor
abufe in their accounts, negotiation, or reckonings, any man
whatfoever, as it may be feen exprefly in R. *Mofes* of *Egypt*, and
R. *Mofeh de Kofi* in *Samag.*

7. Yea, they farther fay, that by reftitutions, there is a refult
to the praife of God, and the facred Law. whence that holy, and
wife man, R. *Simeon Ben Satah,* having bought an affe of a Gentile,
the head ftall whereof was a jewell of great value, which the owner
knew not of, afterwards he found it, and freely, and for nothing,
he reftored it to the feller, that knew not of it, faying, I bought
the affe, but not the jewell. Whence there did accrue honour to
God, and his Law, and to the nation of the *Iewes,* as *Midras Raba*
reports in *Parafot Hekel.*

8. After the fame manner they command, that the oath which
they fhall make to any other nation, muft be with truth, and juftice, and muft be kept in every particular. And for proof thereof, they quote the hiftory of *Zedekias,* whom God punifhed, and
deprived of his kingdome, becaufe he kept not his word, and
oath, made to *Nebuchadnezzar, in the name of God,* though he were a
Gentile, as it is faid, 2 of *Chronicles,* cap. 36.13. *And he alfo rebelled
againft Nebuchadnezzar, who made him fwear by God.*

9. Thefe are the laws and obligations which the *Iewes* hold.
So that the Law that forbids the *Iewes* to *kill* any *Gentiles,* forbids
them alfo to *fteal* from them. Yet every one muft look to it, for
the world is full of fraud in all Nations. I remember a pretty ftory of what paffed in *Morocco,* in the Court of the king of *Mauri-
tania.* There was a *Iew* that had a fort of falfe ftones, &c.—He
making a truck with a *Portugal* Chriftian, for fome Verdigreafe
that he had, which was much fofifticated, (as they are wont to
do there) being all falfified with Earth; one of the *Portugals* friends

E 3   laughed

laughed at him, faying, the *Iew* fitted thee well; he anfwered, If the *Iew* hath ftoned me, I have buried him. And fo they ordinarily mock one another.

This I can affirm, that many of the *Iewes*, becaufe they would not break with other mens goods, were very poor at *Amſterdam*, lived very poorly, and thofe that did break with other mens goods by neceffity, became fo much the more miferable, that they were forced to live on almes.

And whereas in the time of K. *Edward* 1. the *Iewes* were accufed of clipping the Kings coin; it appears that this accufation drew its originall mainly from the fufpicion and hatred the Chriftians bare againft the *Iewes*, as appeares in the ftory, as it is fet forth by Mr. *Prynne, In his fecond part of a Short Demurrer to the Iewes* &c. p. 82. where quoting *Clauf. 7. E. 1. n. 7. De fine recipiendo à Iudæis*, brings in the King, writing to his Judges in Latine, in thefe words. *Rex dilectis, & fidelibus fuis* Stephano de Pentecefter, Waltero de Helyn. *&* Th. de Cobham *Iuſticiariis ad placita tranfgreffionis monetæ audienda, falutem. Quia omnes* Judæi *nuper rectati, & per certam fufpicionem indictati de retonfura monetæ noſtræ, & inde convicti cum ultimo fupplicio puniuntur; & quidam eorum eadem occafione, omnia bona, & catalla fua fatisfecerunt, & in prifona noſtra liberabantur, in eadem ad voluntatem noſtram detinendi. Et cum accepimus, quod plures Chriſtiani ob ODIVM* Judæorum, *propter difcrepantiam fidei Chriſtianæ, & ritus* Judæorum, *& diverfa gratia minus per ipfos* Judæos *Chriſtianis hactenus illata, poſtquam* Judæos *nondum rectatos in indictatos de tranfgrefsione monetæ, per levas, & voluntarias accufationes accufare, & indictare de die in diem nituntur, & proponunt, imponendas eis ad terrorem ipforum, quod de ejufmodi tranfgreffione culpabiles exiſtunt fuper ipfos* Judæos *faciendæ, & fic per minas hujufmodi accufationis, ipfis* Judæos *metu incutiant, & pecuniam extorqueant ab eifdem; Ita quod ipfi* Judæi *fuper hoc, ad legem fuam fæpe ponuntur in vitæ fuæ periculum manifeſtum. Volumus quod omnes* Judæi *qui ante primum diem* Maii *proximo præterit, indictati, vel per certam fufpicionem rectati non fuerunt de tranfgrefsione monetæ predictæ, & qui facere voluerint finem juxta difcretionem Veſtram, ad opus noſtrum facere pro fic, quod non occafiorentur, &c. hujufmodi tranfgrefsionibus factis ante primum diem* Maii

prop-

propter novas accufationes Chriftianorum poft eundem diem inde factas non moleftentur, fed pacem inde habeant in futurum. Provifo, quod Judæi *indictati, vel per certam fufpicionem, rectati de hujufmodi tranf-grefsione ante prædictum diem* Maii, *Iudicium fubeant coram vobis, juxta formam prius inde ordinatam & provifam. Et ideo vobis mane-amus, quod fines hujufmodi capiatis, & præmiffa fieri, & obfervari faciatis in forma prædicto. Tefte Rege apud* Cantuar. 8. *die* Maii.

THE SEVENTH SECTION.

ANd now by this time, I prefume (moft noble Sir) I may have given abundant satisfaction, (fo farre as the nature of an epiftle will permit) to all your objections, without gi-ving juft ground of offence, or fcandall to any. And forafmuch as you are further defirous to know fomewhat, concerning the ftate of this my expedition, and negotiation at prefent, I fhall now onely fay, and that briefly, that the communication and cor-refpondence I have held, for fome yeares fince, with fome eminent perfons of *England,* was the firft originall of my undertaking this defign. For I alwayes found by them, a great probability of ob-taining what I now requeft ; whilft they affirmed, that at this time the minds of men ftood very well affected towards us ; and that our entrance into this Ifland, would be very acceptable, and well-pleafing unto them. And from this beginning fprang up in me a femblable affection, and defire of obtaining this purpofe. For, for feven yeares on this behalf, I have endeavoured, and follici-ted it, by letters, and other means, without any intervall. For I conceived, that our univerfall difperfion was a neceffary circum-ftance, to be fulfilled, before all that fhall be accomplifhed which the Lord hath promifed to the people of the *Iewes,* concerning their reftauration, and their returning again into their own land, according to thofe words *Dan.* 12.7. *When he fhall have accomplished to fcatter the power of the holy people, all thefe things fhall be finished.* As alfo, that this our fcattering, by little, and little, fhould be a-mongft all people, from the *one end of the earth even unto the other;* as it is written *Deut.* 28. 64. I conceived that by the *end of the earth* might be underftood this *Ifland.* And I knew not, but that the Lord

Lord who often works by naturall meanes, might have defign'd,
and made choice of me, for the bringing about this work. With
thefe propofalls therefore, I applyed my felf, in all zealous affection to the *English Nation,* congratulating their glorious liberty
which at this day they enjoy, together with their profperous
peace. And I entituled my book named *The hope of Ifrael,* to the
firft Parliament, and the Council of State. And withall declared my intentions. In order to which they fent me a very favourable paffe-port. Afterwards I directed my felf to the fecond, and
they alfo fent me another. But at that juncture of time my coming was not prefently performed, for that my kindred and
friends, confidering the checquered, and interwoven viciffitudes,
and turns of things here below, embracing me, with preffing importunity, earneftly requefted me not to part from them, and
would not give over, till their love conftrained me to promife,
that I would yet a while ftay with them. But notwithftanding all
this, I could not be at quiet in my mind, (I know not but that it
might be through fome particular divine providence) till I had
anew made my humble addreffes to his Highneffe the Lord Protector (whom God preferve.) And finding that my coming over
would not be altogether unwelcome to him, with thofe great
hopes which I conceived, I joyfully took my leave of my houfe,
my friends, my kindred, all my advantages there, and the country wherein I have lived all my life time, under the benign protection, and favour of the Lords, the States Generall, and Magi-
ftrates of *Amfterdam; in fine* (I fay) I parted with them all, and
took my voyage for *England.* Where, after my arrivall, being very courteoufly received, and treated with much refpect, I prefented to his moft Serene Highneffe, a petition, and fome defires,
which for the moft part, were written to me by my brethren the
Iewes, from feverall parts of *Europe,* as your worfhip may better
underftand by former relations. Whereupon it pleafed his Highneffe to convene an Affembly at *Whitehall,* of Divines, Lawyers,
and Merchants, of different perfwafions, and opinions. Whereby
mens judgements, and fentences were different. Infomuch, that
as yet, we have had no finall determination from his moft Serene
Highneffe. Wherefore thofe few *Iewes* that were here, defpairing
of

of our expected fucceffe, departed hence. And others who defired to come hither, have quitted their hopes, and betaken themfelves fome to *Italy*, fome to *Geneva*, where that Commonwealth
hath at this time, moft freely granted them many, and great priviledges.

Now, O moft high God, to thee I make my prayer, even to
thee, the God of our Fathers. Thou who haft been pleafed to ftile
thy felf *the keeper of Ifrael;* Thou who haft gracioufly promifed,
by thy holy Prophet *Ieremiah*, (cap. 31.) *that thou wilt not caft off
all the feed of Ifrael, for all the evill that they have done ;* thou who
by fo many ftupendious miracles, didft bring thy people out of *E-
gypt*, the land of bondage, and didft lead them into the *holy land;*
gracioufly caufe thy holy influence to defcend down into the
mind of the Prince, (who for no private intereft, or refpect at all,
but onely out of commiferation to our affliction, hath inclined
himfelf to protect, and fhelter us, for which extraordinary hu-
manity, neither I my felf, nor my nation, can ever expect to be a-
ble to render him anfwerable, and fufficient thanks,) and alfo into
the minds of his moft illuftrious and prudent Council, that they
may determine that, which according to thine infinite wifdome,
may be beft, and moft expedient for us. For men (O Lord) fee
that which is prefent, but thou in thy omnifciencie feeft that
which is afarre off.

And to the highly honoured nation of *England*, I make my moft
humble requeft, that they would read over my arguments impar-
tially, without prejudice, and devoid of all paffion, effectually
recommending me to their grace and favour, and earneftly befeeching God that he would be pleafed to haften the time promifed by *Zephaniah*, wherein we fhall all ferve him *with one confent*,
after the fame manner, and fhall be all of the fame judgement, that
as his name is one, fo his fear may be alfo one, and that we may all
fee the goodneffe of the Lord, bleffed for ever, and the confolations of Zion. Amen, and Amen.

From my ftudy, in *London, April* the 10, in the year from the creation 5416, and in the year, according to the vulgar account, 1656.

F

As to give fatisfaction to your worſhip, being defirous to know what books have been written, and printed by me, or elfe are almoſt ready for the preſſe, may you pleafe to take the names of them in this Catalogue.

A Catalogue of ſuch books as have been published by Menaſſeh Ben Iſrael, *in* Hebrew.

Nⁱ *Iſmachaim,* four Books, concerning the Immortality of the ſoul, wherein many notable, and pleafant Queſtions are difcuſſed, and handled, as may be feen by the Arguments of the particular Chapters, prefixed to the book, in *Latine,* dedicated to the then Emperour *Ferdinand* the third.

Pene Rabba, upon *Rabot,* of the Ancient Rabbins, in *Latine* and *Spanish.*

Conciliatoris pars prima in Pentateuchum.

De Reſurrectione mortuorum libri tres.

Problemata de creatione.

De termino vitæ.

De fragilitate humana, ex lapſu Adami, *deque divino in bono opere auxilio.*

Spes Iſraelis. This is alfo in Englifh.

Orationes panegyricæ, quarum una ad Illuſtriſsimum principem, Aurantium, *altera ad fereniſsimam reginam* Sueciorum, in *Spanish* onely.

Conciliator { the fecond part, upon the firſt Prophets.
the third part, upon the later Prophets.
the fourth part upon the Hagiographa.

Humas, or the *Pentateuch,* with the feverall precepts in the margin.

Theſoro de los dirim five books of the rites and ceremonies of the *Iewes,* in two Volumes.

Humas the *Pentateuch,* with a commentarie.

Piedra pretioſa, of *Nebuchadnezzar's* image, or the fifth Monarchy.

Laus orationes del anno, the Iewes prayers for the whole year, tranſlated out of the originall.

Books

Books ready for the Preſſe.

De cultu Imaginum *contra Pontificios Latine.*
Sermois, Sermons in the *Portugal* tongue.
Loci communes Omnium Midraſim, which contains the divinity of the ancient Rabbins, in *Hebrew.*
Bibliotheca Rabbinica, together with the arguments of their books, and my judgement upon their ſeverall editions.
Phocylides in *Spanish* verſe *cum Notis.*
Hippocratis Aphoriſmi in *Hebrew.*
Flavius Ioſephus *adverſus Apionem,* in *Hebrew, ejuſdem Monarchia rationis* in *Hebrew.*
Refutatio libri cui titulus Præadamitæ.
Hiſtoria ſive continuatio Flavii Joſephi *ad hæc uſque tempora.*
De divinitate legis Moſaicæ.
De ſcientia Talmudiſtarum, in ſingulis facultatibus.
Philoſophia Rabbinica.
De disciplinis Rabbinorum.
Nomenclator Hebraius & Arabicus.

I have alſo publiſhed, and printed, with my own preſſe, above 60 other books, amongſt which are many bibles in *Hebrew,* and *Spanish,* with all our *Hebrew* prayers correfted, and diſpoſed in good order.

F I N I S.

NOTES

PORTRAITS OF MENASSEH BEN ISRAEL

(Frontispiece, and pp. 1 and 105)

Pocock, in his biographical introduction to the English translation of Menasseh ben Israel's "De Termino Vitæ" (Lond., 1700), gives the following pen-picture of the author derived from the recollections of English Jews who remembered the days of the Whitehall Conferences :—

"He was of middle stature and inclining to fatness. He always used his own hair, which (many years before his death) was very grey ; so that his complexion being pretty fresh, his demeanour graceful and comely, his habit plain and decent, he commanded an awful reverence which was partly due to so venerable a deportment. In short, he was *un homme sans passion, sans legiereté, mais hélas! sans opulence*" (p. viii).

This description agrees with the portraits of Menasseh. Three of these portraits are extant. Two of them are by Rembrandt, and one is by a Jewish line-engraver, Salom Italia. Curiously enough, although far inferior in artistic merit to the Rembrandts as a portrait, Menasseh prized the Italia engraving highest. He sent a copy to the Silesian mystic Frankenberg in 1643, and he writes in the *Bonum Nuncium Israeli :*—

"Abr. à Frankenberg. . . . effigiem meam, aeri incisam misissem, ubi ad symbolum meum Perigrinando Quærimus, cui ab uno latere Hominis Peregrinantis, ab altero candelæ emblema adscriptum cum hoc dicterio נֵר לְרַגְלִי דְבָרךְ, sic praefatur" (p. 92).

The shield in the left-hand corner of this portrait was used by Menasseh as a trade-mark in his printing-office. It has for this reason been reproduced on the title-page of the present work. Salom Italia's portrait is often found bound up with the first Latin version of the " Hope of Israel," and was roughly copied in the Spanish edition published at Madrid in 1881.

Rembrandt belonged to the distinguished circle of Menasseh's personal friends. He illustrated the *Piedra Gloriosa* published by Menasseh in 1655, and he etched one portrait of the Rabbi, and painted another. The etching, of which a mezzotinted reproduction is presented on the frontispiece of the present work, was produced in 1636 when Menasseh was

thirty-two years old. The painted portrait which is in the Hermitage at
St. Petersburg is of doubtful authenticity as relating to Menasseh, but I am
inclined to regard it as genuine. It represents the Rabbi at a much more
advanced age than the etching. The grey hair agrees with Pocock's description of his appearance in 1656, while the sorrowful expression and full
beard may be accounted for by his troubled experiences in London, and
especially by the death of his son. When he returned to Middleburg in
1657, he was mourning for his son, and hence his beard would be unshaved.
It is not at all improbable that Rembrandt, his old friend of twenty years,
saw him at this tragical moment, and that the portrait is a reminiscence of
the prematurely aged and broken-hearted Rabbi, then tottering on the verge
of the grave.

THE HOPE OF ISRAEL

(pp. 1–72)

BIBLIOGRAPHICAL NOTE

The title is taken from Jeremiah xiv. 8 (see p. 7).

The first edition (pp. xiii, 126, 12mo) was in Spanish, and bore the
following title : —

מקוה ישראל / Esto es, / Esperança / de Israel./ Obra con suma
curiosidad conpuesta / por / Menasseh Ben Israel / Theologo, y Philosopho
Hebreo./ Trata del admirable esparzimiento de los diez / Tribus, y su
infalible reduccion con los de / mas, a la patria: con muchos puntos, / y
Historias curiosas, y declara- / cion de varias Prophecias, / por el Author
rectamen- / te interpretadas./ Dirigido a los señores Parnassim del K.K. /
de Talmvd Tora./ En Amsterdam./ En la Imprension de / Semvel Ben
Israel Soeiro./ Año. 5410.

It was dedicated to the Wardens of the Theological School (Talmud
Torah), Josseph Da Costa, Ishak Jessurun, Michael Espinosa, Abraham
Enriques Faro, Gabriel de Rivas Altas, Ishak Belmonte, and Abraham
Franco. The dedication is dated Shebat 13, 5410 [=Jan. 15, 1650],
and is headed with the significant quotation in Hebrew of part of verse 1
of Isaiah lxi.: "To preach good tidings unto the meek; he hath sent me
to bind up the broken-hearted." This dedicatory epistle is only to be
found in the Spanish edition. In the Latin and English translations it
is replaced by an address "To the Parliament, the Supream Court of
England."

The Latin edition (pp. xii, 111, 12mo), which was printed very shortly
after the Spanish, bore the following title : —

מקוה ישראל / Hoc est, / Spes / Israelis / Authore / Menasseh Ben
Israel / Theologo & Philosopho Hebræo / Amstelodami / Anno 1650.

Notes

It is doubtful whether Kayserling (*Misc. Heb. Lit.*, ii. p. 16 and note 76), following Castro, is correct in his conjecture that this translation is the work of Menasseh himself. There are too many misunderstandings of the Hebrew names and quotations to admit of this view. The deviations from the original suggest that it was hurriedly executed from a first draft of the Spanish version, which was afterwards revised by the author, who omitted to perform the same service for the Latin text.

The English version (pp. xiv, 90, 12mo) was based on the Latin, and reproduced all its faults. It appeared in London towards the end of 1650. The title-page runs as follows:—

The / Hope of Israel: / Written / By Menasseh Ben Israel, / an Hebrew Divine, and Philosopher./ Newly extant, and Printed in / Amsterdam, and Dedicated by the / Author to the High Court, the / Parliament of England, and to the / Councell of State./ Translated into English, and / published by Authority./ In this treatise is shewed the place where the ten / Tribes at this present are, proved, partly by / the strange relation of one Antony Monte- / zinus, a Jew, of what befell him as he tra- / velled over the Mountaines Cordillære, with / divers other particulars about the restoration of / the Jewes, and the time when./ Printed at London by R. I. for Hannah Allen, / at the Crown in Popeshead / Alley, 1650.

The only respect in which this version differs from the Latin is that it contains on pp. xi–xiv an address from "The Translator to the Reader." The name of the translator is not given, but the work was subsequently acknowledged by Moses Wall in a correspondence with E. S. (Sir Edward Spencer); see pp. 66–72.

A second edition, "corrected and amended," sm. 4to, was published in 1651 and reprinted in 1652. It is the latter which is reproduced in the present volume on account of its convenient *format*, and of the Appendices which throw light on the motives by which the publication in England was actuated.

The following is a list of other editions and translations :—

1659. Spanish by Jedidjah Ibn Gabbai (Smyrna).
1666. Dutch by Jan Bara (Amsterdam).
1691. Judeo-German by Mardochai ben Moses Drucker (Amsterdam).
1697. Hebrew by Eljakim ben Jacob (Amsterdam).
1703. *Ibid.*
1712. Judeo-German (Frankfort) reprint of 1691 edition.
1723. Spanish (Amsterdam) reprint of original edition.
1792. English by Robert Ingram (Colchester).
1836. Hebrew (Wilna) reprint of 1703 edition.
1850. English (London) reprint of 1650 edition.
1881. Spanish, by Santiago Perez Junquera (Madrid), reprint of original edition.

Notes

THE EPISTLE DEDICATORY

P. 4, l. 9. "*Not onely by your prayers.*" This, no doubt, refers to the protection extended by the Government to the Marranos in London. (See Introduction, p. xxx.)

TO THE COURTEOUS READER

P. 6, l. 21. "*Others to the Ten Tribes.*" There is a very voluminous literature of the Ten Tribes, a bibliography of which has long been promised by Mr. Joseph Jacobs. Bancroft in his "Native Races of the Pacific States of North America" discusses the theory of the Hebrew origin of the Americans (vol. v. pp. 77–95). Santiago Perez Junquera in his Spanish reprint of "Esperanza de Israel" gives a bibliography of Spanish writers who have dealt with the problem of the Ten Tribes. The Jewish legends on the subject, none of which admit the American theory, have been summarised by Dr. A. Neubauer in the *Jewish Quarterly Review* (vol. i. pp. 14, 95, 185, 408). See also M. Lewin, "Wo wären die Zehn Stämme Israels zu suchen" (1901).

The following selections from the vast literature of the Ten Tribes, especially in its relation to Menasseh ben Israel, may be recommended to investigators of this curious craze :—

Enquiries touching the Diversity of Languages and Religions through the chief parts of the world, written by Edw. Brerewood. London, 1635.

Thos. Thorowgood—Jews in America, &c. 1650.

John Dury—Epistolary Discourse to Mr. Thomas Thorowgood. 1650.

Sir Hamon L'Estrange—Americans no Jews. 1652.

Thos. Thorowgood—Jews in America [with] an accurate discourse [by] Mr. John Eliot. 1660.

Theophili Spizelii—Elevatio Relationis Montezinianæ de repertis in America tribubus Israeliticis. Basle, 1661.

Account of the Ten Tribes of Israel being in America, originally published by Menasseh Ben Israel, with observations thereon. By Robert Ingram, M.A. Colchester, 1792.

The Ten Tribes of Israel historically identified with the aborigines of the Western Hemisphere. By Mrs. Simon. London, 1826.

The Hope of Israel, presumptive evidence that the aborigines of the Western Hemisphere are descended from the ten missing tribes of Israel. By Barbara Anne Simon. London, 1829.

The Remnant Found, or the place of Israel's hiding discovered, being a summary of proofs showing that the Jews of Daghistan on the Caspian Sea are the remnant of the Ten Tribes. By the Rev. Jacob Samuel. London, 1841.

Notes

The Thorn Tree, being a history of thorn worship of the Twelve
Tribes of Israel, but more especially of the Lost Tribes and House
of David. By Theta. London, 1863.

Paläorama. Oceanisch-Amerikanische Untersuchungen und Aufklärun-
gen. Erlangen, 1868.

Ireland, Ur of the Chaldees. By Anna Wilkes. London, 1873.

Ueber die Abstammung der Englischen Nation. Von D. Paulus
Cassel. Berlin, 1880.

P. 6, l. 29. "*Cordillera*," Spanish. A mountain chain, sometimes, as
here, applied in a specific sense to the Andes.

P. 6, l. 32. "*The Sabbaticall River*," or Sambation, a river mentioned
in the Midrash as flowing during the first six days of every week and
drying up on the Sabbath. (Neubauer, "Géographie du Talmud,"
pp. 33–34, 299; Hamburger, "Real-Encyclopädie des Juden-
thums," vol. ii. p. 1071; see also "Hope of Israel," *infra*, p. 35.)

P. 7, l. 15. "*I intend a continuation of Josephus.*" No trace of this
work has been found. From a passage in the *Vindiciæ* there is
reason to believe that it it was completed in MS. (see p. 115 and
note thereon, *infra*, p. 167).

The Relation of Antony Montezinus

P. 11. An earlier translation of this affidavit was published by Thomas
Thorowgood in "Jewes in America," pp. 129, 130. (See Introduction to present work, p. xxv.)

P. 11, l. 13. "*Port Honda*," now Bahia Honda, an inlet at the north-
eastern extremity of Colombia, in 12° 20′ N. and 50° W. It was
first visited by Ojeda in 1502, and named by him Puerto de Santa
Cruz. There is a town named Honda in the interior, and a bay of the
same name on the northern coast of Cuba, 60 miles west of Havana.

P. 11, l. 15. "*Province of Quity*," modern Quito, originally a presi-
dency of the Spanish viceroyalty of Peru, afterwards a division of the
Republic of Colombia, and in 1831 organised with the districts of Asuay
and Guayaquil into a new republic, under the name of Ecuador.

P. 11, l. 17. "*Cazicus*," modern *Cacique* or *Cazique*, used in Spanish to
designate an Indian chief. The word is of Haytian origin. An
early Spanish writer derives it from the Hebrew. (Kayserling,
"Christopher Columbus," p. 154.)

P. 11, l. 29. "*Jonkets*," junket, from Italian *giuncata*, a cream-cheese,
so called because served on rushes (*giuncoa*—a rush):

> "And beare with you both wine and *juncates* fit
> And bid him eat,"
> —Spenser, *F. Q.*, V. iv. 49.

> "With stories told of many a feat,
> How faery Mab the *junkets* eat."
> —Milton, *L'Allegro*, 172.

P. 12, l. 3. "*Carthagenia*": modern Cartagena, a fortified maritime city of the United States of Colombia, on the Caribbean Sea.

P. 12, l. 5. "*Blessed be the name of the Lord that hath not made me an Idolator, a Barbarian, a Black-a-Moore, or an Indian.*" This is an extension of a blessing said in the Hebrew morning service. The original blessing, however, only speaks of "idolator." There is another blessing said on seeing "negroes and redskins," and this, curiously enough, is discussed in the same section of the Talmud as that in which the recital of the blessing in regard to heathens is enjoined (see Schwab, "Le Talmud," vol. i. p. 158).

P. 13, l. 17. "*Duerus*": the river Douro or Duero in Spain. Mr. Wall does not seem to have taken the trouble to delatinise the name. In the Spanish edition it appears, of course, "Duero."

P. 13, l.18. "*Making a sign with the fine linen of Xylus.*" This is a misunderstanding of the original Latin, which says, "factoque ex duabus Xyli syndonibus." The word "Xyli" here is intended for the genitive of Xylon = cotton. The passage should read, "and making out of two pieces of cotton cloth." The original Spanish says, "y haziendo vandera de dos paños de algodon." What Montezinos and his companion did was to construct a flag out of their two cotton waistbands.

P. 14, l. 1. Curious mistake overlooking the identity of Jacob and Israel.

P. 14, l. 22. "*Mohanes*": American-Indian medicine men. (See *infra*, p. 56.)

The Hope of Israel

P. 17, l. 21. For Jewish aspects of the early voyages to America see Kayserling, "Christopher Columbus, and the participation of the Jews in the Spanish and Portuguese discoveries" (Lond., 1894); also the same author's "The First Jew in America," in the John Hopkins University Studies for 1892.

P. 18, l. 32. "*Gomoras*" = Francisco Lopez de Gomara.

P. 18, l. 18. "*Tunes*" = Tunis.

P. 18, l. 22. "*Isaac Abarbanel*," Jewish statesman and theologian (1437–1509), served Alphonso V. of Portugal, Isabella of Spain, and Ferdinand of Naples; author of numerous Bible commentaries and philosophical essays. Headed the emigration of the Spanish Jews at the time of the expulsion (Graetz, *Geschichte d. Juden*, vol. viii. pp. 316 *et seq.*; Kayserling, *Juden in Portugal*, pp. 72, 100). The Abarbanels, whose descendants are numerous in Europe, claimed descent from King David. Menasseh ben Israel's wife was an Abarbanel (see "Hope of Israel," p. 39). Mr. Coningsby Disraeli is a descendant on his mother's side.

Notes

P. 19, l. 30. "*Rabbi Jonathan ben Uziel.*" The author of a free Aramaic paraphrase (Targum) to the Hebrew Prophetical Books. His date is about the beginning of the Christian era. A Targum to the Pentateuch is wrongly ascribed to him; this is properly the Targum Yerushalmi or Jerusalem Targum (see Zunz, "Die Gottesdienstlichen Vorträge der Juden," pp. 66 *seq.*).

P. 19, l. 33. "*Rabbinus Josephus Coen in his Chronology*" (see Bialloblotzky, "The Chronicles of Rabbi Joseph ben Meir the Sphardi," Lond., 1835). Joseph Cohen was born 1496 and died 1575.

P. 21, Sect. 4. The Hebrew in the first case is מׁה תם אל שעלבין מת דע אם, the מ in the second word being regarded as a mistake for ת. In the second case the Hebrew is מהטבאל שעל בן מתדעאל (see "Esperança de Israel," pp. 26, 27).

P. 21, l. 32. "*Collai*" = Callao.

P. 22, l. 7. "*Petrus Cieza*" = Pedro Cieça de Leon.

P. 22, l. 8. "*Guamanga*": modern Ayacucho.

P. 23, l. 30. "*Garracas*" = Caracas.

P. 24, l. 9. "*Alonsus de Erzilla*" = Alonzo d'Ercilla y Zuñiga (1530–1595). The quotation is from "La Araucana," the most famous of Spanish Epics.

P. 24, l. 27. "*Maragnon*" = Marañon, another name for the Amazon.

P. 24, l. 35. "*Farnambuc*" = Pernambuco.

P. 26, l. 14. "*The Isle of Solomon and Hierusalem.*"—Mendaña landed on Isabel Island in 1568, and named the group Solomon, and Bougainville rediscovered the islands in 1768. H. B. Guppy, "The Solomon Islands and their Natives" (Lond. 1887). C. M. Wood in "Proceedings R. Geog. Soc.," 1888, pp. 351–76, and 1890, pp. 394–418, with map (p. 444), on which are given the original Spanish as well as the modern names of the islands.

P. 28, l. 7. "*To this day they privately keep their Religion.*" The Marranos. See *supra*, pp. xii–xiv.

P. 29, l. 9. "*My Reconciler.*" "Conciliador" Segda Parte. Amsterdam, 1641. This work was translated into Latin by Vossius (1687), and into English by Lindo (1842).

P. 29, Sect. 16. A bibliography of the Jews in China has been published in French by Henri Cordier. A useful summary of our knowledge of the Hebrew Settlements in China, brought down to the most recent date, has been written by Mr. Marcus Adler (*Jew. Quart. Rev.*, vol. xiii. pp. 18–41).

P. 33, l. 20. "*David the Reubenite.*" David Reubeni, an Oriental Jew, who visited Europe in 1524, alleging himself to be an envoy from the Ten Tribes. He was received with distinction by the Pope and the King of Portugal, and made a great commotion among the Marranos and Jews (Graetz, "Geschichte," vol. ix. pp. 244 *et seq.*).

Notes

P. 33, l. 23. "*Selomoh Molcho.*" A Marrano disciple of David Reubeni. His name was originally Diogo Pires. He migrated to the East and became a learned Cabbalist. He died a martyr's death in 1532 (Graetz, "Geschichte," vol. ix. pp. 251 *et seq.*).

P. 33, l. 30. "*Abraham Frisol Orchotolam.*" A mistranslation for Abraham Frisol in his book entitled, "*Orhat Olam.*" Abraham Farisol or Peretsol (1451-1525) was a Hebrew geographer, author of "Orchat Olam" (The Path of the Universe), which was edited with a Latin translation by Thomas Hyde (Oxford, 1691). For life of Farisol see Graetz, "Geschichte," vol. ix. pp. 46 *et seq.*

P. 33, l. 38. "*The Hebrew letter (h) and (t) are neere in fashion.*" The letters referred to are ה and ת.

P. 33, l. 39. "*Eldad Danita.*" Eldad the Danite lived in the ninth century. His career was similar to that of David Reubeni (Epstein, "Eldad Ha-Dani," Pressburg, 1891).

P. 34, l. 2. "*Sephar Eldad Danita,*" ספור אלדד הדני. An edition with a French translation was published by Carmoly ("Relation d'Eldad le Danite." Paris, 1838). The best editions are those of Epstein and D. H. Müller.

P. 34, l. 3. "*Rabbi David Kimhi.*" Famous Hebrew exegete, grammarian, and lexicographer (d. 1232). The work referred to as "*etymol suo*" is "The Book of Roots" (ספר השרשים).

P. 34, l. 5. "*Of the name of Rabbi Juda Aben Karis.*" Should be, "in the name of Rabbi Judah ben Koraisch." Rabbi Judah (fl. *circa* 870–900) was a Karaite philologist; lived in North-West Africa. He met Eldad in Morocco (Graetz, "Geschichte," vol. v. p. 261).

P. 34, l. 9. "*Part of the Ten Tribes also live in Ethiopia.*" The Falashas of Abyssinia are here referred to (Halévy, "Travels in Abyssinia"; *Mis. Heb. Lit.*, vol. ii. pp. 175 *et seq.* There are also reports on the Falashas in the Annual Reports of the Alliance Israelite and Anglo-Jewish Association).

P. 35, l. 22. "*Rabbi Johanan, the Author of the Jerusalem Talmud.*" Rabbi Jochanan, son of the Smith, was a disciple of Rabbi Judah the Prince, compiler of the Mishna. He was one of the most famous Hebrew teachers of the third century. The tradition that he was author of the Jerusalem Talmud rests only on the assertion of Maimonides. Modern critics reject it, and date the Jerusalem Talmud in the seventh century. (Hamburger, "Real-Encyclopädie," *sub voc.* "Jochanan" and "Talmud.")

P. 35, l. 34. "*The learned man l'Empereur.*" Constantine l'Empereur, an Hebraist of the seventeenth century (d. 1648), who translated into Latin some tractates of the Mishna and other Hebrew works, including the Itinerary of Benjamin of Tudela.

P. 35, l. 36. "*Sedar Olam.*" The name of two Hebrew Chronologies (see Hamburger, "Real-Encyclopädie," sup. vol., pp. 132, 133).

Notes

P. 35, l. 37. "*In Talmud tractat, Sanhedr.*" "Sanhedrin" is the name of a treatise of the Talmud, the fourth in the fourth book of the Jerushalmi, and the fifth in the fourth book of the Babli. Excerpts have been translated into Latin with elaborate notes by Joh. Coccejus (Amsterdam 1629).

P. 36, l. 9. "*Beresit Rabba.*" The first part of the "Midrash Rabboth," the chief collection of Hagadic or homiletic expositions of the Scriptures. As its name implies, it deals with Genesis (Zunz, "Gottesdienstlichen Vorträge," pp. 184 *et seq.*, 1892.)

P. 36, l. 9. "*In Perasach,*" should be "in Parashah 11" (see original Spanish "Esperança," p. 66). The misprint occurs in the Latin. "Parasha" means section. There are 100 sections in the *Bereshith Rabba.*

P. 36, l. 10. "*Tornunfus*" = Turnus Rufus.

P. 36, l. 12. "*Rabbi Aquebah.*" One of the greatest of the Tanaim or compilers of the Mishna. He became an adherent of the Pseudo-Messiah Bar Cochba, who rebelled against the Romans during the reign of Hadrian, and was put to death after the fall of Bethar. His career has passed into legend (Graetz, "Geschichte," vol. iv. pp. 53 *et seq.*).

P. 36, l. 20. "*Asirim Rabba*" = Shir Ha-Shirim Rabba. Midrashic exposition of the Song of Songs (*supra*, "Beresit Rabba ").

P. 36, l. 27. "*Jalcut.*" A collection of Midrashim covering the whole of the Scriptures, and compiled in the eleventh century by R. Simeon b. Chelbo, whence it is called the Yalkut Shimeoni (Zunz, "Gottesdienst," pp. 183 and 309).

P. 36, l. 31. "*Bamibar Rabba*": misprint for Bamidbar Rabba, the Midrashic exposition of Numbers.

P. 37, l. 12. "*R Selomoh Jarchi.*" Solomon b. Isaac of Troyes, called Rashi (1040–1105), the most eminent Hebrew Bible commentator of the Middle Ages. The name Jarchi was erroneously given to Rashi by Raymund Martini, Munster, and Buxtorf, who imagined that he was a native of Lunel (ירחי = *luna*). Menasseh ben Israel was the first Jewish scholar to adopt this blunder (Wolf, "Biblio. Heb." vol. i. 1057, &c.; Graetz, "Geschichte," vol. vi. pp. 77 *et seq.*; Wolf, "The Treves Family in England").

P. 37, l. 15. "*R. Mardochus Japhe.*" Bohemian Rabbi (1530–1612) (Graetz, "Geschichte," vol. ix. pp. 465–467).

P. 37, l. 26. "*Another worthy of credit.*" In the original Spanish, Menasseh gives his name as Señor H. Meyr Rophé. This is omitted from both the Latin and English editions.

P. 37, l. 34. "*R. Moses Gerundensis.*" Moses ben Nachman (1200–1272), also called Nachmanides, and Ramban. Christian scholars sometimes speak of him as Gerundensis from his birthplace, Gerona. The greatest Talmudic authority of his day, author of a

Bible commentary. His public disputation at Barcelona with Pablo Christiani in 1263 is famous (Graetz, "Geschichte," vol. vii. pp. 131–136, Schechter "Studies in Judaism," art. "Nachmanides ").

P. 38, l. 1. "*Benjamin Tudelensis*," Benjamin b. Jonah of Tudela, famous Jewish traveller (see Itinerary by, translated by A. Asher. Lond., 1840).

P. 38, l. 4. "*The City Lubin*" : misprint for Lublin.

P. 45, l. 14. "*Rabby Simeon ben Johay, the author of the Zoar.*" Rabbi Simeon was a famous doctor of the Mishna and disciple of Akiba. He laid the foundation of the Sifre, the Halachic, or legal exposition of Numbers and Deuteronomy. He figures in Jewish legend as the greatest master of the Cabbala. He was not the author of the Zohar. Internal evidence stamps that work as a product of the thirteenth century, and its authorship is now ascribed to Moses ben Shemtob de Leon (Hamburger, "Real-Encyclopädie," arts. Simon b. Jochai, Sifre, and Sohar).

P. 45, l. 22. "*Rabbi Seadiah*" = Saadja ben Joseph or Saadja Gaon (892–942). The most celebrated of the Geonim, who were the chiefs of the schools of Sura and Pumbaditha, and the ecclesiastical counterparts of the Exilarchs. Saadja was one of the most prolific and versatile writers Judaism has produced (Graetz, "Geschichte," vol. v. pp. 302 *et seq.*).

P. 45, l. 23. "*Moses Egyptius*" = Moses Maimonides.

P. 45, l. 24. "*Abraham bar Ribi Hijah*" = Abraham ben Chijah ha-Nasi of Barcelona (1065–1136), Jewish astronomical and geometrical writer ; was Minister of Police during the Moorish domination in Spain (Graetz, "History," vol. iii. p. 320).

P. 45, l. 24. "*Abraham Zacculo*" : misprint for Zaccuto (d. *c.* 1515). He was a Jewish astronomer employed at the Court of Manuel of Portugal. His works influenced Columbus (Kayserling, "Christopher Columbus," pp. 9, 13, 14, 46–51, 112, 113).

P. 45, l. 30. "*The letter (m) in Isa.* ix. 7." The reference is to the sixth verse of Isaiah ix., in the first word of which, למרבה, the second letter, which should be מ, is written in its final form ם.

P. 47, l. 13. "*Diogo d'Assumean*" : misprint for Diogo da Asunçao (Graetz, "History," vol. iv. p. 711 ; Kayserling, "Juden in Portugal," pp. 282, 292).

P. 47, l. 20. "*The Lord Lope de Veray Alacron*" = Don Lope de Vera y Alarcon. His martyrdom is the subject of a poem by Antonio Enriquez Gomez, " Romance al diuin Martir Juda Creyente" (Kayserling, "Biblioteca Española," p. 50; Graetz, "Geschichte," vol. x. pp. 101, 197).

P. 47, l. 38. "*Isaac Castrensis Tartas*" = Isaac de Castro Tartas (Graetz, "History," vol. v. p. 33).

Notes

P. 48, l. 9. "*Eli Nazarenus.*" His real name was Francisco Meldonado de Silva ("Publications of the American Jew. Hist. Soc.," vol. iv. p. 113).

P. 48, l. 13. "*Thomas Terbinon.*" Doctor Thomas (Isaac) Trebiño de Sobremente ("Pub. Amer. Jew. Hist. Soc.," vol. iv. pp. 124-161).

P. 48, l. 25. "*My booke, De Termino Vitæ*" (English edition by P. T. [Thomas Pocock]. Lond., 1700).

P. 49, l. 8. "*His wife Benuenida*" = Bienvenida Abravanela (Kayserling, "Die Jüdischen Frauen," pp. 77 *et seq.*, 111).

P. 49, l. 16. "*Don Selomo Rophe.*" Rabbi Solomon ben Nathan Aschkenazi, surnamed Rophe, or the Physician, was a diplomatist in the Turkish service who secured the election of Henry of Anjou to the throne of Poland. (Graetz, "Geschichte," vol. ix. pp. 396, 399, 438, 580; Levy, "Don Joseph Nasi," pp. 8 *et seq.*).

P. 49, l. 18. "*D. Ben Jaese, Anancus, and Sonsinos, are of great authority with the Turk.*" These are the names of Jewish families who played an important part in Turkey in the sixteenth century. This is a chapter of Jewish history on which the historians have as yet shed little light. The materials are chiefly in manuscript, and the present author proposes dealing with them in a communication to the Jewish Historical Society. On the Ben Jaese (Ibn Jachya) family, the reader may provisionally consult Carmoly, "Chronica Familiæ Jachya," and on the Soncinos, Mortara, "Indice Alfabetico."

P. 49, l. 20. "*Abraham Alholn*": misprint for Alhulu, treasurer to the Pasha of Egypt. (See *infra*, p. 86.)

P. 49, l. 21. "*Don Josephus Nassi.*" A wealthy Jew, nephew and son-in-law of Donna Gracia Nasi (see note, *infra*, p. 163). He was in the service of the Sultan, and conquered Cyprus for the Turks. In addition to the sources indicated by Menasseh, see Levy, "Don Joseph Nasi, Herzog Von Naxos" (Breslau, 1859), and Graetz, "Geschichte," vol. ix. *passim.*

P. 49, l. 25. "*Jacob Aben Jaes.*" He is sometimes referred to as Don Solomon. He was of the Ibn Jachya family, and was uncle to Joseph Nasi. For a time he was in the service of Queen Elizabeth, and corresponded with her physician Rodrigo Lopez, to whom he was related. The Sultan created him Duke of Mytilene. (MS. materials.)

P. 49, l. 29. "*D. Samuel Palaxe.*" (See Henriques de Castro, "Keur Van Grafsteenen," pp. 91, 94.)

P. 50, l. 6. "*D. Benjamin Mussaphia.*" Dionysius Mussaphia (1605-1674), physician and philologist, court physician to Christian IV. of Denmark, afterwards Rabbi in Amsterdam (Graetz, "Geschichte," vol. x. pp. 24, 26, 202, 227, 243, 244; Kayserling, "Juden in Portugal," p. 298.)

Notes

P. 50, l. 9. " *King Cochini.*" A mistranslation; should be " King of Cochin." The Jews of the Malabar coast settled there in the fifth century. Local tradition gives the colony a much greater antiquity. Menasseh gives further particulars of them in his " Humbler Addresses," *infra,* p. 85 (Graetz, " Geschichte," vol. iv. pp. 470–472; Satthianadhan in the *Church Missionary Intelligencer,* 1871, pp. 365 *et seq.*)

P. 50, l. 12. " *Mardocheas Maisel.*" Mordecai Meisel (1528–1601). The first Hebrew capitalist in Germany. Created an Imperial Councillor by the Emperor Rudolph. His charities were on a princely scale. He built two synagogues at Prague (Graetz, " Geschichte," vol. ix. pp. 477, 478.)

P. 50, l. 14. " *Jacob Bathsebah.*" Jacob Basevi Schmieles (1580–1634), an influential Bohemian Jew, ennobled by the Emperor Ferdinand, receiving the title of Von Treuenburg and a grant of arms. (Graetz, " Geschichte," vol. x. pp. 41–47; Wolf, " Jewish Coats of Arms.")

P. 50, l. 22. " *Moses Amon*" (1490–1565). Physician to Solymon II. Translated the Bible and Hebrew Prayer-Book into Arabic, and was employed by the Sultan on diplomatic missions (Levy, " Don Joseph Nasi," pp. 6–8).

P. 50, l. 23. " *Elias Montalto.*" Felipe Montalto, or Eliahu de Luna Montalto, brother of Amato Lusitano. Portuguese physician. Practised in Italy, and afterwards was appointed physician-in-ordinary to Maria de Medicis; died at Tours 1616, and buried in the Jewish Cemetery at Amsterdam (Kayserling, " Biblioteca Española," pp. 72, 73). Montalto was also known as Don Philipe Rodrigues. Among his descendants is Prof. Raphael Meldola (MS. materials).

P. 50, l. 25. " *Elias Cretensis.*" Better known as Elia del Medigo (1463–1498). Lectured publicly on philosophy in Padua, and arbitrated in a dispute between the professors and students of the university at the request of the Venetian Senate. Pico di Mirandola was one of his pupils. He was a prolific writer (Graetz, " Geschichte," vol. viii. pp. 240–247).

P. 50, l. 26. " *R. Abraham de Balmas*" (d. 1521). Physician, philosopher, and grammarian. Like Del Medigo, he lectured in Padua, and was one of the Hebraists whose teaching influenced the Reformation. Daniel Bomberg, the famous Venetian printer, was one of his pupils, and translated his poems into Latin (Graetz, " Geschichte," vol. ix. p. 215).

P. 50, l. 27. " *Elias Grammaticus.*" Better known as Elia Levita (1498–1549). A German Rabbi who taught in Padua, Venice, and Rome, and who exercised a strong influence on the Hebrew studies which produced the Reformation. Scaliger describes him as " the greatest Hebrew scholar of his age." Among his pupils were the

Notes

Cardinal Egidio de Viterbe, the French bishop and ambassador George de Selve, and the theologians Münster and Fagius (Günsburg, "Masoreth Hamasoreth"; Karpeles, "Geschichte d. Jüd. Lit.," pp. 855 *et seq.*).

P. 50, l. 33. "*David de Pomis.*" Physician, lexicographer, and theologian (1525–1588), translated Koheleth into Italian. Author of "De Medico Hebræo" (Graetz, "Geschichte," vol. ix. p. 483; Karpeles, "Gesch. Jüd. Lit.," pp. 880–881). There is a curious tradition that De Pomis was residing in Hull in 1599 (Symons, "Hull in ye Olden Times," Hull, 1886, pp. 82, 83).

CONSIDERATIONS UPON THE POINT OF THE CONVERSION
OF THE JEWES

Pp. 57–72. This Appendix is, as will be seen, by the English translator, Moses Wall. It does not appear in the first edition, and it is printed here as throwing light on the motives of the English supporters of Menasseh ben Israel.

P. 67, l. 21. "*E. S.*" Sir Edward Spenser, M.P. for Middlesex. See Introduction, p. xxvii.

P. 68, l. 36. "*Did Mr. Broughton gaine upon a learned Rabbi.*" See Broughton, "Ovr Lordes Famile" (Amst., 1608), and "A Reqvire of Agreement" (1611).

THE HUMBLE ADDRESSES

(pp. 73–103)

BIBLIOGRAPHICAL NOTE

For the origin of this tract, and the probable date and circumstances of its preparation, see Introduction, pp. xxxviii–xxxix.

There are two editions, neither of which bears any imprint or date. Both are 4to, but one has 26 pp. and the other 23 pp. It is difficult to say whether, and which, one of these two versions is a revision of the other, as the only difference between them is that the following sentence is added at the end of the 23 pp. text: "Which is the close of Rabbi Menesse Ben-Israel, a Divine, and Doctor in Physick in the Strand over against the New-Exchange in London." The British Museum copy of this edition is dated in MS. "Novemb. 5th (London), 1655." This edition must have been printed after Menasseh's arrival in London, and it is probable that the other is the *Libellus Anglicus* of which he speaks in his letter to Felgenhauer in February 1655, and which, consequently, we may assume was printed in Amsterdam.

The latter was reprinted in Melbourne in 1868, with an introduction by the late Rev. A. F. Ornstien :—

"To / His Highnesse / the / Lord Protector / of the / Commonwealth of / England, Scotland and Ireland / the Humble Addresses / of / Menasseh Ben Israel, a Divine, and / Doctor of Physic, in behalfe / of the Jewish Nation / 1655. / Reprinted by H. T. Dwight, / Bookseller and Publisher, Bourke Street East, Melbourne. / 1868.

English reprints of the 23 pp. text have been published in the *Jewish Chronicle*, Nov.–Dec. 1859, and in Kayserling's "Life of Menasseh ben Israel," with annotations in 1877 (*Miscellany of Hebrew Literature*, Second Series, pp. 35–63). According to Barbosa Machado ("Biblioteca Lusitana," vol. iii. p. 457), a Spanish translation was published in London simultaneously with the first English edition. Its title is given as follows :—

"Las Humildes suplicaciones En nombre de la Nacion de los Judios à su Alteza el Señor Protector Oliver Cromwell de la Republica de Inglaterra, Scocia, y Yrlandia. Traduzido del Original Ingles. En Londres, 1655."

A copy of this translation in MS. existed in the library of Isaac da Costa of Amsterdam (*Misc. Heb. Lit.*, ii. p. 84). Kayserling first translated the tract into German, and published it in his "Menasse ben Israel, sein Leben und Wirken" (Berlin, 1861).

A very large number of the historical references in this tract are taken without acknowledgment from Imanuel Aboab's "Nomologia" (Amst., 1629) and Daniel Levy de Barrios's "Historia Universal Judayca." Kayserling has given many of the original passages in his notes to his "Life of Menasseh ben Israel" (*Misc. Heb. Lit.*, Series II.).

To His Highnesse, &c.

P. 77, l. 9. "*The Ambassadors of England.*" The St. John Mission (see Introduction, pp. xxx–xxxi, and *Vindiciæ*, p. 111).

P. 81, l. 19. "*Merchandizing is . . . the proper profession of the Nation of the Jews.*" In so far as this implies that the Jews have an inborn genius for commerce this is a vulgar error (see Loeb, "Le Juif de l'Histoire et le Juif de la Legende," pp. 7–14).

P. 85, l. 7. "*These in India in Cochin.*" See note, *supra*, pp. 159–160.

P. 85, l. 21. "*In the Turkish Empire.*" See Nicolas de Nicolay, "Navigations, Peregrinations et Voyages faicts en la Turquie," Anvers, 1576, pp. 243 *et seq.*

P. 86, l. 20. "*In this estate some of the Jews have grown to great fortunes.*" The Jewish notabilities referred to in this paragraph are also mentioned in the "Hope of Israel." See note, *supra*, p. 159.

P. 87, l. 6. "*Isaac Iecells.*" Jessel or Joesel is a diminutive of Joseph. The person referred to is probably Asher ben Joseph of Cracow (see Steinschneider, "Bibl. Bodl.," p. 751).

P. 87, l. 9. "*The Cosaques in the late warres.*" The rising of Chmielnicki, 1648–1649. (Graetz, "Geschichte," vol. x. pp. 52–82.)

Notes

P. 87, ll. 22 *et seq.* The references to Jewish families in this paragraph are taken from Aboab and De Barrios. See notes 201–204 to Kayserling's "Menasseh ben Israel" (*Misc. Heb. Lit.*, ii. p. 88).

P. 88, l. 17. "*Seignor Moseh Palache.*" See De Castro, "Keur Van Graafsteenen," p. 93; "Cal. State Papers, Dom.," 1654, p. 91. On the Jews of Morocco, see *Jew. Quart. Rev.*, vol. iv. pp. 369 *et seq.*

P. 89, l. 5. "*Sir Duarte Nunes a'Acosta.*" See Da Costa, "Adellijke Geslachten onder de Israëlieten."

P. 89, l. 8. "*Emanuel Boccaro Rosales.*" See p. lxxx (Menasseh's letter to Felgenhauer); Kayserling, "Sephardim," p. 209; "Biblioteca Española-Portugueza-Judaica," pp. 95–96.

P. 90, l. 16. "*As the Chronicles do declare.*" This paragraph is almost literally translated from Aboab's "Nomologia," p. 290. The story does not appear in the earlier Jewish chronicles, such as *Schevet Jehuda, Emek Habacha,* and *Zemach David,* although the events of the reign of Pedro the Cruel and Don Enrique so far as they affect the Jew are fully dealt with in them. The "Chronicle" referred to by Menasseh is probably that of Pedro Lopez d'Ayala, which is the original authority for the story.

P. 91, l. 27. "*Don Isaac Abarbanel.*" See note, *supra,* p. 154.

P. 92, l. 1. "*They everywhere are used to pray.*" See Singer, "The Earliest Jewish Prayers for the Sovereign" (*Jewish Chronicle,* Feb. 22, 1901).

P. 92, l. 18. "*He that giveth salvation unto Kings.*" This is the first English translation of the Prayer for the Sovereign. See Singer, preceding note.

P. 93, l. 3. "*R. Simon Ben-Iochai in his excellent book called Zoar.*" See note, *supra,* p. 158.

P. 93, l. 26. "*One famous lawyer in Rome, and Osorius.*" The whole of this, and the following paragraphs relating to the expulsion from Spain, is taken from Aboab's "Nomologia." Osorius (Hieronymo Osorio, 1506–1580) was author of a history of the reign of King Emanuel, which was translated into English by Gibbs (Lond., 1752). See notes to Kayserling's "Menasseh" for parallel passages from Aboab.

P. 99, l. 22. "*As Vasquo saith.*" For Vasquo read Usque. Menasseh is quoting from the "Consolacam as Tribvlacoens de Ysrael," by Samuel Usque (Ferrara, 1552), see pp. 198–200. Samuel Usque was one of three brothers, all distinguished Marranos. He fled from the Portuguese Inquisition and settled at Ferrara, whence he emigrated to the Holy Land. He was a protégé of Donna Gracia Nasi (see Note on "Don Josephus Nassi," *supra,* p. 159; also Kayserling, "Jüdischen Frauen," pp. 80–86).

P. 100, l. 5. The narrative as pirated from Aboab's "Nomologia" ends here. For fuller details of the Portuguese persecutions, see Kayserling, "Juden in Portugal," pp. 120 *et seq.*

P. 101, l. 17. "*As for killing of the young children of Christians.*" See *infra*, notes on "Vindiciæ Judæorum," pp. 165–167.

P. 102, l. 9. "*In Araguza*" = Ragusa. For a fuller version of this story see *infra*, "Vindiciæ Judæorum," pp. 116–117.

P. 102, l. 20. "*As for the third point.*" Menasseh himself was largely responsible for the charge of proselytising, inasmuch as in the "Hope of Israel" (*supra*, p. 47) he had boasted of the converts made by the Jews in Spain. There can be no doubt that these conversions were very numerous, but they were probably due in a larger measure to the oppressive policy of the Inquisition than to any active proselytising on the part of the Jews.

P. 103, l. 33. "*In the Strand.*" For a full discussion of the place of Menasseh's abode while in London, see *Trans. Jew. Hist. Soc.*, vol. iii. pp. 144 *et seq.*

VINDICIÆ JUDÆORUM

(pp. 105–147)

BIBLIOGRAPHICAL NOTE

For the origin of this tract see Introduction, pp. lxii–lxiv.

It has often been reprinted and translated, especially on occasions of Jewish persecution. In 1708 it reappeared in the second volume of "The Phœnix; or a Revival of Scarce and Valuable Pieces." In 1743 it was reprinted as an independent pamphlet (Lond., 8vo, pp. 67). Ninety-five years later it was again reprinted by M. Samuels in the prolegomena to his translation of Moses Mendelssohn's "Jerusalem" (Lond., 1838, vol. i. pp. 1–73), together with a translation of Mendelssohn's introduction to the German edition (pp. 77–116).

On the Continent it was first published in 1782 in connection with the Mendelssohnian movement for Jewish emancipation, which was participated in by Lessing and Dohm. The fact that it should have been considered by Moses Mendelssohn worthy to stand by the side of Lessing's *Nathan der Weise* is a striking tribute to its merits. The Mendelssohnian issue is more famous than the original English edition, for in its German form the work became a classic of national Jewish controversy, whereas in English it was only associated with the local history of the British Jews. The following is the full title of the German edition (pp. lii, 64, sm. 8vo) :—

Manasseh Ben Israel / Rettung der Juden / Aus dem Englischen übersetzt / Nebst einer Vorrede / von / Moses Mendelssohn./ Als ein Anhang / zu des / Hrn. Kriegsraths Dohm / Abhandlung : / Ueber / die

Notes

bürgerliche Verbesserung / der Juden./ Mit Königl. Preussischer allergnä-
digster Freyheit./ Berlin und Stettin / bey Friedrich Nicolai / 1782.

This translation is said to have been made by Dr. Herz, the husband of
the famous Henrietta Herz (Kayserling, "Moses Mendelssohn sein Leben
und seine Werke," p. 354), but it was probably done by his wife, who knew
English so well that during her widowhood she was engaged to teach it to
the daughter of the Duchess of Courland. (See "Life" by Fürst, also
Jennings's "Rahel," pp. 19 *et seq.*) The introduction supplied by Moses
Mendelssohn fills fifty-two pages, and is as famous as the *Vindiciæ* itself.

Besides being reprinted in Mendelssohn's collected works, the German
edition of the *Vindiciæ* was republished in 1882, in connection with the
Anti-Semitic agitation, under the title "Gegen die Verleumder," and again
in 1890.

The following editions have also appeared :—

1813. Hebrew by Bloch (Vienna).
1818.   „   with a preface by Moses Kunitz (Wilna).
1837. Polish by J. Tugenhold (Warsaw).
1842. French by Carmoly (Brussels, *Revue Orientale*, ii. pp. 491
       et seq.).
1883. Italian by Nahmias (Florence).

The First Section

P. 108, l. 11. "*The Jews are wont to celebrate the feast of unleavened
bread, fermenting it with the blood of some Christians.*" This accusation, now known as the Blood Accusation, has been for many centuries
the favourite superstition of the Jew-haters. It was revived by
Prynne and Ross during Menasseh's sojourn in London. During
the residence of the Jews in England previously to 1290, it played a
conspicuous part in their persecution. (See Joseph Jacobs' "Little
St. Hugh of Lincoln," *Jew. Hist. Soc. Trans.*, vol. i., especially pp.
92–99. "The Blood Accusation, its origin and occurrence in the
Middle Ages," reprinted from the *Jewish Chronicle*, 1883.) There is
a very voluminous literature of the Blood Accusation (see especially
Zunz's "Damaskus, ein Wort zur Abwehr," Berlin, 1859), but it
has not hitherto been noticed that during the period the Jews were
banished from England (1290–1655) the superstition continued to
haunt the public mind. We have a curious instance of it in 1577.
When John Foxe, the martyrologist, baptized a Moorish Jew named
Nathaniel Menda, on April 1 of that year, at All Hallows, Lombard
Street, he adopted the Blood Accusation in the address he delivered
to celebrate the occasion. "Moreover, if he (Abraham) had seene
your unappeaceable disorder without all remorse of mercy in persecut-
ing his (Jesus's) disciples ; your intolerable scorpionlike savageness,
so furiously boyling against the innocent infants of the Christian

(165)   i

Gentiles : . . . would he ever accompted you for his sonnes." To which the printer's gloss runs thus : " Christen men's children here in Englande crucified by the Jewes, Anno 1189 and Anno 1141 at Norwiche, &c." (John Foxe, " A Sermon at the Christening of a certaine Iew at London," London, 1578 ; p. E. iii.) This sermon, originally delivered in Latin, was translated into English and published *in extenso,* together with the confession of Nathaniel Menda, in 1578. It was dedicated to Sir Francis Walsingham, Principal Secretary of State to Queen Elizabeth.

Thomas Calvert, " Minister of the Word at York," was the next to lend his name to the superstition, and to give vigorous expression to it in his " Diatraba of the Jews' Estate." This was a preface to " The Blessed Jew of Marocco ; or A Blackmoor made White, by Rabbi Samuel, a Jew turned Christian ; written first in the Arabick, after translated into Latin, and now Englished " (York, 1648. The British Museum copy is dated in MS. " July 25, 1649.") His exact words are as follows :—

" So much are they (the Jews) bent to shed the blood of Christians, that they say a Jew needs no repentance for murdering a Christian ; and they add to that sinne to make it sweet and delectable that hee who doth it, it is as if he had offered a *Corban* to the Lord, hereby making the abominable sin an acceptable sacrifice. But beyond all these they have a bloody thirst after the blood of Christians. In France and many kingdoms they have used yearly to steale a Christian boy and to crucifie him, fastning him to a crosse, giving him gall and vinegar, and running him in the end thorow with a spear, to rub their memories afresh into sweet thoughts of their crucifying Christ, the more to harden themselves against Christ and to shew their curst hatred to all Christians " (pp. 18–19).

John Sadler stands out conspicuously for dissociating himself from this baseless prejudice. When he wrote his " Rights of the Kingdom," in 1649, he summed up the matter in a happy and pithy manner : " Wee say, they (the Jews) crucified a child, or more. They doe deny it : and we prove it not " (p. 74). Undaunted by Sadler's championship of the Jews, James Howell followed Calvert, and in the Epistle Dedicatory to his pirated edition of Morvyn's translation of Joseph ben Gorion, " The wonderful and deplorable history of the latter times of the Jews " (London [June 2], 1652), he thus insinuated the truth of the charge :—

" The first Christian Prince that expelled the Jews out of his territories, was that heroik King, our Edward the First, who was such a sore scourge also to the Scots ; and it is thought divers families of those banished Jews fled then to Scotland, where they have propagated since in great numbers, witness the aversion that nation hath above others to hog's flesh. Nor was this extermination for their

(166)

Notes

Religion, but for their notorious crimes, as poysoning of wells, counter-feiting of coines, falsifying of seales, *and crucifying of Christian children,* with other villanies."

Sadler was not the only English contemporary of Menasseh ben Israel who threw doubt on the Blood Accusation. Prynne himself relates in the preface to his "Demurrer" that he met Mr. Nye by the garden wall at Whitehall, when he was on his way to the Conference on the Jewish Question. "I told him," writes Prynne, "the Jews had been formerly clippers and forgers of money, *and had crucified three or four children in England at least,* which were principal causes of their banishment, to which he replied, that the crucifying of children was not fully charged on them by our historians, and would easily be wiped off." (Preface, p. 4.)

It is curious that, as Menasseh himself points out, the Jews were not alone at this period as sufferers from the Blood Accusation. ("Humble Addresses," p. 21.) Apart from the instance quoted by Menasseh, a similar charge was levelled at the Quakers, who were accused of the ritual murder of women. An illustrated tract on the subject will be found in *Historia Fanaticorum.* (See "Historia von den Wider-Tauffern," Cöthen, 1701.)

The Blood Accusation did not again make a conspicuous appearance in Anglo-Jewish history, but it is not improbable that the Damascus trials in 1840 produced a serious effect in retarding the progress of the struggle for emancipation. On the Continent, and in the Levant, it has frequently reappeared during the last thirty years.

P. 109, l. 8. "*In Iad a Razaka.*" Misprint for *Yad Hachazaka* ("The Strong Hand"), also called *Mishneh Torah,* an exposition of Jewish law by Moses Maimonides, written (in Hebrew) 1170–1180.

P. 111, l. 7. "*A particular blessing of the Prince or Magistrate.*" See note, *supra,* p. 163.

P. 112, l. 16. "*And every day the Jewes mainly strike.*" The belief that Jews habitually desecrated the sacramental wafer runs parallel with the Blood Accusation. A curious echo of it was heard in 1822, and the published account of the case was illustrated by George Cruikshank ("The Miraculous Host tortured by the Jews," Lond., 1822).

P. 114, l. 4. "*Wherefore I swear.*" This oath is famous in Jewish history, and has been over and over again quoted and reiterated on occasions of the revival of the Blood Accusation (see *e.g. Trans. Jew. Hist. Soc.,* vol. i. p. 38).

P. 114, l. 20. "*John Hoornbeek in that book which he lately writ.*" The work referred to is *De Convertendis Judæis,* 1655.

P. 115, l. 28. "*In my continuation of Flavius Josephus.*" In the "Hope of Israel" (*supra,* p. 7), Menasseh announced his intention

(167)

of writing this work. From this passage it seems that he had now completed it, and that he had the MS. with him in London. It was never printed, as none of it has survived. It is curious that Menasseh does not mention it among his "Books ready for the Presse," of which he gave a list at the end of the *Vindiciæ* (see p. 147).

P. 116, l. 13. "*One Isaac Jeshurun.*" An account of his persecution was written in Hebrew by Aaron de David Cohen of Ragusa, and translated into Spanish under the title, *Memorable relacion de Yshac Jesurun.* The work is in MS.; a copy was in the Almanzi Library.

P. 118, l. 30. "*That our nation had purchased S. Paul's Church.*" See Introduction, p. xli.

P. 118, l. 34. "*A fabulous narrative.*" Brett, "A Narrative of the Proceedings of a Great Councel of Jews assembled on the plain of Ageda" (Lond., 1655; reprinted in "The Phœnix," 1707, the "Harleian Miscellany," vol i., 1813, and in pamphlet form by Longmans & Co., 1876).

P. 121, l. 27. "*The book called Scebet Iehuda,*" ספר שבט יהודה, by Solomon Aben Verga, a Jewish chronicle of the sixteenth century. See German translation by Wiener (Hanover, 1856). The story related by Menasseh ben Israel will be found on pp. 77–78. It is not told of a "King of Portugal," but of a King of Spain.

P. 121, l. 32. "*Before one of the Popes, at a full Councell.*" For Papal Bulls on the Blood Accusation see "Die Blutbeschuldigung gegen die Juden von Christlicher Seite beurtheilt," Zweite Auflage (Vienna, 1883). Strack's "Blutaberglaube" (several editions) is the classical work on the subject.

THE SECOND SECTION

P. 124, l. 16. "*The Israelites hold.*" This paragraph is a summary of the Thirteen Articles of Faith first drawn up by Moses Maimonides in 1168, and now incorporated in the Synagogue liturgy. Menasseh's summary, though admirably succinct, is not altogether perfect, and was apparently drafted with a view to the susceptibilities of the English Conversionists. A full translation of the thirteen creeds had, however, already appeared in England (see Chilmead's translation of Leo Modena's "The History of the Rites, Customes, and Manner of Life of the Present Jews," Lond., 1650, pp. 246–249).

P. 124, l. 28. "*A French book which he calleth the Rappel of the Jewes,*" Iaac la Peyrère "Rappel des Juifs."

THE THIRD SECTION

The subject matter of this section, the alleged cursing of Gentiles, is, like the Blood Accusation, an obstinate delusion of the anti-Semites. It is

Notes

the burden of a very voluminous literature. See, among recent publications, Jellinek, "Der Talmudjude" (Vienna, 1882); Daab, "Der Thalmud" (Leipzig, 1883); Hirsch, "Über die Beziehung des Talmuds zum Judenthum" (Frankfort, 1884); and Hoffmann, "Der Schulchan Aruch und die Rabbinen über das Verhältniss der Juden zu Andersgläubigen" (Berlin, 1885).

P. 127, l. 31. "*Prayers for Kings and Princes.*" See note, *supra,* p. 163.

P. 128, l. 6. "*The form of prayer in the book entitled The Humble Addresses,*" *supra,* p. 92.

P. 133, l. 25. "*Wise and vertuous Lady Beruria.*" The most famous of the women mentioned in the Talmud. She was the daughter of Rabbi Chanina ben Tradjon, and wife of Rabbi Meir (Kayserling, "Jüdischen Frauen," pp. 120–124).

P. 133, l. 26. "*R. Meir.*" A distinguished pupil of the great Rabbi Akiba, and one of the most famous of the authors of the Talmud. He lived in the second century (Levy, "Un Tanah," Paris, 1883; Blumenthal, "Rabbi Meir," Frankfurt, 1888).

THE FOURTH SECTION

P. 134, l. 14. "*Buxtorphius.*" Johann Buxtorf the Elder (1564–1629), the greatest Christian Hebraist of his day. Professor of Hebrew at Basle.

P. 136, l. 22. "*R. David Gawz.*" David Gans (1541–1631), a Jewish chronicler, mathematician, and astronomer, author of *Zemach David.* He lived in Prague, and was a friend of Tycho Brahe and Keppler (Klemperer, "David Gans's Chronikartige Weltgeschichte," Prague, 1890).

P. 136, l. 25. "*Antonius Margarita.*" His name was Aaron Margalita. He was an ignorant Polish Jew, who became converted to Christianity and placed his services at the disposal of the Jew-haters (Graetz, "Geschichte," vol. x. pp. 313–314).

THE FIFTH SECTION

P. 137, l. 18. "*I have held friendship with many great men.*" Menasseh's circle of Christian friends was large and distinguished. His intimacy with Rembrandt has already been referred to (*supra,* pp. 149–150). Among his other friends were Hugo Grotius, the learned family of Vosstus, Episcopius, Vorstius, Meursius, Cunæus, Blondel, Chr. Arnold, Bochart, Huet, Sobierre, Felgenhauer, Frankenberg, Mochinger, and Caspar Barlæus.

P. 137, l. 23. "*Many verses in my commendations.*" The poem by Barlæus here referred to was prefixed to Menasseh's treatise "De Creatione" (Amsterdam, 1636), together with congratulatory

(169)

sonnets by Himanuel Nehamias, Mosseh Pinto, Jona Abravanel, and Daniel Abravanel. It ran as follows :—

EPIGRAMMA,
IN
PROBLEMATA
Clarissimi viri Manassis Ben-Israel,
DE CREATIONE.

Qvæ cœlos terrasq̃; manus, spatiosaq̃; Nerei
Æquora, & immẽsas, quas habet orbis opes,
Condiderit, mersuniq̃; alta caligine mundum
Iusserit imperijs ilicet esse suis :
Disserit Isacides. Et facta ingentia pandit;
Et nondum exhaustum contrahit arte Deum.
Hîc atavos patresq̃; suos & verba recenset,
Sensaq̃; Thalmudicæ relligiosa Scholæ.
Vera placẽt, placet egregijs conatibus author,
Et pietas fidei disparis ista placet.
Cunctorum est coluisse Deum. Non unius æví,
Non populi unius credimus, esse pium.
Si sapimus diversa, Deo vivamus amici,
Doctaq̃; mens precio constet ubiq̃; suo.
Hæc fidei vox summa meæ est. Hæc crede *Menasse*.
Sic ego Christiades, sic eris Abramides.

C. BARLÆVS.

THE SEVENTH SECTION

P. 144, l. 37. "*Wherefore those few Jewes that were here, despairing of our expected successe departed hence.*" This can only refer to Menasseh's companions on his mission. With two exceptions all the Marranos in London at the time of Menasseh's arrival remained in the country.

P. 145, l. 34. "*From my study in London.*" See *Trans. Jew. Hist. Soc.*, vol. iii. pp. 144–150.

INDEX

Index

Augustus Cæsar, 129, 130
Auns, 32
Austin, cited, 56
Austine the Monk, 68
Austria, 115
Ayacucho = Guamanga 155 (notes)
Ayala, Pedro Lopez d', 163 (notes)
Azahel, Rabbi Jacob ben, xxxvii *n.*
Azores, 21

" BABLI, The," Talmud, 157 (notes)
Babylon, 35, 39, 40, 42, 64, 92 ; captivity of, 41, 43, 93 ; redemption from, 42 ; rivers of, 36
Babylonian Talmud, cited, 36, 43, 157 (notes)
Bagdad, 85
Bahia Honda = Port Honda = Puerto de Santa Crus, 153 (notes)
Bairos, Johannes de, 38
Bajaseth, Bajazet, Sultan, 50, 97
Baker, Richard, lxxi *n.*
Balaam, 46
Balboa, Basco Nunez de, 19
Balmas, R. Abraham de, 50, 160 (notes)
Baltasar, 129
" Bamibar Raba " = Bamidbar Rabba, 36, 157 (notes)
Bancroft, cited, 152 (notes)
Banishments from England, France, Spain, 46
Baptist, John the, 30
Baptists, xviii
Bar Cochba, the Pseudo-Messiah, 157 (notes)
Bara, Jan, 157 (notes)
Barbadoes, xxxi, xxxvii
Barbary, 49 ; Kingdom of, 88
Barcelona, Disputation of Grundensis at, 157 (notes)
Barleus, Gaspar, 137 = Barlæus, Caspar, 169 (notes)
Barlovent, Isle of, 18 ; Islands of, 54
Barlow, cited, l. liv
Barrios, Daniel Levy de, cited, 162, 163 (notes)
Baruch, cited, 129
Basle, 169 (notes)
Bathsebah, Jacob = Jacob Basevi

Schmieles, received title von Treuenburg, 50, 160 (notes)
Batueca, 39
Bazalel, 75
Beleeving Judas, 47 (*see* Alacron)
Belmonte, Ishak, 150 (notes)
Benhadad, King of Assyria, 111
Ben Jaefe, D., 49
Benjamin, tribe of, 7, 36, 39, 40, 52, 66, 70, 85
Benjamin, R., cited, 32
Benjamin of Tudela, 156 (notes)
Benn, William, xlviii
Benuenida, wife of Samuel Abarbanel, 49, 159
" Beresit Rabba," 36, 157 (notes)
Bergarensis, Caspar, 25
Berkshire, Earl of, lxxiv
Bermuda Company, xlvii
Beruria, daughter of Rabbi Chanina ben Tradjon, wife of Rabbi Meir, 133, 169 (notes)
Bethar, 157 (notes)
Bialloblotzky, cited, 155 (notes)
" Bibliotheca Rabbinica," 134, 147
Biddle, xl
Blake, xl
Blood Accusation, 108, 165 (notes), 166, 167 (notes) ; the Pope declared false, in full Council, 102
" Bloudy Tenent of Persecution," xix
Blumenthal, cited, 169 (notes)
Bochardus, Samuel, 40
Bochart, 169 (notes)
Bodleian Library, xli
Bohemian Jews, lxx
Bomberg, Daniel, famous Venetian printer, 160 (notes)
Bondel, 169 (notes)
Bondi, Abraham de, Ambassador for Alphonso II., 88
Bordeaux, lxxi
Borja, St. Franciscus de, 25
Boterus, 33 ; cited, 34, 49
Boyle, Robert, l *n.*
Bozara, 48
Bozius, 54
Brahe, Tycho, 169 (notes)
Brasil, Seignory of, 91
Brazil, xxxiii, xxxvii ; Negroes of, 101

Index

Index

Elhazar, 49

Eliezer, David ben, xxxvii *n.*

Eliot, John, xxiv, 152 (notes), 166

Elisha, 64

Elizabeth, Queen, xiv, xv, 159 (notes), 166 (notes)

Emanuel, King of Portugal, 51, 94, 95, 97, 163 (notes); cruelty of, 99

Embassies in London, xl; in Holland, xl

"Emek Habacha," 163 (notes)

l'Empereur, Constantine, 35, 156 (notes)

England, banishments of, 46

Enrique, Don, 163 (notes)

Ephraim, 41, 42, 69, 70; Tribe of, 43

Epicureans, 125

Epiphanius, 76

Episcopius, 169 (notes)

Epstein, cited, 156 (notes)

Erzilla, Alonsus de = Alonzo d'Ercilla y Zuñiga, 24; cited, 155 (notes)

"Esdras," 37; cited, 56; quoted by Genebrardus, 20

"Esperanza de Israel," 152 (notes); cited, 155 (notes), 157 (notes)

Espinosa, Michael, 150 (notes)

Esquilache, 25

Essex, Earl of, xiv

l'Estrange, Sir Hamon, 152 (notes)

Estrozi, Seignor Philip, 96

Ethiopia, 6, 34, 40; Ten Tribes, 156 (notes); Ethiopian ships, 34 (*see* Almadiæ)

Eucharistical sacrifices, 130

Euphrates, 20, 35, 39, 40, 41, 44, 56

Eurgetes, Ptolomy, 130

Europe, 6, 21, 35, 42, 82; Menasseh has friendships with eminent men of, 137

Eusebius, cited, 55

Evelyn, John, lvi

Everard the Leveller, xxi

Expulsion of Jews, lvii, 154 (notes); from England, xi; from Spain, xiv, 163 (notes)

Ezion-Geber, 19

Ezra, Aben, cited, 109

Ezras, 136

FAGIUS, 161 (notes)

Fairclough, Samuel, xlviii

Fairfax, Lord, xx

Falashas of Abyssinia, 156 (notes)

Famian, 47

Fano, Lord Joseph de, Marquis de Villependi, 87

Farisol or Peretsol, Abraham = Abraham Frisol Orchotolam, author of "Orchat Olam," 156 (notes) (*see* Frisol)

Farnambuc = Pernambuco, 25, 28, 48, 155 (notes) (*see* Fernambuc)

Farnesia (*see* Paul III.), 94

Faro, Abraham Enriques, 150 (notes)

Felgenhauer, xxv, xxxviii, xxxix, lxxix, 161 (notes), 169 (notes)

Felibert, Emanuel, Duke of Savoy, 97

Ferdinand, xi, 51, 91, 93, 102, 138; King, 94; Bathsebah knighted under reign of, 160; of Naples, 154 (notes); Emperor, 160 (notes); of Spain, 39

Ferdinandus, 17

Ferrara = Ferrare = Ferraria, 87; Alphonso II., Duke of, 88; Hercules, Duke of, 34, 97, 163 (notes) (*see* Usque)

Fez, King of, 91

Fifth Monarchy men, xv, xxi

Finch, Sergeant, xxi

Finicus, Marcilius, cited, 54

Firth, cited, xx *n.*

Firuz, 31

"Flavius Josephus adversus Apionem," 147

Flemburgh, 109

Florence, Duke of (*see* Cosmo the Great), 97

Forbes, 68

Founders of the Protectorate, xlvii

Foxe, John, 165 (notes); cited, 166 (notes)

"Fragmenta Sacra," 68

France, xxix, lxii, lxxiii, lxxx, 33, 166 (notes); banishments of, 46; King of, 124; Philip of, 51; Loysia de Medici, 50

Francis I. of France, 33

Franciscus de Borgia, St., 25

Franco, Abraham, 150 (notes)
Frankenberg, Abraham, a Silesian mystic, lxxx, 149 (notes), 169 (notes)
Frankfort, Franckfurt, 151 (notes); Jews in, 86
Frederick, Emperor, cited, 115
Frisol, Rabbi Abraham, cited, 34, 38 (*see* Farisol)
Fullana, Nicholas de Oliver y, xiii
Fuller, xxi *n.*, xxii, xxvii

GABBAI, Jedidjah Ibn, 151 (notes)
Gad, tribe of, 29
Galatine, Peter, 72
Galilee, 29
Ganges, 38, 39
Garcias, 23
Gardiner, xxix, xxx, lviii, lxxxiv
Garracas, 23
Garzoni, Thomas, 50
Gath, 125
Gawz, R. David = David Gans, 136, 169 (notes)
Gazim, 125
Gehazi, 64
Geluckstadt, 84
Genebrardus, 20, 21
Geneva, xvii, xviii; Jews go to, 145
"Geographie du Talmud," 153 (notes)
Gerizim, Mount, 128
German-Austrian Beast, the, 57
Germany, Jews in, 77, 86; usury in, 120
Gerona, birthplace of Gerundensis, 157 (notes)
Gerundensis, R. Moses = Moses ben Nachman = Nachmanides = Ramban, 157 (notes); cited, 37, 45
Gibbs, 163 (notes)
Gibeonites, the, 111
Gilead, 69; Hazor-Gilead, 29
"Glory of Jehudah and Israel, The," lxxx, 103
Glynne, Sir John, xlvii, xlix
Gog, Battle of, 44; War of, 43, 52
Golden Chersonesus, the, 19
Golden Land, the, 19
Goleta, 95
Gomara, cited, 54 (*see* Gomoras)

Gomaza, 22
Gomez, Antonio Enriquez,158(notes);
Gomez, Gabriel, agent for King of Denmark, 89
Gomoras = Francisco Lopes de Gomara, 20, 21, 154 (notes)
Gonzales, Abraham Coen, lxxxvi
Goodwin, xlvii, l
Gorion, Joseph ben = Gorionides, 128, 129, 166 (notes)
Goropius, 53
Gozan, 37–38; river, 32, 33, 38, 39
Gracias, Gregorius, 22
Graetz, cited, xii, xiii, xiv, xxiii, xxvii, xxxvii, xxxix, lix, lxx, 154–162 (notes), 169 (notes)
Grammaticus, Elias = Elias Levita, 50, 160 (notes)
Granada, 93
Grecians, 7
Greece, Monarch of, 131
Greenland, 20
Grotius, Hugo, 20, 169 (notes)
Guainacapacus, 22
Guamanga, 22
Guariaga = Indians living near river of that name, 25; River, 24, 25
Guatemala, Indians of, 23
Guayaquil, 153 (notes)
Guinea, negroes of, 101
Günsburg, cited, 161 (notes)
Guppy, H. B., cited, 155 (notes)
Guz, 37

HABOR, 33, 39
Habyssins, 34; kingdom of the = Abyssinia, 34, 40
Hadrian, 157 (notes)
Hagarens, the, 125
Haggai, 136
Haghe, the = Hague, the, xxiv, xxxi, 49
Halah, 33, 39
Halévy, cited, 156 (notes)
Hamath, 40, 41
Hamborough, 116
Hamburg, 89, 100; Bank, xxx; Jews at, 49; Marranos founded congregations at, xiv
Hamburger, cited, 153 (notes), 156 (notes), 158 (notes)

Index

Hamchen, 30

Hara, 39

Hartlib, Samuel, 63

Havana, 153 (notes)

Hazor-Gilead, 29

Hebræus, Jacobus Rosales, lxxx

Hebraism of English religious thought, xv

Hebrew Cazici, 17

Hebrew tongue, the, 47

Hebrews, 7 ; laws and customs of the, 22

Heliodorus, 128

Henrique, Don, 90

Henry VIII., xv

Hercules, Duke of Ferraria, 34, 55, 97

Herrera, Alonzo de, xiv ; cited, 56

Heschel, Rabbi Joshua ben Jacob, xxxvii *n.*

Heseah, cited, 131

Hierome, S., 119

Hierusalem, 26

Hijah, Abraham bar Ribi=Abraham ben Chijahha-Nasi of Barcelona, 45, 158 (notes)

Hindostan, Jewish settlers in, xii

" Hippocratis Aphorismi," 147

Hircanus, High Priest, 129

Hirsch, cited, 169 (notes)

Hispaniola, 23

" Historia sive continuatio Flavii Josephi," 147

" History of the Jews," 51

Hoffmann, cited, 169 (notes)

Holland, xxx, xxxi, xxxii, xxxiii, lxii, lxxiii, 82, 100, 120, 137 ; embassies in, xl ; Jews of, 77, 83 ; Royalist spies in, xviii

Holmes, Nathaniel, xxv, xxvi, lxxx, lxxxii

Holstace, 89

Holstein, Duke of, 49, 50

Holy Land, 41, 42, 66, 163 (notes), (*see* Usque)

Holy Mount at Jerusalem, 44

Holy Office, Tribunals of, xiii

Honan, 29

Honda, 11 *n.*, 12, 16 ; Port, 153 (notes) (*see* Bahia Honda)

Hoornbeek, John, 114 ; cited, 136, 167 (notes)

" Hope of Israel, The," xvii, xviii, xxvi, xxxix, lxxviii, 7, 17, 65, 144, 149-154 (notes), 157 (notes), 164 (notes), 167 (notes) ; translated into Dutch, Spanish, Judeo-German, Hebrew, 151 (notes)

Hord-Jerida, 31

Hord of Naphtali, 31

Howell, James, 166 (notes)

Huarte, Johannes, 54

Huet, 169 (notes)

" Humas," 146

" Humble Addresses, The," xxxvi, xxxviii, xl, xlii, xliv, xlv, 73, 75, 128, 160, 162, 167 (notes); cited, 169 (notes) ; Bibliographical note, 161 (notes)

Hungaria, 18

Huns, 32

Huza, Elhazar, 85

Hyde, Thomas, 156 (notes)

" Iad a Razaka "=" Yad Hachazaka "=Mishneh Torah, 109, 167 (notes)

Iaes, Jacob ben, Governor of Tiberiades, 86 (*see* Jachya, Ibn)

Ian, David, 85

Idumean, 101

Iecells, Isaac=probably Asher ben Joseph of Cracow, 87, 162 (notes)

Ijon, 29

Inde Maienses, Province of, 25

Independents, xix, xlviii ; extreme, xx ; Messianic beliefs held by, xxi ; rise of, xviii

India, 15, 19, 20, 21, 26, 33, 41, 50, 162 (notes); Jews in, 85 ; Upper, 38

Indian, 154 (notes)

Indian Company, West, xxx, 88

Indian Sea, 19

Indians, 6, 17, 22, 28, 38, 54, 56 ; American, xxiv ; Carybes, 27 ; countries of the, 24 ; first baptized and then murdered by Spaniards, 113 ; forced to swear fealty to King of Spain, 25 ; of Guatemala, 23 ; of Jucatan, 22 ; of New Spain and Peru, 18, 23 ; of Oronoch, 27 ; of Peru, 23

Index

Index

Meldola, Prof. Raphael, 160 (notes)
Menasseh ben Israel, Rabbi of Amsterdam, author of "Spes Israelis" and other works; son of Marrano of Lisbon; educated under care of Rabbi Isaac Uziel; became Rabbi at age of eighteen; accomplished linguist, writer, and preacher; married into the Abarbanel family, xxii, xxiii, xxxiii, xlv, lxviii, lxxxvi, 6, 69, 71, 157 (notes), 161 (notes), 169 (notes); arrives in London, xxxvii; campaign of, lxxv; catalogue of books of, 146; Christian friends of, 169 (notes); connection with members of the St. John Mission, xxxi; contemporary with Sadler, 167 (notes); death of, lxix; Declaration to the Commonwealth of England, 78; "De Creatione," 169 (notes); demands presented to Cromwell, lxxxiii; "De Termino Vitæ," 149 (notes); formally opens negotiations with the Government of the Commonwealth, xliv; "Hope of Israel," xxvi, 65; dedication of "Hope of Israel" to Parliament and Council of State, 3; "Humble Addresses" printed, xxxviii, 73, 75, 162 (notes); close of "Humble Addresses," 103; invited to England by Cromwell, xxxvi; letter, lxxvii; letter to Dury, lxxviii; letter to Felgenhauer, lxxix, 163 (notes); Mission to Cromwell, xvi, lxxiii; motives of his English supporters, 161 (notes); negotiations with Thurloe, xxxii; petition not favoured by the clergy, xlvi; petition sprung on Council, xlvi; petition to Cromwell, lxxxvi, lxxxvii; his portraits, 149 (notes); Menasseh's proposals read, xlviii; Menasseh's reply to Prynne and Ross, "Vindiciæ Judæorum," lxiii; sends Dormido to England, xxxiii; signs petition, lxii; Menasseh's sojourn in London, 165 (notes); Menasseh's summary of the Thirteen Articles of Faith, 168 (notes); Menasseh's "Vindiciæ Judæorum," 105; wife of, 154 (notes); with relation to the Ten Tribes, 152 (notes)
Menda, Nathaniel, 165 (notes), 166 (notes)
Mendaña, 155 (notes)
Mendez, Alvaro = Jacob Aben Jaes, 49
Mercado, Abraham de, xxxvi, xxxvii
Mercado, Raphael de, xxxvii
Messiah, xxiii, xxv, xxvi, lxxviii, lxxix, 7, 45, 46, 52, 53, 63, 79, 118, 124; son of David, 43, 44; son of Ephraim, 43; son of Joseph, 43, 44; Bar-Cochba, the Pseudo, 157 (notes)
Messianic beliefs, xxi, xxviii
Meursius, 169 (notes)
Mexico, 22, 23, 48
Michael, Isle of St., 21, 55
Michesius, Joannes = D. Josephus Nassi, 49
Middelburg, lxix, 150 (notes)
Middlesex, E. S., xxvii n.
Middleton, General, lxxviii
"Midras Rabba," cited, 141
"Midrash, The," cited, 153 (notes)
Millenarians, xxiii, xxv, xxvii, xxix, xl, 67, 70
Millennium, xxxi, xxxiii
Milum, Lord of = D. Josephus Nassi, 49
Mirandola, Pico de, 50, 160 (notes)
"Mishna, The," 156 (notes)
Mochingerius, Joh., lxxx, 169 (notes)
Modena, Leo de, xlii, 168 (notes)
Modena, State of, 88
Modina, Duke of, 85
Mohanes = magicians = American-Indian medicine men, 28, 56, 154 (notes)
Molho, Selomoh = Diogo Pires, 33, 156 (notes)
"Monarchia Ecclesiastica," 120
Monarchia Ingasonum, 22
Monarchies, The Four, 45, 46
Monarchy Men, Fifth, xv, xxi
Monk, xl, lxxiii
Montalto, Elias = Felipe Montalto = Eliahu de Luna Montalto = Don Philipe Rodrigues, 50, 160 (notes)

Montanas, Arias, 18
Montezinos, Antonio de = Aaron Levy, xxiv, xxvii, 6, 12, 15, 17, 20, 27, 28, 54, 56, 151, 153, 154 (notes) ; goes with Cazicus, 13 ; relates his story, 11
Montezinos, Ludovicus, 12
Montfort, Marquis of, xiii
Moorish domination in Spain, 158 (notes)
Moors, 39
Mores, the, 94, 98
Morines, 91
Morocco, 127, 141, 156 (notes)
Mortara, cited, 159 (notes)
Morvyn, 166 (notes)
Moses, R., of Egypt, 109, 110, 123, 125, 140 ; cited
Münster, 157 (notes), 161 (notes)
Mussaphia, D. Benjamin = Dionysius Mussaphia, physician and Rabbi, 50, 159 (notes)
Mysketa, 37

NACCIA = D. Josephus Nassi, 49
Nachman, Moses ben, 157 (notes), (*see* Gerundensis)
Nahomi, 102
Naphtali, Hord of, 31 ; war with Zeno, 31
Naphtali, tribe of, 32
Naphtalites, 32 ; war with Zeno, 31
Naples, 49
Nasi, Donna Gracia, 159, 163 (notes)
Nassi, Don Josephus = Joannes Michesius, nephew and son-in-law of Bienvenide Abravanela, 49, 86, 159 (notes)
Nation of the Jews, 90
National Conference, xlvi
Navigation Act, xxx, xxxi, xxxii, xli, lxxiii
Naylor, James, xl
Nazarenus, Eli = Francisco Meldonado de Silva, turned Jew, was burnt at Lima, 48, 158 (notes)
Nebuchadnezzar, 40, 42, 51, 76, 129, 141 ; dream of, 75 ; image of, 52, 57
Nebuchadnezzar's tree, 59
Nehamias, Himanuel, 170 (notes)

Nephussim, 52
Nero, 101, 130
Netherlands, xxx, xxxiii
Neubauer, Dr. A., cited, 152 (notes), 153 (notes)
Neve, Le, lxxv
New Africa, 34
New Christians or Marranos, xii
New Exchange, xxxvii
"New Model," xix
New Spain, 18, 22, 31, 54 ; Indians of, 18, 23 ; Ten Tribes in, 20
New World, xiv ; inhabitants of, 6
Newcomen, xlviii, xlix
Nicanor, 128
Nicaraguazenses, 22
Nicholas, Sir Edward, xxii, xli ; cited, 103
Nicolay, Nicholas de, cited, 162 (notes)
Nieupoort, cited, xli *n.*, lx *n.*
Nile, The, 19, 34, 39, 41, 44
Nisa, 84
Nisebor, 32
"Nismachaim," 146
Nizza, 82
"Nomenclator Hebraius and Arabicus," 147
"Nomologia," 163 (notes)
North Sea, 21
Norway, 6, 54
Norwich, 112, 166 (notes)
Nova Granada, 24
Novæ Angliæ, lxxxi
Nuevos Christianos (*see* Marranos), lix, lxi
Nye, Philip, xlviii, xlix, l

OG, 57
Ogay, 29
Ojeda, 153 (notes)
Omeguas, 23
Onias, the High Priest, 76, 128
Onkelos, cited, 135
Ophir, 19, 53, 54 ; son of Jokton, 18
"Orationes Panegyricæ," 146
"Orchot Olam," 38, 156 (notes)
Orchotolam, Abraham Frisol = Abraham Farisol or Peretsol, author of "Orchot Olam," 33, 156 (notes)
Origen, 54 ; cited, 55

Index

Ornstein, Rev. A. F., 162 (notes)
Orœnsis, 30
Oronoch, the Indians of, 27
Orosius, cited, 55
Orpa, 103
Orsna, Petrus de, killed by Aquirre, 24, 25
Ortelius, 31 ; cited, 33, 53, 54
Osorius, Hieronymus, 28 ; cited, 98, 99, 100, 138, 163 (notes)
Otteman race, 52
Ottoman family, 97
Owen, Dr., xxix, xlviii
Oxford University, xlviii

PACK, Sir Christopher, xlvii, li
Padua, 50, 160 (notes) ; Jews in, 87 ; Mounts of Piety at, 101
Palache, Seignor Moseh, 88, 163 (notes)
"Paläorama," 153 (notes)
Palatine, Prince, 28
Palaxe, Samuel, 49, 159 (notes)
Paliciano, Monsegnor Monte, 95
Pampelona, 24
Panama, 18, 31
Para, Great, 27
"Parasa Aazinu," 37
Paris, Matthew, cited, 112
Paris, Parliament of, 97
Parisius, Cardinal, cited, 96
Parliament, of England, 157 (notes) ; dedication of " Hope of Israel " to, 3, 144 ; dedication of Latin edition of " Hope of Israel " to, xxvi ; Long, lviii ; pamphlet, probably read in, xxvii ; of Paris, 97
Parthia, 40
Parvaim, 18
Pathros, 40
Paul III. of the House of Farnesia, 94, 95, 96
Paul IV., Pope of Rome, 98
Paul's, St., Cathedral, xli ; Church, 118
Paz, Enriquez de, xiii
Paz, Seignor Duarte de, 95
Pedro the Cruel, Don, 90, 163 (notes)
Peka, 29
Pelham's " Jew Bill," xx
Pelu, 19

Pelusium, 40
" Pene Rabba," 146
Pequin, 29
Pequinenses, 29
Perasach, 36
Pernambuco, xxxiii, xxxvii
Peroza, 31
Persia, 32, 39, 40, 42 ; Kings of, 31 ; Monarch of, 131
Persians, 32
Peru, 18, 20, 22, 24, 25, 31, 53, 54, 153 (notes) ; Indians of, 23 ; chronicles of, 22
Pesria, Guebia ben, 141
Peters, Hugh, xix, xxviii, xl, xliii, l, lix
Petition, for burial-ground, lxvi ; to repeal " Statute of Banishment " against Jews, xx
Petra, 40
Petronius, 129
Peyrère, Iaac la, 168 (notes)
Pharaoh, 76
Pharaonica, Isle, 55
Phenicians, 6
Phes, Governors of, 49 (see Rutes)
Philadelphus, Ptolomeus, 124, 130
Philip II., King of Spain, 91
Philip III., 26
Philip, King of France, 51
Philo, 129 ; cited, 130, 131, 135
" Philosophia Rabbinica," 147
" Phocylides," 147
Pickering, Sir Gilbert, xlvi, xlvii
" Piedra Gloriosa," 149 (notes)
" Piedra Pretiosa," 146
Pineda, Thomas de, Marrano Jesuit Father, xiii ; cited, 54, 120
Pinto, Mosseh, 170 (notes)
Pires, Diogo (see Molcho), 156 (notes)
Pisarrus, Gonzalus, 24
Pizarrus, Franciscus, 17
Placentia, 39
" Plain Dealing," lxvi
Plancius, 130
Plato, 54
Pliny, 20 ; cited, 37, 55
Plutarch, 55, 58 ; cited, 118, 127
Pocock, cited, 149 (notes), 159 (notes)
Poland, xxxix ; Jews in, xlv, lxx, 77, 87 ; King of, Henry of Anjou elected, 159 (notes) ; usury in, 120

(185)

(186)

Index

"Remnant Found, The," 152 (notes)
Republican Government, xix, lxxiv, xxvii ; triumph, xxiii
Resettlement, petition, xxxv ; question, Holmes's treatise on, xxvi
Restoration, lxx ; Cromwell's maritime and commercial policy carried out after, lxxiii
Retio, 85
Reuben, tribe of, 29
Reubenita, David, 33
Reubenite, David the (*see* Reubenita) = David Reubeni, 33, 155 (notes)
Reuchlin, 72
"Revelation Revealed, The," 63
"Revelation Unrevealed, The," 67
Revolution, xx
Ribera, Franciscus de, 19
Ricaut, lxxiv
Riccards, Alderman, xlvii
Riccius, P. Matthæus, 29, 30
Richardson, Samuel, lxvi
"Rights of the Kingdom," 166 (notes)
Rios, Amador de los, xiv
Robles, Don Antonio Rodrigues, lx, lxi, lxii, lxiii ; Robles's petition to the Protector, lxiv ; reinstated, lxvi
Rocamora, Vicente.de, xiii
Rodriques, Don Daniel, 88
Rofe, Selomo, ambassador to Venice, 86 (*see* Rophe)
Roman, 22 ; empire, 101
"Romance al diuin Martir Juda Creyente," poem by Gomez, 158 (notes)
Romans, 32, 35, 90, 97 ; Bar Cochba rebelled against the, 157 (notes) ; the kingdom of the, 126
Rome, xiii, 26, 48, 50, 57, 95, 96, 160 (notes), 163 (notes) ; a famous lawyer of, 93 ; Habyssins at, 34 ; Jews in, 87 ; monarch of, 131 ; Paul IV. of, 98 ; people of, 129 ; Pope of, 94
Rophé, Señor H. Meyr, 157 (notes)
Rophe, Don Selomo (*see* Rofe)= Rabbi Solomon ben Nathan Aschkenazi, 49, 159 (notes)
Rosales, Immanuel Bocarus Frances

y, a Count Palatin, lxxx, 89, 163 (notes)
Ross, Alexander, xlii, xliii, lvii, lxiii, 165 (notes)
Rothschild, Baron Lionel de, lxxvi
Rous, Francis, xlvii
Rowe, Owen, xlvii
Royalists, xl, xli, lxxi ; letter, lix ; spies, lx ; spies in Holland, xviii ; treat with Jews, lxxiii
Rudolph, Emperor, 160 (notes)
Ruffinus, 119
Rupert's Horse, xlii
Rutes, the Lords, 49
Ruthes, 88
Rycaut, xv *n.*, liii *n.*

SABBATH, 37 ; Jewish, 37
Sabbathion or Sabbathian River, 35, 37, 38, 40 (*see* Sabbatical River)
Sabbatical River, 35–38, 66, 69, 153 (notes)
Sabellicus, Marcus Antonius, cited, 97
Sadler, John, contemporary of Menasseh ben Israel, xxii, xxvii, xl, xliii, lviii, lxii, lxiii *n.*, 166, 167 (notes)
Sagredo, xli
Saladin, King of Egypt, 50
Salamanca, xiv, 39
Salamanque, Synagogues of, 86
Salines, Captain, 25
Salmanassar, captivity of, 69 ; Salmanaster, 20 ; Salmaneser, 33, 37, 42
Salvetti, xli *n.*, lix
Samaria, 29, 130
Samaritans, 128
Sambation, 153 (notes), (*see* Sabbatical River)
Samuel ben Israel, xxxvi
Samuel, Jacob, 152 (notes); Rabbi, 166 (notes)
Sanhedrin, 35, 156 (notes)
Saracen, 115
Saragoci, grandson of Ferdinand and son of Emanuel, 51
Saragossa, xii
Saraph baxas, Jews as, in Egypt, 49
Sarazens, 30

Sasal, Prince of, 88
Sasportas, Jacob, xxxvii *n.*
Satah, R. Simeon ben, 141
Satthianadhan, cited, 160 (notes)
Savoy, Duke of, 51, 84, 97 (*see* Felibert)
" Scala de Spalatro," 82
Scaliger, cited, 160 (notes)
Scandia, Marquis of, 88
" Scebet Jehuda," 121, 168 (notes)
Schemtob de Leon, Moses ben, 158 (notes)
Schikhardus, cited, 31
Schmieles, Jacob Basevi, 160 (notes), (*see* Bathsebah)
Schwab, cited, 154 (notes)
Scythia, 20, 42
Seadiah, Rabbi = Saadja ben Joseph = Saadja Gaon, 158 (notes)
Seba, Fernando Jacob ben, 86
Sebastian, King, 51
Second Temple, 46, 53
" Sedar Olam," 35, 156 (notes)
Seignor of Millo = Joseph Nasino, 86
Sekes, Governors of, 49 (*see* Rutes)
Selencus, 128
Selim, Sultan, 49, 113, 135 ; peace with Venetians, 49
Selve, George de, 161 (notes)
Senensis, Sixtus, cited, 125
Separatists, xviii, xix
" Sepher Eldad Danita," 34, 156 (notes)
" Sermois," 147
Setuval, 99
Seven Islands, Lord of the, 49
Seville, xii
Sextus V., Pope, 50
Shalmaneser, King of Assyria, 29, 32
Shinar, 40
" Shir Ha-Shirim Rabba " = " Asirim Rabba," 157 (notes)
Shulamite, 58
Shunamite, the, 64
" Sicilian Constitutions," cited, 115
" Sifre," 158 (notes), (*see* Johay)
Silesia, lxxx
Silva, Don Francesco Meldonado de = Eli Nazarenus, a Marrano (*see* Marquis of Montfort, 158 (notes), 159 (notes)

Simeon the Just, 128
Simon, Barbara Anne, 152 (notes)
Simon, Rabbi, cited, 36
Simon, Petrus, cited, 23
Sina, 29, 40, 41
Sinai, Mount, 114
Sinear, 40
Sinim, Land of, 31 (*see* Sina)
Singer, Rev. S., cited, 163 (notes)
Sion, 46, 61, 62
Sisbuthus, the end of, 51
" Smectymnuus," xlviii
Smyrna, xv, 151 (notes)
Sobierre, 169 (notes)
Soeiro, Semvel ben Israel, 150 (notes) (*see* Samuel Ben Israel)
" Sohar " = " Zohar " = " Zoar," 158 (notes)
Soliman, Sultan, 97
Solime, Sultan, 86
Solinus, cited, 33
Solis, Eliazar de, 117
Solis, Simao Pires, 117
Solomon, Isle of = Isabel Island, 115 (notes)
Solomon and Hierusalem, 155
Solon, 98
Solymon II., 160 (notes)
Sonsinos, 49, 159 (notes)
Southern Sea, 16
South Sea, De Quieros enters, 26
Spain, xi xii, xiii, 51, 54, 84, 90, 154 ; banishments of, 46 ; banishment of Jews from, 93 ; cruelties to Jews in, xlv ; Inquisition in, lxix ; Indians compelled to swear fealty to King of, 25 ; Jews in, 83 ; King of, lxi, 28, 49, 91, 93, 121—*see* Alfonso, 168 (notes) ; *see* King Alphonso the Wise of, 102 ; King of, present at an " act of the faith " at Madrid, 117 ; Papistry of, xxix ; struggle with Elizabeth, xv ; trade of, xxx ; war with, lx ; when possessed by the Moors, 39
Spaniards, 17, 18 ; in America, 25 ; baptized Indians and then murdered them, 113 ; cruelty of, to Indians, 11 ; dwelling in the Indies affirm that the Indians come of the Ten Tribes, according to Menas-

Index

Index

Westminster Assembly, xlviii
Whitchcote, xlviii
Whitehall, xvii, xliv, xlvi, xlvii; meeting of Council of Mechanics at, xix
Whitehall Assembly, xvii, lvii, 144
Whitehall Conference, xix, xlviii, l *n.*, li, lii, liii, lviii, lix, lxvi, lxxxiv, 149 (notes); adjourned, xlix; meeting between Nye and Prynne at, 167 (notes)
Whitelock, xxi *n.*, xli
Wicofortius, Jaochimus, 31
Wiener, cited, 168 (notes)
Wilkes, Anna, 153 (notes)
Wilkinson, Henry, xlviii
Williams, Roger, xix, xxii, xl
Wilna, 151 (notes)
Wolf, Lucien, cited, xii *n.*, xv *n.*, xix *n.*, xxxiii, xxxviii, lxxv, lxxvi, 157 (notes), 160 (notes)
Wolseley, Sir Charles, xlvi, xlvii
Wood, C. M., cited, 155 (notes)

XARITES, 91
Xenophon, cited, 55

Xylus, 154 (notes)

YAD Hachazaka = Iad a Razaka, 167 (notes)
York, Marrano settlements in, xiv

ZACCULO, Abraham = Zaccuto, 45, 158 (notes)
Zaduces, 125
Zarate, cited, 54
Zealand, 27
Zebulon, tribe of, 32
Zeeland, lxix
"Zemach David," 163 (notes), 169 (notes)
Zeno, Emperor, 31
Zevi, Sabbethai = Pseudo-Messiah, xv
Zidan, Mulai or Mulet = King of Maracco, 49, 127
Zion, 60, 114, 145
"Zoar" = "Zohar" = "Sohar," 45, 93, 158 (notes), (*see* Johay), 163 (notes)
Zuñiga, Alonzo di Ercilla y (*see* Erzilla), 155 (notes)
Zunz, cited, 155 (notes), 157 (notes), 165 (notes)

THE END

Printed by BALLANTYNE, HANSON & Co.
Edinburgh & London

For EU product safety concerns, contact us at Calle de José Abascal, 56–1°, 28003 Madrid, Spain or eugpsr@cambridge.org.

 www.ingramcontent.com/pod-product-compliance
Ingram Content Group UK Ltd.
Pitfield, Milton Keynes, MK11 3LW, UK
UKHW010345140625
459647UK00010B/845